The Legacy of Ruth Klüger and the End of the Auschwitz Century

Perspectives on Jewish Texts and Contexts

───

Edited by
Vivian Liska

Volume 20

The Legacy of Ruth Klüger and the End of the Auschwitz Century

Edited by
Mark H. Gelber

DE GRUYTER

ISBN 978-3-11-151873-2
e-ISBN (PDF) 978-3-11-079323-9
e-ISBN (EPUB) 978-3-11-079327-7
ISSN 2199-6962

Library of Congress Control Number: 2022936936

Bibliographic information published by the Deutsche Nationalbibliothek
The Deutsche Nationalbibliothek lists this publication in the Deutsche Nationalbibliografie;
detailed bibliographic data are available on the internet at http://dnb.dnb.de.

Cover image: Many thanks to Dan Angress, Ruth Klüger's son, for providing the photograph
of her (ca. 2010) for the cover image.
Typesetting: Integra Software Services Pvt.

www.degruyter.com

Acknowledgements

I would like to thank sincerely the scholars who submitted their essays in order to make this volume a reality. I owe special thanks to Irène Heidelberger-Leonard for her advice and help. Vivian Liska, editor of the series "Perspectives on Jewish Texts and Contexts," has been enthusiastic about this project since its inception, for which I am grateful. Nathan Marcus, Director of the Center for Austrian and German Studies at Ben-Gurion University supported this project in diverse ways. Also, I wish to thank Katja Lehming at De Gruyter for her reliability, prompt communications, and good work, which facilitated the editing and production of this volume. Dan Angress, Ruth Klüger's son, always responded promptly to my requests for information or material. And, my wife Jody has been a constant source of support on this project from start to finish. We were both good friends of Ruth Klüger for decades. Her friendship was a special gift to us, as was her professionalism and colleagiality for me personally.

Mark H. Gelber

https://doi.org/10.1515/9783110793239-202

Contents

Mark H. Gelber
Introduction – The Legacy of Ruth Klüger and the End of the Auschwitz Century

When Ruth Klüger passed away in October 2020, I thought it would be very fitting and important to organize an international conference in honor of her legacy. Given the worldwide pandemic which raged at that time, it appeared to me to be prudent to set the date for this meeting well in advance, in fact in a year's time, which would have also marked her "yahrzeit," the annual Jewish commemoration of the day of death, as well as her 90th birthday. Ruth Klüger was not one for whom birthdays meant all that much; I think she would have preferred to forget her own birthday every time it came around. Perhaps each birthday appeared to her to be one of several harbingers of her eventual death, a reminder that she had one year less to live. Still, she had been very much determined to come to terms personally with the Jewish concept of "yahrzeit" and how to mark it fittingly, first and foremost, in the case of her father. She addressed this issue in her writing and in her poetry. Consequently, I decided to entitle the conference tentatively: "Kaddish for Ruth Klüger and the End of the Auschwitz Century," and I began to organize the event. Some colleagues and friends of hers responded positively to this concept, which on one hand aimed to focus on her literary and scholarly legacy, while on the other hand it purported to invite a discussion beyond the person and career of Ruth Klüger on the basis of her contribution to specific areas of concern related to understanding the Shoah and the end of the Auschwitz century.

As far as I have been able to determine, the term "Auschwitz century" was coined by one of the contributors to this volume, Irène Heidelberger-Leonard, Professor Emerita of the Université Libre de Bruxelles, who was a close friend of Ruth Klüger and who is presently writing her biography. What Heidelberger-Leonard means by this particular formulation is that the century or the period of time which began with the Nazi genocide formally comes to an end when the last of the survivors finally dies. It is a term that has not been widely accepted as yet. Still, one must ask what is at stake when there are no victims of Nazi atrocities alive to testify regarding the horrible crimes committed during the Shoah and concerning their own experiences of survival and suffering? Would the claims of deniers of the Shoah somehow become more cogent or believable after the end of the Auschwitz century?

These questions bring to mind some of the talks and responses given at an international conference, entitled "Belated or Timely Memories: the Last Phase

https://doi.org/10.1515/9783110793239-001

of Survivor Literature," which I organized at Ben-Gurion University in Beer Sheva in May, 1996. Ruth Klüger was one of the principal speakers and active participants at this meeting. Others who lectured at this meeting included Geoffrey Hartman, Freddie Rokem, Sara Horowitz, Shlomo Breznitz, Henry Greenspan, Vivian Liska, Alan Rosen, Fanya Gottesfeld Heller, myself, and others. Cordelia Edvardson, Alvin Rosenfeld, Sigrid Bauschinger, Jakob Hessing, Shimon Redlich, Efraim Sicher, Norman Simms, to name just a few of the better known attendees, also participated actively. My motivation for organizing this conference had to do with my sense that a new phase of Shoah-related literature had commenced already by the early 1990s with the appearance of several autobiographical accounts, written by survivors of the Shoah, who had survived the camps or in hiding as children. At that time, more than fifty years had elapsed since the liberation of the concentration camps and the end of the war. Some of the youngest survivors who were still alive, like Ruth Klüger, were beginning finally to write about their experiences as child survivors, despite the gap in time and the challenge of remembering or reconstructing the past, especially given the traumatic events and ordeals that characterized their survival and the dislocations and disorientations many of them suffered during their subsequent lives following the Shoah. Complicating issues concerning the form and content of this literature included: relocation, coming to terms somehow with the death of immediate family members, the search for lost family members who were possibly alive, readjusting or creating new family or support structures, negotiating new human relationships, processes of finding paths to a more or less normal existence often in a different or new culture and language, which may have included education or reeducation and finding means of employment.

However, the opening lecture at this conference, entitled "The Dilemma of the Child Survivor," given by Rabbi Joseph A. Polak, who at that time served as a Justice of the Rabbinical Court of Massachusetts and as director of the Hillel House at Boston University, probably confounded most of the conference attendees. At the very least, it astounded me, but it also helped me to revise partially my original conception of what this conference might accomplish. Polak, born in 1942, was an infant and then a toddler who together with his mother survived the Westerbork transit camp and the Bergen-Belsen concentration camp. In Beer Sheva, he stated that although he certainly was to be classified as a survivor, as this term is commonly understood in connection with the Shoah, he had no specific personal memories of the experience or of hardships or of survival *per se*. His father and thirty members of his family were murdered during the tragic ordeal. Polak reported that in 1945 during the final days of the war, he and his mother and other inmates of Bergen-Belsen were loaded onto a transport train which departed from the camp heading towards an unspecified destination. But, at some point during the journey the train just stopped in the middle of nowhere, and the personnel in charge of the train abandoned it and took flight. He first wrote about this experience in a short piece entitled "The Lost Transport" (published in *Commentary* in 1995).

In the meantime, Rabbi Polak has written in detail and elaborated on his particular case in a book entitled *After the Holocaust the Bells Still Ring* (2015). Because he had no specific memories about his experiences as a child survivor, owing to his tender age at the time, he had to piece together belatedly the puzzle of his survival from the bits and pieces of what he had been told, together with information he subsequently collected from his reading and research.

The case of Rabbi Polak appears to call into question some of the standard categories and terminology used to discuss the phenomenon of Holocaust survival. While the conference in Beer Sheva attempted to analyze and focus on "the last phase of survivor literature," which I claimed had already come into existence by the early 1990s, I could have never guessed that this last phase would last for decades. Now, some thirty years later, "the end of the Auschwitz century" is being bruited, although when the real end of the Auschwitz century – in the sense that Irène Heidelberger-Leonard has proposed – will truly come to pass, is uncertain and perhaps ultimately indeterminate.

Originally, I did not intend, by employing the term "the end of the Auschwitz century," to connect it polemically or otherwise to another phrase which has gained currency in the last decade or even longer, namely: "the end of the Holocaust." This phrase, which has been been in the air for a while now and is still very much present in diverse discussions today, can be understood as a call for ending the alleged "hegemonic position" of the Holocaust in different intellectual, cultural, historical, and political discussions and frameworks. Alvin Rosenfeld, who attended the conference in Beer Sheva in 1996, has written critically and cogently about the voices which call for "the end of the Holocaust," and he has linked this phenomenon to the end of the "era of the survivor." (Rosenfeld 2011, 238) He claims that there has been general indifference to the testimony of Holocaust survivors and an unwillingness to learn from them. What Rosenfeld has deemed most pernicious in this context are the widespread attacks on Holocaust memory, while at the same time observing general Holocaust fatigue and Holocaust resentment, as well as persistent Holocaust denial or minimalization as recurrent anti-Semitic tropes. As it turns out, survivors themselves, in addition to so-called "Holocaust professionals" have been the targets of these types of vicious and specious attacks. (Rosenfeld 2011, 252) What concerns Rosenfeld is the way in which this phenomenon of calling for "the end of the Holocaust" has also had a net effect of "calling into question the value of any serious ongoing engagement with the Holocaust." (Rosenfeld 2011, 269)

The writings of Ruth Klüger, which concern the Shoah and extend into several other areas of concern beyond it or unrelated to it, provide excellent examples or paradigms of "serious engagement," regarding confronting and comprehending the Shoah and virtually every other area she reflected on critically. This tendency is an important aspect of her general legacy, whether or not it can be martialed in support of those who decry others who call for "the end of the Holocaust." Her specific legacy, in its various expressions, is the central topic of this volume, and it stands to outlast or continue beyond "the end of the Auschwitz century." It should last as long as readers continue to encounter her writings, and perhaps as long as viewers continue to encounter her in documentaries or on YouTube and in video clips, which present her in dialogue with others or giving lectures and talks, especially at American and European universities or in public forums, like the talk on forced child labor she gave at the Bundestag in Berlin in January 2016.

Several longtime friends and colleagues of Ruth Klüger have contributed essays for this volume. Sander Gilman, whose own career intersected with hers, is able to trace his friendship and colleagueship with her over five decades, while focusing in his essay on the topic of naming. He is specifically interested in the particular significance of Ruth Klüger's different names. He considers "Ruth" to be a "magic name." Thus, he is able to illuminate aspects of her career, which pertain to gender, memory, and identity – both American and Jewish. By understanding naming as a reflection of context and of the morality in that context, he argues that "names become identity" for Ruth Klüger, as well as for himself and others. He identifies two cultural wars being waged at present: a memory war and a naming war. And, they are intimately related to each other. These insights provide a framework for a subtle understanding of the tension between the "narrator I" and the "narrated I" in her autobiographical writings. While Gilman agrees with Ruth Klüger's provocatory claim that German is a Jewish language, he concedes that they do not understand this claim in the same way, and also that "Jewish" means something different to each of them.

Heinrich Detering, a second longtime friend and colleague of Ruth Klüger represented in this volume, aims to analyze her style of writing and thinking. Drawing on the methodology and model provided by a leading Germanist and literary critic of the previous generation, Richard Alewyn (1902–1979), Detering offers a sophisticated close reading of a sentence and formulations in her writing, in order to extrapolate Ruth Klüger's poetics. He probes the *Spannung*, – a sense of tension or suspense – which characterizes her authorial style. Detering identifies the hermeneutic dialectic at work in her writing and thinking, drawing on the hermeneutical tradition represented by the German theologican, Biblical scholar, and philosopher Friedrich Schleiermacher (1768–1834). Commensurately, Detering suggests that the sense of tension or suspense, which he has elaborated on in regard to her writing, can also be seen as a principle at work in her life.

In his essay in this volume, Stephan Braese focusses on the special status of the German language owing to the Shoah, which includes the changes in German language usage during and after the Nazi period, and the attempt to foster a dialogue between Germans and Jews in German following the genocide, as exemplified by Ruth Klüger's *weiter leben*. Gershom Scholem's notion of the "restitution of language between Germans and Jews" informs Braese's argument. Ruth Klüger originally wrote her memoirs, *weiter leben*, in German, and she dedicated the book to her German friends, even calling it a German book. According to Braese, conditions had to change radically in Germany in order for the spectacular success of *weiter leben* to take place. Numerous obstacles, many of which were difficult and painful to confront, had prevented the possibility of initiating the kind of a dialogue the book aspired to achieve.

Irène Heidelberger-Leonard is the third longtime friend and colleague of Ruth Klüger represented in this volume. She is presently (in 2022) at work on a biography of her mentor. Heidelberger-Leonard's monograph on *weiter leben. Eine Jugend,* published in 1996, established the guidelines and high standards for approaching this text, as well as situating it within larger literary and philosophical frameworks beyond the literature of Holocaust survival. Heidelberger-Leonard is interested in how Holocaust Studies have changed over the last decades and what will happen at the end of the Auschwitz century, when the literature of the Shoah passes from memory to history. She argues that the writings of Jean Améry, Imre Kertész, and Ruth Klüger inaugurated a fourth stage in the development of Holocaust Studies characterized by much more complex and self-reflective texts. According to Heidelberger-Leonard, their works are "solely driven by the Jewish experience" and they represent diverse Jewish voices. In effect, she understands their major works – Améry's *At the Mind's Limits*, Kertész's *Fateless*, and Klüger's *Still Alive* – as "Bildungsromane in reverse" that delineate different paradigms of testimony in dialogue with one another.

In her contribution, Ulrike Offenberg presents a detailed discussion of the Jewish prayer of mourning, the Kaddish, as a response to Ruth Klüger's lengthy explanation in *weiter leben* and *Still Alive* of why she rejected the notion of reciting this prayer in memory of her father. Offenberg, as a congregational rabbi, historian, and Jewish scholar, is well-positioned to view this text and the issue of Klüger's rejection of it in all of its complexity – from its origins and uses in the distant past up until its function in contemporary Jewish communal life. Offenberg views the Kaddish prayer as the quintessential Jewish expression of mourning, which traditionally has been viewed as a prayer to be said only by men in a quorum of ten Jewish males, according to guidelines stipulated in Jewish sources, including the Talmud, Midrash, and commentary literature. However, Offenberg presents many interesting cases and little-known precedents which in fact include women reciting the Kaddish in public over centuries. She also reviews the various pro's and con's which have been advanced in Jewish religious sources through the ages and in different locales regarding the women's issue. Given Ruth Klüger's estrangement from Jewish religion, it may be contradictory or at the least somewhat inconsistent that she decided to light "Yahrzeit" candles annually in memory of her father. However, those candles were lit in the privacy of her home; in Judaism lighting "Yahrzeit" candles is not a public act. Nevertheless, Offenberg suggests that by writing poetry pertaining to loss and the death of her father, for example, Klüger substituted poetry for Jewish prayer. At the same time, the specific process of her composing poetry in memory of her father can be understood as a thoroughly Jewish practice.

Another longtime friend and colleague of Ruth Klüger, Mark H. Gelber, the editor of this volume, summarizes and analyzes in his essay her relationships to Judaism and Zionism in an American context. He ponders the significance of her late decision to be buried in a Jewish cemetery in Los Angeles, whereas she consistently rejected both Jewish ritual and organized Jewish religion during her adult life. Her experiences during the Shoah and her feminism certainly played important roles in this regard. Gelber employs the concept of "Jewish sensibility" as a methodological tool, in order to refute claims often found in the secondary literature that Ruth Klüger is to be understood primarily as an assimilated Jew, one that had no particular interest in Judaism, Zionism, or the fate of the State of Israel. Additionally, Gelber illuminates numerous aspects and common views that Ruth Klüger, who immigrated to the U.S. at the age of sixteen, shared with American Jewry at large.

Monica Tempian's contribution to this volume examines examples of poetry and diary entries written by children during the Shoah. The children authors she cites are pre-teens and teenagers invariably aged twelve to eighteen, and they write in different languages about their ordeals. Tempian sheds light on the variety and complexity of the figurative discourse of young people, as they responded in multilingual writings to the atrocities they endured. Most of the writing samples she presents are authored by less-well known or virtually unknown teens. But, as Tempian demonstrates through close analysis of the poetical language in this corpus, an argument may be advanced to the effect that this specific children's literature often evidences "eloquence and philosophical depth." Ruth Klüger, who as a girl composed poems in captivity in her mind or recited poetry committed to memory before deportation, claimed that the writing of poetry stimulates and encourages clarity of thought. According to Tempian, the writing of poetry and diaries by children victims during the Shoah may be understood as acts of resistance, to the extent that they assert the identity and humanity of the authors. In the face of evil and suffering, and given the threats to their lives, violence, and the need for protection, many of these children expressed their responses to their plight in poetical language. Not all of them survived.

In the first part of his contribution to this volume, Daniel Reynolds considers the place of Ruth Klüger in Holocaust memory culture. Klüger only valued Holocaust representation, according to Reynolds, if it engendered critical reflection. Interestingly, he places the burden of responsibility regarding memory both on the creators and consumers of Holocaust representation. At the same time, he explains that Klüger argued against Adorno's famous dictum against poetry after Auschwitz and instead in favor of poetry, including, for example, the abstruse poems of Paul Celan, because for her, poetry could serve as an effective and necessary means to stimulate critical thought concerning the Shoah. In the second section of his essay, Reynolds turns his attention more squarely to the issue of Holocaust tourism, which Ruth Klüger tended to doubt as an educational tool, because of its superficiality and tendency toward kitsch. Also, she rejected individual identification with the inmates or survivors as a strategy employed by memorial sites and museums, since it tended to elicit emotional and unreasoned responses on the part of visitors. Following his in-depth historical and critical depiction of the most visited Memorial and Museum of the Shoah, Auschwitz-Birkenau in Poland, Reynolds formulates an argument against Ruth Klüger and in favor of Holocaust tourism. He lists the positive aspects for tourists of visiting the concentration camps, basing his view partially on a concept of the "implied tourist." Reynolds also considers the potential impact and efficacy of Holocaust documentaries, for example *Austerlitz* (2016) by the Ukrainian filmmaker Sergei Loznitsa.

In her personal and poetic meditation composed for this volume, Vera Schwarcz utilizes numerous examples from Chinese literature and especially Chinese poetry that incorporate ghosts and mourning as frameworks for contextualizing Ruth Klüger's legacy. Several of the Chinese authors and poets who are cited in her essay are depicted as iconoclasts and dissidents within the political arena in China, but in general, they are sympathetic to individual Jews and seem to understand the historical trauma suffered collectively by the

Jewish people during the Shoah. Schwarcz claims that one of Ruth Klüger's major goals was to encourage those who encounter and read her poetry and other writings to become better "Ghost Seers." What Schwarcz means by this term is that Klüger's readers would hopefully become more open to untold stories and unseen presences, after becoming familiar with her writing. China, for Schwarcz, is the locus where weaving ghosts and poetry together is a prized cultural accomplishment. In addition, by foregrounding herself as a daughter of survivors of the Shoah, Schwarcz, who grew up in Transylvania, establishes a personal link to Ruth Klüger, while mediating between Jewish and Chinese sensibilities, given the historical traumas experienced by both peoples in the twentieth century. Whether these traumata were fated or not, Schwarcz views Klüger's demonstration of "writing against fate" to be her most compelling legacy at the end of the Auschwitz century.

Bibliography

Alvin H. Rosenfeld, *The End of the Holocaust* (Bloomington and Indianapolis: Indiana University Press, 2011).

Sander L. Gilman
Poetry and Naming in Ruth Klüger's Works and Life

R.K. Angress

In the late 1960s the humanities were "hot" in the United States. They were seen as an essential part of the university, having been accepted, at least in the Anglophone world, as the moral center of Higher Education. And German Studies seemed to have a high status among the humanities – not quite as important as English or French but certainly morally superior to Spanish. (That was more on account of the *Caudillo*, Francisco Franco, as peninsular Spanish then defined the field, rather than any evaluation of the new and extraordinary writing exploding in the Americas.) In 1968, with a freshly minted doctorate, I was offered a position at the newly merged Case Institute and Western Reserve University in a post-apocalyptic Cleveland, Ohio. Indeed, the most momentous public event of my time in Cleveland was the day the Cuyahoga River caught on fire, one of the iconic ecological disasters of the age. My mandate in the German department was to teach courses from early German literature to the moderns, in addition to the required course "German language for engineers," Saturday mornings at 8 a.m. German still had the aura of being the language of science in the American academy, something that it had acquired in the nineteenth century, and that it would lose, along with its privileged status in the humanities over the next decades. Among my new colleagues was one who became a life-long friend. Ruth Angress had survived Terezín and Auschwitz, and, as I later learned, had written poems in Christianstadt, a satellite camp of Groß-Rosen. She came, with her two sons, Percy and Danny, from a failed marriage to another "refugee," the historian Werner "Tom" Angress. She had arrived in Cleveland a few years before me from the University of California, Berkeley, where she had just finished her Ph.D.

We bonded on a number of fronts. I had returned from a summer in West Berlin, having bought a number of new books at the Heinrich-Heine Book Store in East Berlin with my required twenty-five Marks *Zwangsumtausch*. My booty included an anthology of poetry written in the concentration and death camps, which she saw lying on my desk. She mentioned that a poem of hers was in the volume, but when I could not find it, she said it was under her maiden name of Ruth Klüger. Many years later she began to send me drafts for an autobiography, which I critically commented on, and which, to her great credit she published in 1992 under the title *weiter leben*, having ignored all of my protestations.

https://doi.org/10.1515/9783110793239-002

Names matter. Naming conventions matter. For "Ruth Angress" was still in name but not in reality the wife of "Tom." Divorce, certainly in the 1960s, rarely led women to abandon their married name or indeed to abandon their honorific title of "Mrs." Ruth's feminism, quite apparent in our earliest time together, was moderated by her need to maintain an academic identity not with "her" name but with Tom's. She eventually joined the Modern Language Association's "Women's Caucus" and The Coalition of Women in German in the 1970s as Ruth Angress. But was such naming, forced upon women in bourgeois culture, a truly involuntary, an unconscious labeling as a "victim?" Later she imagined, thinking of her life in New York City as a newly arrived immigrant, such naming to be equivalent to the tattoo that she bore on her forearm: "Man kann ja Verschiedenes wollen zu verschiedenen Zeiten. Warum die Vorschriften, die doch, wie jede Form von Zwang, suspekt sein sollten? Es ist wie mit angeheirateten Namen, wenn man geschieden ist: Manche wollen sie loswerden, manche wollen sie behalten. Die Wahl, scheint mir, ist moralisch neutral. Als ich Kellnerin war, haben mich die Kunden öfter gefragt, was das für eine Nummer sei. Ich mußte lachen, weil sie es nicht wußten oder vorgaben, es nicht zu wissen, und zwischen Küche und Stammtisch ist nicht der Platz für Aufklärung. Um die Frager loszuwerden, sagte ich gelegentlich, das sei die Telephonnummer von meinem Freund, meinem boyfriend. Der hat's gut, sagte ein Gast. Ich sehe meine Leser befremdet die Köpfe schütteln. Tut mir leid. Ich war frei, ich konnte sagen, was ich wollte, das hat mich gefreut." (Klüger 1992, 238) Names matter; tattoos matter. But their reading was truly not up to the individual, but the individual embedded in a world of social conventions about naming – and beginning in the 1960s, about tattoos, which were slowly becoming the mark of a body counterculture not of victimhood.

But, perhaps I should begin again: among my colleagues in Cleveland, in that decrepit building that housed the German department, was a very productive scholar by the name of "R.K. Angress." Names matter. Names are unstable. And if I were shocked that poems by Ruth Klüger were in a book on my desk, I was equally puzzled when Ruth handed me, as was our want, offprints of her first articles, under the name "R. K. Angress." We called offprints "akademische Postkarten," in retrospect an odd tradition that seems to have vanished without much of a trace. We published without recompense in academic journals read almost exclusively by our colleagues and subvented those journals (admittedly badly) by buying over-priced offprints to send to those self-same colleagues who read precisely the journals in which we published. And it turned out that "R.K." was productive as well as engaged with many of the same projects as I was. There were essays on Wolfram von Eschenbach, (Angress 1969) and then, Lessing, (Angress 1971b) and double Grillparzer (Angress 1971c and 1972). "R.K.'s"

Berkeley dissertation, written with Blake Spahr, on the Baroque Epigram appeared with the University of Kentucky Press in 1971. (Angress 1971a) My own work at the time quite paralleled hers: an edition of Johannes Agricola von Eisleben's proverb collections, (Gilman 1971b) articles on Novalis (Gilman 1970a) and fantasies of Blackness in Enlightenment Germany. (Gilman 1970b) And my dissertation on Klabund, novel theory, and the cinema, then also appeared in 1971. (Gilman 1971a) We were both turning to Kafka: R.K., trained by Heinz Politzer, on Kafka and Sacher-Masoch (Angress 1970) and I, trained by Eberhard Lämmert, on narrative strategies in Kafka. (Gilman 1971c)

Notice any similarity between "R.K." and me? Most of our work at the beginning of our mutual careers was mainstream in a world of German Studies that was still in the thralls of an Imperial German (and Austrian) nationalism, even in programs that were critical of such approaches. It was more than merely canonical; it was not terribly different from what scholars in the field had done before 1933. Like much of the study of things German at the time, we managed to leap across the period from 1933 to 1945 as an aberration, not to be studied, but to be avoided. How could you argue that literature provided some sort of moral training and study the writers, some major, some trivial, many still writing in the 1960s, whose moral center was defined by Nazi ideology? Yes, our work started to move ever so slowly towards new questions, if hesitantly. Things "Jewish," which for complex reasons shaped both of our psyches and, more importantly, our eventual choice of profession, were avoided, even when writing about that most Jewish of German-language writers, Franz Kafka. Kafka had had the "Gnade des frühen Todes," even if his beloved sisters were murdered in the camps. "Jewish" meant something very different to Ruth and to me; but both of us, for better or worse, were shaped by that very term. (Angress, 1985) And both of us held, for very different reasons, German to be (also) a Jewish language.

One major difference, which you immediately noted, was that while Ruth transformed herself into "R.K." I remained "Sander L." in my professional writing. And this rang home to me immediately. When I asked her about this she was very straightforward in her answer. Getting published as a woman in our field was hard; indeed, getting a job as a woman with a family had been complicated and conflicted. That this was the case was oblivious to me. All of my colleagues in New Orleans and Munich and Berlin were men. Virtually all of my teachers too, with the real exception of Margaret Groben, who had written her dissertation on Friedrich Schlegel with Paul Hankamer and Ernst Bertram in Cologne in 1934. (Groben) She taught at Newcomb College, the coordinate woman's college at Tulane. She became my advocate and advisor when I returned with half a dissertation from Berlin. Her own experience in what had quickly become a very fascist

Cologne, working on a topic quickly beloved by German nationalists, shaped her advice, and her focus helped me complete my thesis while I was teaching at a HBCU, Dillard University, the year before I left for Cleveland. Ruth helped me understand the barrier that Margaret Groben had faced and the very limits on her career in the 1930s and 1940s. Indeed, there was one moment that was telling for me. Mid-year Ruth came to me with an odd request. Her car had broken down for the very last time; would I go with her to a car dealership to help her purchase a new (used) one? Puzzled, I, of course, agreed, telling her that she should know that I didn't actually know how to drive. Would this be a problem? Just wait, she said. We arrived there in order for Ruth to buy a car. The conversation was triangular. Ruth said what she wanted; the car salesman answered ME, and then I nodded at Ruth who responded to the salesman. Eventually a deal was struck, we left the showroom with a car, and I turned to Ruth, who needless to say was driving, and said: That was weird. Yes, she said, but I paid hundreds less because you were there.

Ruth – A Child from Auschwitz

Ruth and I both left Cleveland – she in 1970 for the University of Kansas, me the year before for Cornell. And like me, Ruth began to move in directions frowned upon when we were being trained. As I noted, I had "discovered" Ruth's poems when I read them, unknowingly, in Heinz Seydel's *Welch Wort in die Kälte gerufen: Die Judenverfolgung des Dritten Reiches im deutschen Gedicht*. (Seydel 1968) She had then marched back to her office, having identified herself as Ruth Klüger, and plopped a sheaf of papers on my desk. Poems, including versions of the fragmentary two, "Auschwitz" and "Der Kamin," that I had already read. They were, at least to my practiced eye reading "classical" German poetry, extraordinary in their evocation of her own "Jewish" experience in the camps and thereafter. Not the radical modernism of a Paul Celan, but of a more naïve and perhaps thus truer voice. The poems too had their own history.

What I did not know then was that Seydel's East German anthology was heavily indebted to the first anthology comprised exclusively of poems from the concentration camps, Manfred Schlösser's *An den Wind geschrieben: Lyrik der Freiheit, 1933–1945*. (Schlosser 1960) The record goes back yet further to 1956 when her poems appeared in a West German literary journal entitled *Ariel* under the title "Gedichte aus Auschwitz" with the author's date of birth (October 30, 1931) and 1944 as the date of composition. (Euler 1956, 12) The poems were fragmentary yet still extraordinary in their voice. They had appeared first in newspapers issued by the Allied authorities, mainly by German Jewish members of the American army intelligence corps, as part of the very beginnings of German "re-education," a superficial approach that would soon degenerate into a systematic whitewashing of West Germans to create a German bulwark against Soviet expansion westward. A single stanza of her poem "Auschwitz" had appeared in 1945 in the *Münchener Zeitung: alliiertes Nachrichtenblatt für die deutsche Zivilbevölkerung / Die Amerikanische 12. Heeresgruppe* and subsequently in the identical form in the Hessian version of the same newspaper. It was entitled "Ein Kind schrieb aus Auschwitz . . ." and it was accompanied by an "illustration [that] shows a starved and terrified young girl, behind her we see what we assume must be a crematorium, flames shooting out the side, with smoke from the tall chimney descending in a black serpentine cloud to reach in front of the girl almost as if to strangle her. Clearly, she cannot escape the smell of the burning bodies." The text reinforces the image: the "small young girl, not yet fourteen years old" had been at "possibly the worst of the concentration camps, the death camp Auschwitz," . . . "day and night the air was full of the smell of burning human flesh." (Nader 2010, 55–56) The child is identified as Jewish and as having been born in Germany.

Yet, names matter here too; "the reader is constantly reminded of the young age of the writer – who is referred to as 'small young girl,' 'child,' 'Ruth,' or 'thirteen-year-old Ruth' – of her lack of guilt and that of her countless fellows (Kameraden und Kameradinnen) who did not survive. The paper reports that this 'child' regained her freedom, and goes on to claim that that 'freedom cannot make good the crime committed against a child, not even against a child who escaped' (Die Freiheit kann nicht gut machen, was an einem Kind verbrochen wurde – an einem Kind das noch entkam)." (Nader 2010, 55–56)

I am quoting this description here from a 1999 dissertation, revised as a first-rate, prize-winning book, by one of my students at Cornell, Andrés Nader. Published later as *Traumatic Verses: On Poetry in German from the Concentration Camps, 1933–1945*, Nader had completed his work after I left for the University of Chicago. I am doing so because he had come to me for a thesis topic, while I had been struggling with the real question of how to deal with the fragmentary, often nameless, work that had appeared in these early anthologies. Part of my own task at recoupment was to ask Ruth whether I could use the draft of her "Der Kamin" poem and then translate it into English for a chapter I had written in 1983 for a textbook on *Contemporary Germany: Politics and Culture*. (Gilman 1984a) I subsequently included the essay with many revisions in my book *Inscribing the Other*. (Gilman 1991) There I named the author as "Ruth Klüger," giving her back the name denied her in 1945 in the initial publication of the texts. As Nader quite correctly describes, the initial publication, a form of reeducation *avant le lettre*, was an appeal to the guilt of murdering the innocent, rather than the acknowledgment of the culpability of the German readers in the mass murders, not yet labeled the Holocaust.

Ruth Klüger

Names matter. Names are unstable. Ruth began to send me drafts from her autobiography. Large envelopes full of xeroxes arrived on my desk. I knew that she had survived a massive head injury while she was supervising the California program in Göttingen and was only marginally surprised with her turn from criticism to creative writing, which is, of course, exactly what an autobiography is. What she warned me was that she was writing this "secretly" as she did not want her mother in California, and with whom she had a complex relationship, to know about it. What she asked me in particular was did I feel that she was being too difficult in her presentation of her father, Viktor, in the account of what she had experienced as his abandonment of her when, although she was also on his passport, he left Vienna for Italy without her. Mirroring, of course, the opposite event with her mother, who later removed her from the "Kindertransport" because she could not be separated from her. According to a phone call with her mother, as she reported, he was weak, he had "no elbows." When her older son was born, following Jewish custom, she had felt obligated to name him after her dead father, but refused to do so. Rather she chose "einen für uns unbedeutenden englischen Name." (Klüger 1992, 26) Her father had been prosecuted as an abortionist, stripped of his medical license, incarcerated in a concentration camp. He fled eventually from Italy to Paris, was rounded up at Drancy, from where he was eventually transported, as a foreign Jew, to Auschwitz, where he was murdered. Her older half-brother, Jiri, whom she adored, was deported from Prague to Terezín and then to Riga, where he too was murdered. Ruth was quite right: her treatment of his father was harsh, I thought, he too had suffered and died. Speak not ill of the dead, I was taught. Ruth evoked Sophocles' Antigone: ". . . hab ich mich in eine Antigone verwandelt, aber bitte, in eine Antigone in Kolonos, deren Vater gar nicht stirbt, sondern in eine Apotheose steigt. Ich hatte mir einen Tochter-Vater-Mythos gefunden, wo der Vater den Tod nie erleidet." (Klüger 1992, 37) Freud's Electra seemed to me a better fit. My response was too long, too convoluted, and perhaps too revealing of my own conflicted relationship with my own father, whom I would love to have blamed for everything while quite aware that the tension between us was also of my own making. As I said, Ruth ignored everything I wrote in my protestations.

In writing these autobiographical drafts, Ruth too looked back at that moment in 1945, when the first poems appeared. At a moment when that world that she had experienced still did not have a name: ". . . Endlösung, Holocaust, die jüdische Katastrophe, immer neue Namen, weil uns die Worte dafür sehr schnell im Munde faulen." (Klüger 1992, 300) Names matter, as they give us hold on a world perpetually in flux just as they are always changing. Certainly, Adam's task to name all the beasts in Genesis 2:19 is the first moment when this was tried. The "Churban," the term with which I was raised, that is, the Yiddish term my grandparents used for the destruction of their own extended families in Poland and Belorussia, gave way to the various namings, each incomplete, each fragmentary, until, recently, the very naming of the mass murders has become part of the memory wars, used by Left and Right for their own purposes.

Susi

We, in the early twenty-first century, are not only in a memory war but equally in a name war: how are we to be located in time and space, in gender and in identity? We dismiss "dead names" or "slave names" with equal fervor. In *weiter leben* Ruth looks back at our acts of naming as always situated in history. On August 17, 1938 the "Executive Order on the Law on the Alteration of Family and Personal Names" required German Jews as well as those in the newly integrated Austria (Ostmark) bearing first names of "non-Jewish" origin to adopt an additional name: "Israel" for men and "Sara" for women, before January, 1939. What exactly is a "non-Jewish" name? As Dietz Bering long ago argued, Jewish-sounding names meant those names sounding Jewish to the ears of those in 1938. (Bering 1987) "Non-Jewish" names too were a problem. As a graduate student I was appalled to read the same in Old High German extracts from the best known encyclopedist of the Middle Ages, Isidore of Seville, whose anti-Judaism was front and center. And then to think how many European Jews shifted their too Jewish Biblical name of "Isaac" to the very European name of Isidore, only to find Isidore becoming "too Jewish" when they immigrated to New York or Johannesburg or being in Berlin in 1938. (Think of Goebbels' 1927 attack on Bernard Weiss, the Jewish head of the Berlin police. It was simply entitled "Isidor.") (Goebbels 1927) Were then "Biblical" names too Jewish for the Nazis? Susannah Heschel's reading of the Evangelical theologians in the Third Reich certainly would argue that they were. (Heschel 2008)

Names matter. But names come suddenly to be identity. At the time, Alfred Döblin stated that the Nazis had made him into a Jew. But "Alfred" was too "non-Jewish" a name to bear, evoking Alfred the Great, so if Döblin had gotten a passport with a large red "J" stamped on it after 1938, he would have been Alfred Isaac Döblin. (He couldn't, as he had fled to Paris already in 1933.)

In an Austro-fascist Vienna the young Ruth Klüger too suddenly felt herself as visibly Jewish: "Und nun, als mein ungefestigter Glaube an Österreich ins Schwanken geriet, wurde ich jüdisch in Abwehr. Bevor ich sieben war, also schon in den ersten Monaten nach dem Anschluß, legte ich meinen bisherigen Rufnamen ab. Vor Hitler war ich für alle Welt die Susi, dann hab ich auf dem anderen Namen bestanden, den ich ja auch hatte, warum hatte ich ihn denn sonst, wenn ich ihn nicht benutzen durfte? Einen jüdischen Namen wollte ich, den Umständen angemessen." (Klüger 1992, 41) But what "Jewish" name? "Niemand hat mir gesagt, daß Susanne genau so gut in der Bibel steht wie Ruth. Wer war schon bibelfest bei uns zu Haus?" (Klüger 1992, 41) But "Ruth" is also a name found in those gold-lettered volumes of "great poetry" that bourgeois Jews had on their shelves in their "gute Stube," proving that their "Bildung" was the equivalent of, if not more deeply felt (or at least shown), than that of their non-Jewish neighbors. For the tale of Ruth echoes through the melancholy of John Keats's "Ode to a Nightingale," a text we all learned in school:

> Die Stimme, die ich höre, sang den Ohren
> Von Narr und Kaiser einst dieselben Lieder:
> Vielleicht was es der gleiche Klang,
> Zum Herzen Ruths sich stahl, als heimwehkrank
> Inmitten fremden Korns sie weinend stand;
> Oft war es deine Weise,
> Die ins Gemach des Zauberslasses drang,
> Das meerumrauscht ins Feeland verbannt.
> (Gothein II, 238)

Well, I and generations of school children in the United States learned it by heart in school, as:

> Thou wast not born for death, immortal Bird!
> No hungry generations tread thee down;
> The voice I hear this passing night was heard
> In ancient days by emperor and clown:
> Perhaps the self-same song that found a path
> Through the sad heart of Ruth, when, sick for home,
> She stood in tears amid the alien corn;
> The same that oft-times hath
> Charm'd magic casements, opening on the foam
> Of perilous seas, in faery lands forlorn.
> (Bryant 1880, 317)

Ruth is thus a magic name, evoking poetry, open to all, Emperor and clown, Jew and Gentile, alike. M. H. Abrams, in his *Natural Supernaturalism*, resurrected Keats and the Romantics from T. S. Eliot's dismissal as poetry reflecting the comfortable pathos of such a gold-bound Victorianism, nature imagined by the bourgeoisie. Our generation after the Holocaust read Keats radically as the text that "through the midnight of suffering, and that, like the song of the nightingale in the darkness, only then, in our deep pain, does the world's song of life sound out divinely to us." (Abrams 1973, 438) It is an evocation of poetry, a mitigation as well as evocation of home. Texts matter; names matter.

Abandoned names also have histories. Goethe and Uhland tell Susanna's tale, of course, but reading the Book of Daniel (Chapter 13) was one text too many. Iconic in the art of Western Europe, it had a precarious hold as a marginal narrative in Protestantism and was "Jewish" only well after the first compilation of the Tanach. And even if the young Susi had read it, the tale of Susanna and the Elders would have only reenforced the notion that it takes a man (Daniel) to rescue a falsely accused woman, lusted after by two aged men. Susi's demand to be renamed, to declare her birthname a dead one becomes a pivotal point in Ruth's retrospective account of the development of her self-consciousness: "Ich hab die Erwachsenen mit großer Sturheit ausgebessert, wenn sie mich beim alten Namen riefen, und siehe, man gab nach, lächelnd, ärgerlich oder anerkennend. Es war das erste Mal, daß ich etwas durch reine Hartnäckigkeit durchsetzte, und so hab ich mir den richtigen Namen ertrotzt, ohne zu wissen, wie sehr er der richtige war, den Namen, der 'Freundin' bedeutet, den Namen der Frau, die ausgewandert ist, weil sie die Freundschaft höher schätzte als die Sippschaft. Denn Ruth ist ausgewandert, nicht um des Glaubens, sondern um ihrer Schwiegermutter Naëmi willen, die sie nicht allein ziehen lassen wollte. Sie war einem Menschen treu, und dieser Mensch war eben nicht der geliebte oder angetraute Mann, sondern es war eine frei gewählte Treue, von Frau zu Frau und über die Volkszugehörigkeit hinweg." (Klüger 1992, 41) Names matter: we are given them and then they become us, or do they?

This is the birth moment of "Ruth Klüger." But this is also the account that the author in the 1990s gives of her own sense of self as a feminist. And a feminist bound to the world of women in conflict with the patriarchy. And here the patriarch stands for not merely Biblical society but for the society in which now the adult "Ruth Klüger" writes. And this voice within a narrative voice suddenly appears to confirm this: "(Diese Lesart des Buches Ruth wird mir kein Theologe rauben und schon gar nicht ein männlicher. Dafür schenk ich euch das Buch Esther und Makkabäer dazu. Die brauch ich nicht, diese Fabeln vom Sieg durch Sex und Gewalt, die könnt ihr so nationalistisch und chauvinistisch lesen, wie ihr wollt.)" (Klüger 1992, 41) But it is also the non-Jewish Ruth who says to Naomi, her Jewish mother-in-law, that she will follow her whither she goes and abide whither she abides. (Ruth 1:16) A cruel reversal of our Ruth's mother who demands that her daughter remain with her and not wander far from her.

But naming, as I have already noted, is a reflection of context and of the morality, or its absence, implicit in that context. All of the adults but one acquiesce. "Nur meine alte Großmutter nannte mich bis an ihr Ende Susi. Sie starb in Theresienstadt, keines ihrer neun Kinder war bei ihr, nur ihre einstmals verwöhnte, aber in dieser Situation rührend töchterliche Schwiegertochter, meine Mutter. Die anderen, die ausgewandert waren, hatten ja alle geglaubt, daß niemand einer alten Frau was antun würde. Oder einem Kind, wie ihrem jüngsten Enkel, der Susi." (Klüger 1992, 41) For the moral order demanded by the very notion of *Bildung* which underpinned Jewish integration into European society, was a moral order that respects the fragility of age and the innocence of youth and where, following Martin Luther King, Jr., "the arc of the moral universe is long, but it bends toward justice." But it was not just King who claimed this. So did Ruth's beloved Schiller. As Caroline Schaumann notes: "She names Schiller's ballads, generally interpreted as declarations of Christian ethics and Hellenistic ideals, as a bulwark against despair. These ballads express trust in a pure, inviolable soul and belief in ultimate justice and freedom. In Auschwitz, these ballads offered an escape from brutal reality and furthermore symbolized hope for eternal justice. Klüger refers specifically to . . . [Schiller's] "Die Kraniche des Ibykus". . . . In the poem, which was clearly of crucial importance to Klüger, justice is ultimately reinstated on the basis of testimony." (Schaumann 1994, 56) This was and is a powerful fantasy, then as it is now. It was certainly not true in German Southwest Africa; it was not true during WWI; it certainly was not true in Weimar, if you read Hanns Johst or *Der Stürmer*; and after 1933, it was clearly not true at all. Moral order is defined, and Jeremy Bentham said this long ago, by our self-awareness as human beings about our obligations to the world around us. Denial of such self-awareness, as Thomas Hobbes said well before Bentham, is why human beings need the coercive state. But even in Hobbes' world, the state was both protector and hangman, a dilemma that he never resolved. The moral order that we imagine inhabits the books we read, the moral order represented by Thomas Mann's "good German," exists only as our collective fantasy of the unimpeachability of human endeavor, a utopian order never achieved but always sought after. It was the moral order we ascribed to poetic texts in the academic world that Ruth and I had entered in the 1960s, which centered student's moral education in the humanities. We learned quickly that this was not true, had never been true, and its claim merely obfuscated the role of the university in perpetuating rather than questioning itself as an institution.

The reaction to the industrialized killing of the Third Reich shaped our post-war thought about the moral role of the humanities in higher education. In New York City, two very different Jewish intellectuals, Hannah Arendt in "Crisis in Education" (1954) and Lionel Trilling in *Sincerity and Authenticity* (1972), cast about for new models and means of critiquing the moral obligations of the humanities in American Higher Education. In occupied Germany, the "reeducation" of the Germans, including the restructuring of the humanities in the universities, was the stated goal of the Allies. Some thinkers, such as C. P. Snow, answer the debates about the moral force of the humanities in the moment when the humanities still seem to be ascendant and yet were grappling with the legacy of the Third Reich. Snow, in his 1959 "The Two Cultures and the Scientific Revolution," countered the perceived dominance of the humanities and their claim to make better people as simply a falsehood proven by their failures. He demanded a recalibration of the universities to balance the role of the humanities with a new and robust role for the sciences, with their expanded moral force reinforced by the debates following the dropping of the atomic bomb. Snow's argument, an answer to the Nazis' idea of the humanities in the service of a totalitarian state, *pace* Goebbels, prefigured the entire reevaluation of the humanities as no longer central to modern education, in which we now find ourselves.

ΟΥΤΙΣ

"Bildung" demands analogies. We are (or seem to be) educated when we can gesture towards texts that show our cultural and moral superiority. In the ninth book of the *Odyssey*, Odysseus lands on the Island of the Cyclops. There he finds a cave full of provisions and he and his men are surprised by its inhabitant, the one-eyed giant Polyphemus. They are trapped and the giant proceeds to eat two of Odysseus's men a day until he is brought down by having his wine drugged. He had asked the leader of the group, Odysseus, his name and promised him a gift if he would reveal it. Οὖτις, "No One" is my name, Odysseus says, and then blinds the giant in his drugged stupor. Awake and asked who has harmed him, the giant states that "No one has." You all know the tale. You also know that the crime of Polyphemus was one of the most basic ones in the world of the Greeks and indeed all Mediterranean peoples, the violation of ξενία, of guest friendship. Throughout *weiter leben* the violation of this basic principle is evident. The redefinition of the Jews as a foreign people and then their isolation and destruction, to the point, as Ruth stated, that even violates the rights of the aged and the very young to succor.

At one point, having escaped from a transport from Groß-Rosen, Ruth's mother appeals to the "Dorfpastor," the Lutheran pastor in the tiny village where they have hidden themselves away, for exactly that succor. He immediately provided her with the necessary papers to allow them to claim to be good Christian parishioners. He is nameless in the narrator's memory: "Er, der uns neue Namen gab, hat keinen Namen in meinem Gedächtnis hinterlassen, noch kann ich mich an den Namen seines Dorfes erinnern." (Klüger 1992, 181) But so, in a remarkable turn, are mother and daughter: "Auch unsere Namen habe ich vergessen. Nach Kriegsende nie wieder daran gedacht. Das ist keine Verdrängung, das ist ein Hintersichlassen." (Klüger 1992, 181) Here is, in the nameless pastor the antithesis of Polyphemus, the individual who respects the universal demand that one succor the traveler and help the stranger. He was the embodiment of Immanuel Kant's demand for a *Weltbürgerrecht* (law of world citizenship) in the Third Article of his *Perpetual Peace* (1795), to which all humans would be entitled. For Kant the "use of the right to the earth's surface which belongs to the human race in common" would "finally bring the human race ever closer to a cosmopolitan constitution." (Kant, 358) This is rooted in the assumption that there is an innate rule of hospitality to the stranger, the Greek idea of ξενία, guest-friendship, that defines his understanding of the cosmopolitan, for "cosmopolitan right shall be limited to conditions of universal hospitality." (Kant 1999, 357) Hospitality is defined here as "the right of a foreigner not to be treated with hostility because he has arrived on the land of another." (Kant 1999, 357–8) Nameless perhaps because unlike all of those named, he acted selflessly as a human being.

And that brings us back in complex ways to Cleveland, Ohio in 1968. For Ruth's best friend then (and later) was our colleague Maria Alter, who also was a member of the German department. She too had recently arrived at Case with her husband Jean Alter, who was a structuralist professor of French. Early on in my stay I had all three over for drinks in my tiny apartment across from the Cleveland Museum of Art. After a few glasses of wine, I remarked on Jean's last name, as it was quite an important one in the lives of my Bundist Polish family. Indeed, the one thing I rescued from my grandfather's library was his three-volume, annotated Yiddish translation of Marx's *Capital*. But Jean did not really respond; rather he deflected to the unpleasantness of Cleveland and the rather stodgy nature of the French department. But I was right: Jean was the son of Wiktor Alter, one of the leading Bundists of the interwar years, murdered by Stalin in Soviet exile. Jean survived because on a fluke he was with his Belgian mother in Belgium on holiday when the Germans invaded Poland, and they went underground. Let Ruth narrate the rest of the tale: "Ich kenne einen polnischen Juden, heute Professor für Romanistik in den Vereinigten Staaten, der als Kind in der Nazizeit in Belgien vier Jahre lang unter einem Decknamen lebte. Der weiß auch seinen falschen Namen nicht mehr, obwohl er ihn so lange benutzt hat. Seine amerikanische Tochter sagt, das sei ein Musterbeispiel für Verdrängung. Ich sehe das eher als ein gesundes Vergessen. Was man sich nicht wiederholt, das vergißt man eben. Der Mann hat ja nicht verdrängt, daß er sich umnennen mußte. Doch der Name selbst ist wie die Telephonnummer einer Wohnung, die man nicht mehr bewohnt. Sicher weiß man, daß man dort Telephonanschluß hatte, aber die Reihenfolge der Zahlen ist unerheblich, daher verwischt, gelöscht. Wenn man endlich wieder so heißen kann, wie man wirklich heißt, warum sich die falsche Identität ins Gedächtnis zurückrufen?" (Klüger 1992, 181) A wrong number or, as his daughter, the comparatist Nora Alter observed, a repressed one? Numbers, like names, can be repressed, but not those tattooed on one's forearm. Perhaps like names they need to be present to be absent. That the "Good Germans" and Ruth, speaking parenthetically to her present-day German audience, note how pleased they must be with the actions of the pastor, knows that ξενία cannot be the exception in receiving the stranger, but rather the rule. Nameless, like Odysseus wandering the world, one is always, to paraphrase Tennessee Williams, thrown on the mercy of strangers.

By this point the reader has figured out that there is a problem with names in *weiter leben*. Names given are not names narrated. The fictionality of autobiography lets the present voice take the name of the narrated persona. Is Boswell the author or is it Boswell the character interacting with Dr. Johnson? Yes and no. For all we have of that earlier Boswell are the tales of the later one. Decades ago, I published a book of J. P. Eckermann's aphorisms, not particularly because of their literary merit, but because if you know them, suddenly his creation, Goethe, appears to be a creation of Eckermann's obsession with gnomic utterances. (Gilman 1984b) Compellingly so. Are we to take the narrated Ruth as identical to the narrator Ruth, who seems to bear the same name? What about all of the other names? I would say that we need to be respectful but skeptical. For the trace of the child is in the eye of the adult, as with all of us. Or in my case, the trace is in the memory of the colleague and friend, distanced by time and space.

Ruth begins in the early drafts of her autobiography to grapple with this flux in her own retelling of her life and, equally important, of the function of her poetry in that moment, in that place. In *weiter leben* she reconstructs her poetic education before the camps. Now, one revelation about Ruth as a colleague, one that I experienced over and over again, and that my wife, Marina, who had been her student still marvels at, was her uncanny ability to – seemingly off the cuff – quote broad swatches of poetry in Germany, English, and

French. I write this as one also raised in an educational system where rote memorization was still part of studying literature and one who can still mangle the opening of Longfellow's "Hiawatha" on occasion. But Ruth's obsession with poetry was, as she later wrote "eine Angewohnheit, die bei mir bis zur Manie gedieh und zweifelsohne ebensosehr neurotischen als kunstliebenden Ursprungs war." (Klüger 1992, 13) Ruth's teenage poetic imagination was, as she wrote in *weiter leben*, stocked with such fragments as she was "leider belesen, hatte den Kopf voll von sechs Jahren Klassik, Romantik, Goldschnittlyrik. Und nun dieser Stoff. Meinem späteren Geschmack wären Fragmentarisches und Unregelmäßigkeiten lieber, als Ausdruck sporadischer Verzweiflung zum Beispiel. Aber der spätere Geschmack hat es leicht. Jetzt hab ich gut reden." (Klüger 1992, 127) But that was a true artifact of the German-Jewish bourgeois experience in Central Europe. Emigrants' libraries, such as that of Marina's family, if they had paid the "Fluchtssteuer," were full of the gold-bound "Klassiker": Schiller and Goethe most of all. And, of course, numerous anthologies of the very best poems. These were the books at home as well as the texts in school. "Erhobene Literatur" had created the educated members of the German and Austrian middle class in the course of the late eighteenth and nineteeth century. This was quite evident to the "Ruth Klüger" who authored *weiter leben* in the 1990s. She understood her family as "großbürgerlich" (Klüger 1992, 42) but also as "ritually Jewish," rather than observant. "Die Sederabende in Wien" (Klüger 1992, 44) marked the calendar: "Viertage Juden," rather than "Dreitage Juden." The Jews, more or less simultaneously "emancipated," were also weaned on the very same notions of "Bildung" as a moral force. This was the same motivation that had put the Humanities in the latter half of the twentieth century so very central to the American educational experience in which she and I taught. Serious literature was the center of not only a moral culture but of an identity crafted out of that implied moral stance. For Jews in Vienna and New Orleans an important sign of belonging to a higher culture. The irony of this was not lost on any of us teaching exactly these texts in the 1950s and 1960s, no matter how much Thomas Mann had tried to persuade us that the real Germans, the good Germans, had fled to Los Angeles and New York after 1933 with their libraries and their values.

Her childhood poems, which I greatly admired, were thus dismissed by Ruth Klüger retrospectively as "in aalglatten Kinderversen eine Sprache zu finden" (Klüger 1992, 106) and a mechanism to externalized "kindischer Verblendung und Todesangst." (Klüger 1992, 106) Yet such mechanisms can (and I believe do) lead to new and startling readings for even in her "Der Kamin", ". . . trotz und wegen ihrer Unbeholfenheit. Man muss die abgenützten Worte auf die Waagschale legen als wären sie neu." (Klüger 1992, 126) A creative reconstruction is the only possible use of poetic clichés.

Ruth recognized this. They seemed from the perspective of the 1990s to have been initially thought of a weapon. But a weapon to be brandished not only in the camps but thereafter in now defeated Germany. "Aber an dem Abend hab ich vor dem Publikum meiner Zimmergenossen mein 'Kamin'-Gedicht aufgesagt, in dem die personifizierte Todesmaschine prophezeit: Keiner ist mir noch entronnen,/ Keinen, keinen werd ich schonen./ Und die mich gebaut als Grab/ Schling ich selbst zuletzt hinab./ Auschwitz liegt in meiner Hand,/ Alles, alles wird verbrannt./ Ich rezitierte kühn, mit dem Hintergedanken: 'Es wird ihn schon erwischen, den Kerl, der mich geschlagen hat, früher oder später wird es ihn erwischen.' Das war damals ein Trost, aber es war auch ein Unsinn, denn es hat ihn sicher nicht erwischt. Wenn er nicht in Südamerika eine bequeme Villa hat, so lebt er vielleicht in Göttingen und ist der Rentner, der mir neulich in Schmidts Drogerie-Markt aufgefallen ist, als er sich zusammen mit einer jungen Verkäuferin den Mund über die schmarotzenden Aussiedler aus Polen zerrissen hat. 'Die Ausländer, die sollt man vergasen, und die Politiker gleich dazu', meinte er. Ich war im Begriff, zwischen zwei Tuben Zahnpasta zu wählen, die fielen mir fast aus der Hand. Ich schau hin zu ihm, schätze sein Alter, ja, der ist alt genug, der weiß, was er sagt. Er merkt meinen Blick, er mustert mich seinerseits. 'Solche Sprüche!' sag ich zu ihm, wir sehen einander in die Augen, Freunderl, wir kennen uns, da sagt er mit festem, höhnischem Blick: 'Ja, ja, Sie haben schon richtig gehört.'" (Klüger 1992, 163–164) Poetry as acting out. Poetry as fragments of half-remembered normality. "Wer nur erlebt, reim- und gedankenlos, ist in Gefahr, den Verstand zu verlieren, wie die alte Frau auf dem Schoß meiner Mutter. Ich hab den Verstand nicht verloren, ich hab Reime gemacht." (Klüger 1992, 128) Poetry as defensive or offensive weapon? Perhaps like a belief that writing poems would persuade God to spare the poet? (Klüger 1992, 138) This was not only Ruth's remit as Andrés Nader observed in his dissertation: "Inmates with a 'großbürgerlich' background or with a liberal intellectual biography, as in Jean Améry's example, turn to the traditional canon of German poetry as a possible source of succor during their harrowing experience, or seek expression for their suffering by writing about it in poetic forms which were familiar to them, going back to the Classicist and Romantic models of the eighteenth and nineteenth centuries. Even as a failed cultural resource, Hölderlin's poetry remains [Jean] Améry's frame of reference. Klüger refers to Schiller and Uhland; the Dutch Nico Rost entitles his camp-memoirs 'Goethe in Dachau.'" (Nader 1999, 41)

Critics seem in an odd way to agree with the Ruth Klüger of *weiter leben*, indeed using her own voice. Irène Heidelberger-Leonard finds in "Auschwitz," the poem that Ruth labels as the earlier of the two, a "helpless revolt that turns into a hope that is just as clumsy." (Heidelberger-Leonard 1996, 124) The poetic appeal to an absent God is a trope not merely of the much later work of Death-of-God theologians such as Richard Rubinstein, but it is already quite present in the poetry written during WWI: think of Wilfred Owen's poem on the Akedah. Heidelberger-Leonard also points out that "Der Kamin" is much less conciliatory because it is "gottlos." (Heidelberger-Leonard 1996, 37) Eva Lezzi stresses that Ruth's own distancing of her poetry gains a level of control over the texts and their reception. (Lezzi 2001, 234) She labels the poems "Kindergedichte" and "aalglatte Kinderverse" marked by "Unbeholfenheit." (Lezzi 2001, 107 and 126) Yet Ruth herself in another voice seems to argue against a reading that tried to place the reader, even those who read what they wrote in the camps, in the time rather than as a distanced observer: "Je grosser die zeitliche Distanz, desto unverstandlicher wurde das Geschehen jener Jahre. Auch mir scheint es manchmal, dass die Erinnerungen, die ich im Gedächtnis herumtrage, mir fremd sind, nämlich sie sind der Person fremd, die ich seither geworden bin. Wenn das stimmt, so nähert sich das Lebensgefühl der Überlebenden der KZs immer mehr dem Lebensgefühl derer, die nicht dabei waren." (Klüger 1996, 33) Memory wanes; poetry remains.

We have to remember that by the 1990s Theodor Adorno's comment of 1949 on writing poetry after the Holocaust had become a cliché. Early on in the book, she observed that: "Ich meine nicht, daß man 'keine Gedichte nach Auschwitz' schreiben dürfe. Ich meine nur, daß Gedichte neben ihren Schaukelrhythmen und unreinen Reimen auch aus sinnträchtigen Sätzen bestehen, und hinter diesen lauert oft wieder ein anderer Sinn, der in meinem, in diesem Fall aus einer zähneklappernden Angst besteht, sich der Wahrheit zu stellen. Was hier nicht zur Sprache kommt, ist die knirschende Wut, die unsereiner irgendwann haben muß, um den Ghettos, den KZs und den Vernichtungslagern gerecht zu werden, die Einsicht, daß sie eine einzige große Sauerei waren, der mit keiner traditionellen Versöhnlichkeit und Märtyrerverehrung beizukommen ist." (Klüger 1992, 38) She returns to that caveat much later observing that "So gut reden hab ich wie die anderen, Adorno vorweg, . . . man möge über, von und nach Auschwitz keine Gedichte schreiben. Die Forderung muss von solchen stammen, die die gebundene Sprache entbehren können, weil sie diese nie gebraucht, verwendet haben, um sich seelisch über Wasser zu halten." (Klüger 1992, 127) Claudia Liebrand writes that Ruth counters Adorno by exorcising the idea of the unspeakable. "Auschwitz" is not like the known but never articulated name of God; Auschwitz can be, indeed must be represented. No "Bilderverbot" for her. Comparisons are vital to who we are as human beings, or at least as poets. But she also rejects the very patriarchal religion that places Abraham and

Isaac on Mount Moriah. (Liebrand 2003, 110, 204) In *weiter leben* both concepts, the poetic and the father's voice, are elided.

Weiter leben is thus an answer to Adorno, who, it will be remembered left Germany in 1934 for Oxford, New York City, and finally became Mann's neighbor in Los Angeles. Can poetic language thus have another function besides evoking the aesthetic of *edle Einfalt, stille Größe*? Can it have a compensatory effect, providing a resource that may mask or perhaps moderate lived experience? Not the beautiful but the comforting; not "Bildung" but refuge. All of us read, if you like it, through the experience of being read to as children. The more terrifying the tales, the warmer and more comforting the lap upon which we sat. Even bad poems, crude stories, Kitsch are the stuff of nostalgia. For reading and remembering are linked to private spaces for all readers.

For Ruth the poetic is also a type of individual affective truth-telling:

> Und was sollen sich Leser oder Betrachter solcher Dokumente dabei denken? Gedichte sind eine bestimmte Art von Kritik am Leben und könnten ihnen beim Verstehen helfen. Warum sollen sie das nicht dürfen? Und was ist das überhaupt für ein Dürfen und Sollen? Ein moralisches, ein religiöses? Welchen Interessen dient es? Wer mischt sich hier ein? Das Thema wird brennender Dornbusch auf heiligem Boden, nur mit nackten Füßen und unterwürfiger Demut zu betreten. (Klüger 1992, 127)

We can thus dismiss reading as an act of piety or aesthetic experience. What we cannot do is to ignore the simple fact that reading *in extremis* is different. And doubly so, if we understand that while remembering one's reading may enable you to flee momentarily from the world in which you are to one in which you were, it also returns you at some moment to that brutal reality without escape.

In *weiter leben* Ruth also reads Primo Levi's reading in his immediate post-camp text *Se questo è un uomo* (1947). She, however, cites him not as a reader but as a (perhaps *the*) classic text that reveals through individual experience, the truth of the camps: "Das Autoritätsgebaren in Auschwitz war stets auf Aberkennung gerichtet, Ablehnung der menschlichen Existenz des Häftlings, seines oder ihres Rechts dazusein. Primo Levi hat das in seinem Buch "Ist das ein Mensch?" beschrieben." (Klüger 1992, 112) But the heart of *Se questo è un uomo*, like Ruth's reading of her early poems in *weiter leben*, deals with memory and the acts of reading more than anything else.

At the core of Levi's account is the chapter "The Canto of Ulysses" with its motto from Dante's *Inferno*: "*. . . fatti non foste a viver come bruti. Ma per seguir virtute e conoscenza. . . .*" The account is grim. A young French deportee, whom Levi baptized the Pikolo, the little one, shows up on morning in the IG Farben factory at Monowitz and is assigned with Levi to carry food to the outer reaches of the camp. To alleviate the boredom, Levi decides that to teach him Italian would be a task that might liberate them both, at least psychologically. He recalls the account of Ulysses' (Odysseus') punishment for betraying Troy through the trick of the Trojan horse as narrated by Dante in the eighth circle of Hell. "Who knows why or how it comes into my mind":

> Jean pays great attention, and I begin slowly and accurately . . . Here, listen Pikolo, open your ears and your mind, you have to understand, for my sake:
>
> *Think of your breed; for brutish ignorance*
> *Your mettle was not made; you were made men,*
> *To follow after knowledge and excellence*
>
> As if I also was hearing it for the first time: like the blast of a trumpet, like the voice of God. For a moment I forget who I am and where I am.
> . . . but still more, something gigantic that I myself have only just seen, in a flash of intuition, perhaps the reason for our fate, for our being here today. . . . Pikolo begs me to repeat it. How good Pikolo is, he is aware that it is doing me good. Or perhaps it is something more: perhaps, despite the wan translation and the pedestrian, rushed commentary, he has received the message, he has felt that it has to do with him, that it has to do with all men who toil, and with us in particular and that it has to do with us two, who dare to reason of these things with the poles for the soup on our shoulders.
>
> (Levi 1963, 113–14)

Can we, in our imagination, flash back to Levi's Jewish home in Turin during that Silver Age of Italian Jewry, as Stuart Hughes labeled it? (Hughes 1983) Levi's father, Cesare, a voracious reader; the family surrounded by books. Like the bourgeois Jewish families in Ruth's Vienna, perhaps there is a massive, gold-bound three volume set of Dante, with plates by Gustav Doré. Devoured by the chronically home-bound Primo, not only the text, but the terrifying images of Doré imprinted themselves on the child's imagination. Later reading Dante at the *Massimo d'Azeglio* Royal Gymnasium, the only Jewish student there, must have sealed this sense of the text as binding him to a culture that transcended everything else. (Gilman 1989)

More than a decade passes. Levi finds himself at a reunion of the few of his colleagues who had worked at Monowitz. "Jean" is there and Levi goes into detail about his meeting with the "Pikolo" in his *La tregua* (*The Reawakening*) of 1963. There is an appendix to the volume, basically a list of the people whose names appear in this memoir, including "Jean, the 'Pikolo' of the Canto of Ulysses, [who] is alive and well. His family had been wiped out. . . . Strange as it may seem, he has forgotten much of his year in Monowitz." (Levi 1963, 224) We learn much later that Jean Samuel had read Levi's chapter on Ulysses before its publication in 1947. (Samuel 2007) That is his "forgetting" in the early 1960s, prior to Levi's global fame, and his remembering Dante well after Levi's death in 1987, places reading and memory and poetry in the same flux of history.

Ruth notes too that she writes poetry "überall, wo ich war, Gedichte aufsagt und verfaßt. Viele KZ-Insassen haben Trost in den Versen gefunden, die sie auswendig wußten." (Klüger 1992, 123) But in Auschwitz she writes, she wrote two poems that she recited for the "Häftlinge, die nicht unbedingt davon erbaut waren." (Klüger 1992, 124) Poetry may promise redemption, but it is always read (or in the case of Ruth and Levi, heard) in a specific context that shapes the reader/listener's affect.

There is one more poetic name that appears in Ruth's text and that is Paul Celan, also a person of many names, AKA: Paul Antschel or Ancel or indeed earlier Paul Aurel, as a successful translator from Russian into Romanian; later as A. Pavel. (Roditi 1992, 13) (I discovered another "Paul Celan," when on board a freighter from Bremerhaven to Wilmington DE, I read a German translation of a Maigret novel translated by Paul Celan.) Ruth recounts that she was teaching in Göttingen and had mocked in a kind but critical manner the self-conscious artifice of his poetry. Parody is not permitted, a student shouted, there is something holy in such an approach: "Man solle eigentlich den Holocaust ausschliesslich mit solcher hermetischer Lyrik [of the late Celan] verarbeiten. Ich geb zu bedenken, dass diese Lyrik Vorkenntnisse vorrasusetzt, die sich nicht jeder aneignen kann. . . . Ich verfasste eine harmlose Parodie auf ein abstruses Gedicht von Celan. Leute, die ich noch nie schockiert habe, sind schockiert. Über Gott und Goethe darf man lästern, der Autor der "Todesfuge" is unantastbar. Und nicht etwa, weil er ein so guter Dichter ist, das war Goethe auch." (Klüger 1992, 126–7) This prefigures what has recently come to be the new "Historikerstreit." A. Dirk Moses, in *Geschichte der Gegenwart,* reframed this in an essay on the uniquely German "catechism" concerning the Holocaust, a new civic religion that forbids any discussion of the nature of German culpability and Jewish victimhood. In this he echoed not too obliquely the views of my late colleague and friend Peter Novick, concerning how the Holocaust among American Jews had become a "civic religion." Moses stressed that the German political elite believed that the Holocaust proved that German anti-Semitism was unique; that the special relationship with the State of Israel was foundational to a new moral Germany and that, therefore, anti-Zionism is de facto anti-Semitism. What Ruth found in her Celan seminar was a prefiguration of such views, views that dominated both of our interactions in teaching about the Holocaust in German-speaking lands. Sara R. Horowitz has noted: "Between verisimilitude and veracity yawns a wide gulf. . . . Unlike a bare chronology, which aspires to the facts as such, the literary text, in avowing its own artifice, rhetoricity, and contingent symbol-making – threatens to shift and ultimately destroy the grounds by which one measures one set of truth claims or one historical interpretation against another." (Horowitz 1997, 20) Names, too.

Bibliography

Abrams, M. H. *Natural Supernaturalism: Tradition and Revolution in Romantic Literature.* New York: W.W. Norton, 1973.

Angress, R. K. *The Early German Epigram: A Study in Baroque Poetry.* Lexington: University Press of Kentucky, 1971a.

Angress, R. K. "Interrogation in Wolfram's *Parzival*," The *German Quarterly*. 42, 1 (1969): 1–10.

Angress, R. K. "Kafka and Sacher-Masoch: A Note on *The Metamorphosis*." *MLN*, 85:5, German Issue (1970): 745–6.

Angress, R. K. "Dreams that were more than dreams' in Lessing's Nathan," *Lessing Yearbook* 3 (1971b): 108–27.

Angress, R. K. "'Weh dem, der lügt': Grillparzer and the Avoidance of Tragedy." *The Modern Language Review*, 66, 2 (1971c): 355–364.

Angress, R. K. "Das Gespenst in Grillparzers *Ahnfrau*," *The German Quarterly* 45, 4, Tribute to the Memory of Franz Grillparzer (1972): 606–619.

Angress, R. K. "A 'Jewish Problem' in German Postwar Fiction," *Modern Judaism* 5 (1985): 215–233.

Bering, Dietz. *Der Name als Stigma: Antisemitismus im deutschen Alltag 1812–1933.* Stuttgart: Klett-Cotta, 1987.

Bryant, William Cullen. (Ed.) *The Family Library of Poetry and Song.* New York: Fords, Howard and Hulbert, 1880.

Euler, Walter. *Ariel* 3. Darmstadt: Darmstädter Echo, 1956.

Gilman, Sander L. (Ed.) *Johannes Agricola, Die Sprichwörtersammlungen: Eine historisch-kritische Ausgabe.* 2 vols. Berlin: De Gruyter, 1971a.

Gilman, Sander L. *Form und Funktion: Eine strukturelle Untersuchung der Romane Klabunds.* Frankfurt a. M.: Athenaeum, 1971b.

Gilman, Sander L. "Friedrich von Hardenberg's Twelfth 'Geistliches Lied'." *Seminar* 6 (1970a): 225–236.

Gilman, Sander L. "A View of Kafka's Treatment of Actuality in *Die Verwandlung*." *Germanic Notes* 2 (1971c): 26–30.

Gilman, Sander L. "The Image of Slavery in Two Eighteenth-Century German Dramas." *Germanic Review* 45 (1970b): 26–40.

Gilman, Sander L. "Literature in German, 1933–1945." In Charles Burdick, et al. (Eds.) *Contemporary Germany.* Boulder, Colorado: Westview Press, 1984a, 276–297.

Gilman, Sander L. *Inscribing the Other.* Lincoln: University of Nebraska Press, 1991, 211–37.

Gilman, Sander L. (Ed.) *J. P. Eckermann: Aphorismen.* Berlin: Erich Schmidt, 1984b.

Gilman, Sander L. "To Quote Primo Levi: 'If You Don't Speak Yiddish, You're Not a Jew'." *Prooftexts* 9 (1989): 139–160.

Goebbels, Joseph. "Isidor." [August 15, 1927] *Der Angriff. Aufsätze aus der Kampfzeit* (Munich: Zentralverlag der NSDAP., 1935), 308–310.

Gothein, Marie. Trans. *John Keats. Leben und Werk.* Bd. 2. Halle: Max Niemeyer, 1897.

Groben, Margaret. *Friedrich Schlegels Entwicklung als Literarhistoriker und Kritiker*. Diss. Köln, 1934.

Heidelberger-Leonard, Irène. *Ruth Klüger. weiter leben; Eine Jugend: Interpretation*. Oldenbourg Interpretationen 81. Munich: Oldenbourg, 1996.

Heschel, Susannah. *The Aryan Jesus: Christian Theologians and the Bible in Nazi Germany*. Princeton: Princeton University Press, 2008.

Horowitz, Sara R. *Voicing the Void: Muteness and Memory in Holocaust Literature*. Albany: State University of New York Press, 1997.

Hughes, H. Stuart. *Prisoners of Hope: The Silver Age of the Italian Jews, 1924–1974*. Cambridge: Harvard University Press, 1983.

Kant, Immanuel. "'Toward Perpetual Peace' in Practical Philosophy." In: *Cambridge Edition of the Works of Immanuel Kant*. Eds. Günter Zöller and Robert B. Louden. Cambridge: Cambridge University Press, 1999, 107–120.

Klüger, Ruth. *weiter leben: Eine Jugend*. Göttingen: Wallstein, 1992.

Klüger, Ruth. *Still Alive. A Holocaust Girlhood Remembered*. New York: Feminist Press at the City University of New York, 2001.

Klüger, Ruth. *Von hoher und niedriger Literatur*. Gottingen: Wallstein, 1996.

Lezzi, Eva. *Zerstörte Kindheit: Literarische Autobiographien zur Shoah*. Cologne: Böhlau, 2001.

Levi, Primo. *Survival in Auschwitz: If this is a Man?* Trans. Stuart Woolf. New York: Collier, 1959.

Levi, Primo. *The Reawakening*, Trans. Stuart Woolf. New York: Little and Brown, 1963.

Liebrand, Claudia. "'Das Trauma der Auschwitzer Wochen in ein Versmaß stülpen' oder: Gedichte als Exorzismus; Ruth Klügers *weiter leben*." In *Jüdische Intellektuelle im 20. Jahrhundert: Literatur- und kulturgeschichtliche Studien*. Eds. Ariane Huml and Monika Rappenecker. Würzburg: Königshausen & Neumann, 2003, 237–48.

Moses, A. Dirk. "The German Catechism," *Geschichte der Gegenwart* https://geschichtedergegenwart.ch/the-german-catechism/

Nader, Andrés José. Emergency Poetry: Lyric Production in the Concentration Camps. Diss. Cornell 1999.

Nader, Andrés José. *Traumatic Verses: On Poetry in German from the Concentration Camps, 1933–1945*. Rochester, N.Y.: Camden House, 2010.

Novick, Peter. *The Holocaust in American Life*. Boston: Houghton Mifflin, 1999.

Sander, Gabriele. "'. . . A Banner I Could Not Hold Aloft': Alfred Döblin and Judaism." *European Judaism: A Journal for the New Europe* 34, 1 (2001): 94–113.

Roditi, Edouard. "Paul Celan and the Cult of Personality." *World Literature Today*, 66, 1 (1992): 11–20.

Schaumann, Caroline. "Remembering Nazi Germany: Trauma and Testimony." Diss. University of California, Davis, 1994.

Schlösser, Manfred. (Ed.) *An den Wind geschrieben: Lyrik der Freiheit, 1933– 1945*. Darmstadt: Agorà, 1960.

Seydel, Heinz. (Ed.) *Welch Wort in die Kälte gerufen: Die Judenverfolgung des Dritten Reiches im deutschen Gedicht*. Berlin: Verlag der Nation, 1968.

Samuel, Jean. *Il m'appelait Pikolo. Un compagnon de Primo Levi raconte*. Paris: Laffont, 2007.

Heinrich Detering

Spannung: Remarks on a Stylistic Principle in Ruth Klüger's Writing

Spannung as Wordplay

"Authors speak one language, we another, they are saturated by their and we by our experiences, with their books they throw us a rope, pulling on the one end, we on the other, the tension is suspended between us." (Klüger 1994, 7)[1] It would be hard for anyone to resist being enchanted by a Ruth Klüger sentence such as this one. And for those who are even remotely familiar with her work, her style of writing and thinking is instantly recognizable. Pithy and witty, vivid and inviting, the sentence sparks the reader's curiosity for what is to come.

In an essay originally published in 1957, Richard Alewyn, a master in the analysis of literary style, practically demonstrated what Roland Barthes would proclaim in 1974 at the beginning of *S/Z*: "There are said to be certain Buddhists whose ascetic practices enable them to see a whole landscape in a bean." (Barthes 1990, 3) In "Eine Landschaft Eichendorffs" [An Eichendorff Landscape], Alewyn examined a single sentence that is representative of the poet and writer's landscape portrayals, led by the assumption: "that Eichendorff's landscapes are simply composed of varying combinations of a limited number of elements, in short, that they are nothing more than modifications based on a single proto-landscape which serves as background to his narratives and is ever-present like soft music." (Alewyn 1982, 205f.)

If this observation is accurate, a single landscape depiction – even a single sentence surveying the landscape – would suffice to expose the fundamental features of the landscape pattern. Alewyn found this particular sentence in a lesser-known novella; he may have considered others, but this particular one paves the way to the desired points of exploration as well as any other might have.

Following his example, I will attempt to expose the poetics in the work of literary scholar and critic Ruth Klüger using the sentence quoted at the start. My

---

1 Unless an English-language source is cited, translations were made for this publication. This particular translation is kept purposefully close to the original.

(Translated by Ingrid Lezar)

https://doi.org/10.1515/9783110793239-003

choice is however not as random as Alewyn's, because the sentence concludes the first passage in *Katastrophen: Über deutsche Literatur* (1994), Klüger's first book of essays, which was published two years after the international success of her autobiography *weiter leben*. And it is – in my estimation – the most programmatically articulated sentence in all of her literary theory or criticism. This is how the collection opens:

> That which a treasured or even just somewhat stimulating book says is not the same thing as what "the author wants to tell us." Each of us has our own language, and these languages are as varied as our handwriting and our fingerprints. Authors speak one language, we another. They are saturated by their and we by our experiences. With their books they throw us a rope, pulling on the one end, we on the other. The tension is suspended between us.
> (Klüger 1994, 7)[2]

The final sentence will be considered here as exemplary of Ruth Klüger's literary-theoretical style. Its suspended syntax delivers the high point and conclusion to the passage – both in what it says and in how it says it.

We are clearly dealing here with a hermeneutic principle that is described as a hermeneutic *event*. Ruth Klüger captures the event in a pithy metaphor that does not stop at telling the reader something – it simultaneously shows it, by describing a language-based occurrence through playing with language itself. The metaphor thus operates self-reflexively. The wordplay is of course based on the convergence of an everyday image from the world we know; in a tug-of-war the rope is pulled taut, and we have tension or "Spannung." It is a term from literary theory, "Spannung," in the sense of tension or suspense. Working backwards from the ambiguity established in this word, we can reinterpret the preceding figurative elements as a metaphorical explication of a particular phenomenon in the study of literature. The image of a tug-of-war thus takes the ambiguity in the "Spannung" pun to literally pull a whole series of terms through defamiliarization into new perspective: book, writer, wanting-to-say, and saying, authors, language, experience, tension, and suspense.

In so doing, the sentence follows a stylistic principle that was developed during the Enlightenment, termed by Paul Böckmann in his classic essay as the "Formprinzip des Witzes." This formal principle of the *Witz* is based on the

---

2 "Was uns ein geliebtes oder auch ein nur anregendes Buch sagt, ist nicht dasselbe wie das, was 'der Dichter uns sagen will.' Wir haben jeder und jede unsere eigene Sprache, und diese Sprachen sind so unterschiedlich wie die Handschriften und die Fingerabdrücke. Die Autoren sprechen eine Sprache, wir eine andere, sie sind gesättigt von ihren, wir von unseren Erfahrungen, sie werfen uns mit ihren Büchern ein Seil zu und ziehen an dessen einem Ende, wir am anderen, zwischen uns ist die Spannung."

historical double meaning of the word: as a playful punchline (joke) and a surprising insight (wit). In demonstrating what it describes, the sentence also takes to heart Horace's call for poetry to instruct as it delights and delight as it instructs.

Spannung as Hermeneutic Event

But how does the hermeneutic event, encapsulated in this manner, unfold? It takes place between two languages and two sets of experiences, both of which are tied to their respective individual subjects. If texts are born from a particular set of experiences just as much as they are from a particular language, which Ruth Klüger's assumption seems to hold as self-evident, then individual subjectivity comes to the fore as the driving force in the creation of texts and as the mediator of interpersonal contexts and literary texts. Accordingly, the sentence manages to express the converse of both an exclusively formalistic and an exclusively culturalistic conception of literature. At the same time, as is demonstrated with this book and its opening remarks, she construes the work of literary theory as conducting a reading just as it would have been done before the existence of the academic discipline, though with the simple yet crucial addition of critically reflecting on one's methods. The form of the literary criticism essay occupies a transitional space between regular reading and literary theory as an academic discipline. The aim is neither to analyze formal characteristics, regularities, or irregularities in a text, nor to reconstruct the active discourses, narratives, or social conditions that played a part in constructing the text and were written into it. Rather the goal is to comprehend such characteristics and conditions in the ontological mode of an author-subject's experiences, whose individuality shows itself in a text just like "handwriting" and "fingerprints."

This individuality that the author brings to the text is however not the same thing as controlling the work as a whole. Because, as has been posited, "that which a treasured or even just somewhat stimulating book says is not the same thing as what 'the author wants to tell us.'" Indeed, from the following sentence, through a change that almost seems to have been made merely in passing, the subjects involved are constituted quite differently. We are no longer dealing with only a single writer and a single reader. Now we have groups, formed around a common language and common experiences, which could include shared gender, cultural, ethnic, or other identities: "Authors [plural] speak one language [singular], we another." The "us" in the statement – "the tension is suspended between us" – does not denote individuals; rather it denotes groups, two distinct communities with a shared language and shared experiences.

Ruth Klüger thus not only (but also) poses the question of what the author deliberately wants to say. Beyond that, she also asks what the author actually says. At the intersection of these arguments we can clearly see connections to the cultural and socio-historical but especially the psychoanalytic[3] and gender-theoretical considerations (especially in the aforementioned collections *Frauen lesen anders* and *Gemalte Fenster* as well as in the collected literary criticism columns *Was Frauen schreiben*) that play such an important role in Ruth Klüger's writings as a whole. Moreover, we are able to trace her study of aesthetic form in poetry (collected in Klüger 2007 and 2018).

There is a charged relationship between the experiences an author intentionally or unintentionally articulates in the text and the experiences of the readers. If the tension in this relationship sparks competition between the two sides, it can only be ascribed to the fact that the different sets of experiences are each tied to a respective *worldview* that must be enforced or defended. The text as the tug-of-war rope first *brings together* both groups but then sets them against each other in pull and counter-pull, the movements drawing both sides into a *reciprocal change in position* (and thereby a shift in perspective).

If we have not made the observation yet, at this point we can certainly see that Ruth Klüger's sentence is a pointed dialectical expression of what Schleiermacher's lectures on *Hermeneutics and Criticism* explore in more detail. Indeed, in the introduction to a contemporary German-language edition of these lectures, Manfred Frank proposed that this method could be adopted to mediate between hermeneutic and (post) structuralist approaches to texts. (Frank 1977, 63)[4] Schleiermacher lays out one of his central considerations as follows:

> As every utterance has a dual relationship, to the totality of language and to the whole thought of its originator, then all understanding also consists of the two moments, of understanding the utterance as derived from language, and as a fact in the thinker. . . .

---

3 To name only a few examples: in her Hofmannsthal lecture on *Freuds Ödipus*; in her essays on Heinrich von Kleist (Klüger 1994, 133–162, and Klüger 1996, 129–176) and on Adalbert Stifter (Klüger 1994, 107–132); in her essay on Else Lasker-Schüler, Nelly Sachs, and Gertrud Kolmar (Klüger 2007, 198–227); or in her essays on Erich Kästner, Grimmelshausen, and Goethe. (Klüger 2007, 63–82, 185–190, 105–128)

4 According to Manfred Frank in his detailed introduction, Schleiermacher's work "especially in the current situation, marked by a fruitless dispute over methods, namely structuralist versus hermeneutic language-analysis categories of interpretation" proves to be "a highly topical approach."

> According to this every person is on the one hand a location in which a given language forms itself in an individual manner, on the other their discourse can only be understood via the totality of the language. But then the person is also a spirit which continually develops, and their discourse is only one act of this spirit in connection with the other acts.
>
> (Schleiermacher 1998, 8–9)

And this is exactly how I understand the reading process in Ruth Klüger's sentence. On one hand, it is the movement of an agent-like language through the *places* the individuals involved can be comprehended as (what the text "says" is different from what the author "wants to tell us"). On the other hand, it is a contest between people, each person "has" their respective language, for enforcing the worldview conceived within it. I think it would not be going too far to make the observation that this dialectic reflects Ruth Klüger's experience of engaging with European and American literary theory in the 1990s: hermeneutic subjectivity (and with it the concept of "interpretation") being asserted on the one hand, while simultaneously being questioned by post-structuralism on the other.

Understood in this manner, the suspenseful hermeneutic event as a tug-of-war is simultaneously agonistic and *amorous*; the competition has the features of amorous play. But rather than fully and finally asserting an entrenched worldview, the goal of the event is to enjoy the thrill of competing for its own sake. The book that is being read starts off by throwing the end of the rope as a challenge to be pulled against, as an invitation to relish an agonistic *togetherness*. "We" accept the invitation, if we feel amorous (or at least somewhat stimulated). The hermeneutic tug-of-war parallels, astonishingly closely, another encounter in two of Ruth Klüger's essays – also dialectically linked – on Kleist's *Penthesilea* and *Das Käthchen von Heilbronn*. In these essays she portrays a struggle for love, fought with a wide variety of means, including "Küsse, Bisse" – kisses [and] bites. (Klüger 1996, 129–156 and 157–176; cf. Klüger 1982)

In another logically consistent move, tension also determines the flow in Ruth Klüger's sentence. Syntactically we are actually faced with four sentences, and it is only through the punctuation choices that we arrive at a single rhetorical unit. The effect this achieves becomes clear if we experiment (as per Ruth Klüger's suggestion[5]) with doing the exact opposite:

---

5 In one of her essays on Kleist, she experimentally switched the names in the first sentence of Kleist's *Die Verlobung in St. Domingo* with the names of the protagonists in his work "Die Hermannschlacht." (Klüger 1994, 142)

> Authors speak one language, we another. They are saturated by their and we by our experiences. With their books they throw us a rope, pulling on the one end, we on the other. The tension is suspended between us.

This succession of sentences resembles a syllogism. What happens in the third sentence follows from the preconditions in the first two sentences, before the fourth sentence concludes by naming the phenomenon in our midst: "Spannung." The words make a rather different impact when the four sentences are punctuated as one:

> Authors speak one language, we another, they are saturated by their and we by our experiences, with their books they throw us a rope, pulling on the one end, we on the other, the tension is suspended between us.

Here the stylistic principle is not determined by a string of separately stated facts but by the dynamics of a single, flowing, uninterrupted event.

Spannung and Essayistic Tradition

The texts of literary theory that are born out of such an understanding of the hermeneutic event, that is to say brought into being as both record and result of the process, will not claim to be "academic" in the conventional sense; indeed, they emphasize the subjective involvement of the theorist instead. Ruth Klüger's metaphorical explanation of hermeneutics outlines the principles of an academic style that is essayistic *as such*.

Anyone who pages through her writings on literature will quickly notice that her contributions occupy a liminal space between literary theory and literary criticism. This is clear, first of all, from the topics she wrote on and the places she published. After she completed her dissertation on Baroque epigrams, Ruth Klüger did not produce any additional real monographs; her books that followed were collections of shorter essays centered around a theme. A few of the texts first appeared as articles or contributions in journals and anthologies, some were originally public lectures, but most were written as literary criticism for newspapers and journals.

Given these external conditions, her texts largely do without discussions of secondary literature or footnotes, though without sacrificing any air of learned expertise. At the end of her foundational essay, "Gegenströmung: Schreibende Frauen. Entwurf einer alternativen Literaturgeschichte," first published in 1990, Ruth Klüger explicitly gives a reason for this choice. (Klüger 1996, 220–234) This essay, like most of her others, contained no academic references or remarks in notes. However, in this case, under the heading "Statt Anmerkungen" [In lieu of notes], she explained her reasons in small print. The note closes the collection *Frauen lesen anders*, and it continues what the opening passage in *Katastrophen* had initiated. It is a concise poetic reflection on a literary theory that conducts itself in an essayistic manner:

> *In lieu of notes.* This text is the result of considerations that have emerged over many years of engaging with German literature. Therefore they are not "findings" in the strict sense of the word. The facts on which they are based . . . are familiar to me and others with extensive knowledge of German literature and can be verified in common reference works. For this reason I find it incongruous to take the thoughts presented here – intended to prompt contemplation and provoke counterargument – and disfigure them with the use of a "device." (Klüger 1996, 234)

This note, too, implies the making of decisions with far-reaching consequences, and it, too, does so in a succinct compression that exemplifies what it means to say. First, it assumes an opposition between "'findings' in the strict sense of the word" and "considerations that have emerged over many years of engaging with German literature." The argumentation is not based on secondary literature but grounded in having *expertise*, which connects Ruth Klüger with the aforementioned "others with extensive knowledge of German literature." Second, the note sees the essence of the considerations in their purpose to express thoughts that "prompt contemplation and provoke counterargument." And third, she expects a text of this nature to be able to make an *aesthetic impact*. If footnotes could do no more than serve as a "device" that would "disfigure" the text, the reverse argument must be that the text is finer and more accessible without them. "Device," set in quotation marks, takes the place of the aforementioned "notes." The polemical difference lies in the free, flexible, lively communication that "notes" as well as "considerations" imply, whereas "device" implies a stiff, rigid, lifeless machine. In this seemingly incidental yet far-reaching differentiation of terms, "findings" and "device" go together on the one hand, while "considerations" and "thoughts" or "contemplation" and "counterargument" go together on the other. The aesthetic impact she calls for (which a device would "disfigure") is apparently the exact characteristic of the text that enables it to prompt contemplation and provoke counterargument.

And here, like before, she takes up the same hermeneutic dialectic. Whereas a device predictably produces that which it was made to produce, it is natural for thoughts and considerations to "emerge" throughout the course of "engaging" with texts. That is to say: a connecting third element arises between text and reading, and it takes on an unpredictable, vital dynamic life of its own. And Ruth

Klüger's book, too, may say something different from what "the author wants to tell us."

The principle, according to which Ruth Klüger's thoughts are intended "to prompt contemplation and provoke counterargument," repeats word-for-word in 1990 what she had written three years prior in an essay on Kleist's relationship to the Enlightenment. (Klüger 1994, 163–188) There it had sprung from a comparison of such provocatively inhumane texts as Kleist's *Germania an ihre Kinder* with the nationalistic poems of Theodor Körner. Klüger claims in an accusatory manner that Körner's verse "does not prompt contemplation, nevermind provoke counterargument." (Klüger 1994, 183) According to her analysis, Kleist's outrageous verse does this purposefully:

> It is not the poet who speaks, it is Germania. The speaker and the poet are not identical even in a fictional sense, and the degree of agreement necessarily remains questionable in such cases. Kleist's anti-French position thus directly assumes an indignant, Enlightenment-minded reader. (Klüger 1994, 182)

His text throws this reader a rope, pulls on the one end, while the indignant, enlightened reader pulls on the other end, and the tension is suspended between them. Provoking counterargument is, as "an alternative to Schiller's all-encompassing idealism," indeed "a challenge" or even "a declaration of war": "Who was the provocation aimed at? A public who had grown used to the rhetoric of eternal peace and understanding among nations." (Klüger 1994, 182)

In adopting the sentence originally applied to Kleist's writing in justifying decisions made in her own work, Ruth Klüger takes up the tension between fierce provocation and enlightened indignation as a perfect example for the tension that she wishes to emerge once more between her own essays and those who read them.

Should alternative viewpoints and provocation not automatically yield an agonistic constellation, Ruth Klüger's texts stir it up explicitly and with rhetorical verve. Faced with a book emblazoned with a thesis statement as its title, she questions this very thesis right at the start. Similarly, in the first line of the collection *Frauen lesen anders* [Women read differently] (1996), she asks: "Do women read differently? Yes, but in what way?" (Klüger 1996, 7) The title essay, located in the middle of the collection, starts by rationalizing the thesis: "Books have a different effect on women compared to men." However, after twenty pages, it reads: "And thus the title of this essay is perhaps false, because. . . ." (Klüger 1996, 83 and 103) The point here is not the content of the argument but its form: the ultimate result of the discussion is a critique of its original premise.

This is the only time that I have understood Ruth Klüger herself to describe this method in dialectical terms. Had she opted for an alternate title, namely the thesis "Men read differently," this would have been "the same thesis in the guise of an antithesis." Thus: "Synthesis may be a long time coming." She closes the book with this sentence, akin to an appeal to readers to follow the example of Brecht's theater audience and figure out their own ending.

Spannung as Ethos

In the second part of her autobiographical work *weiter leben*, translated (and partly rewritten) by the author as *Still Alive*, Ruth Klüger describes a breakdown in conversation:

> During a discussion with some youngsters in Germany I am asked (as if it was a genuine question and not an accusation) whether I don't think that the Jews have turned into Nazis in their dealings with the Arabs, and haven't the Americans always acted like Nazis in their dealings with the Indians? When it gets that aggressive and simple, I just sputter. Or I sit in the student cafeteria with some advanced Ph.D. candidates, and one reports how in Jerusalem he made the acquaintance of an old Hungarian Jew who was a survivor of Auschwitz, and yet this man cursed the Arabs and held them all in contempt. How can someone who comes from Auschwitz talk like that? the German asks. I get into the act and argue, perhaps more hotly than need be. What did he expect? Auschwitz was not an instructional institution . . . . You learned nothing there, and least of all humanity and tolerance. . . . No one agrees, and no one contradicts me. . . . Germany's young intellectuals bow their heads over their soup plates and eat what's in front of them. Now I have silenced them, and that wasn't my intention. There is always a wall between the generations, but here the wall is barbed wire. Old, rusty barbed wire.   (Klüger 2001, 65)

This is a key passage in the book, because it makes a plea for continuing the conversation through walls and barbed wire. But if her counterpart has been silenced, how can communication proceed? Her answer follows the previously quoted passage: "And yet they could easily have objected. Don't I often insist that" – and then she formulates objections against herself. (Klüger 2001, 65) Elsewhere in the same book she remarks, ". . . instead of God I believe in ghosts. To conjure up the dead you have to dangle the bait of the present before them, the flesh of the living, to coax them out of their inertia." (Klüger 2001, 69) This is a different version of Ruth Klüger's *Spannung* poetics – here not as a maxim that guides the act of reading, but as an ethos that can be applied to everyday life. This is formulated as an appeal to the reader in the middle of *weiter leben* (only in the German version):

> You needn't relate to me; in fact, I would prefer if you didn't . . . . But let yourselves at the very least be provoked, don't hide away, don't start out by saying it doesn't concern

you or it only concerns you within a neatly defined . . . framework . . . . Seek out argument, enter into confrontation. (Klüger 1992, 141)[6]

In such explicit reflections and in tiny performative details – like an interjecting
question dashed off to the reader ("But hadn't I been in a quandary?", Klüger
2001, 49) – *Still Alive* also means not letting the rope fray in the tug-of-war of
conversation. And here at last we can see why the hermeneutic battle was
styled as an amorous act. Both variations of the *Spannung*-concept operate in
this manner, because "reason . . . is the greatest of all goods, except love. Reason is a way of turning towards the world, even as love is." (Klüger 2001, 141)
Reason, which is realized in a communicative practice that is agonistic by necessity, is revealed to be – just as in Ruth Klüger's essayistic discussion of Lessing (Klüger 1994, 189–227) – an analog of love.

This ethos may be considered central not only to *Still Alive* but also to Ruth
Klüger's books of literary criticism.[7] It was there in the opening sentence of her
first essay collection, revealing itself as a basic yet fundamental stylistic principle: "Authors speak one language, we another, they are saturated by their and
we by our experiences, with their books they throw us a rope, pulling on the
one end, we on the other, the tension is suspended between us."

Bibliography

Alewyn, Richard. "Eine Landschaft Eichendorffs." In: Richard Alewyn, *Probleme und Gestalten: Essays*. Frankfurt am Main: Insel [1957] 1982, 203–231.
Barthes, Roland. *S/Z*. Transl. Richard Miller. Oxford: Blackwell [1974], 1990.
Böckmann, Paul. "Das Formprinzip des Witzes in der Frühzeit der deutschen Aufklärung." *Jahrbuch des freien deutschen Hochstifts* 1932/33: 52–130.
Frank, Manfred. "Einleitung." F. D. E. Schleiermacher. In: *Hermeneutik und Kritik: Mit einem Anhang sprachphilosophischer Texte Schleiermachers*. Ed. Manfred Frank. Frankfurt am Main: Suhrkamp, 1977, 7–67.
Klüger, Ruth. *Frauen lesen anders*. Munich: dtv, 1996.
Klüger, Ruth. "Kleist's Nation of Amazons." In *Beyond the Eternal Feminine: Critical Essays on Women and German Literature*, Ed. Susan L. Cocalis and Kay Goodman. Stuttgart: Akademischer Verlag Hans-Dieter Heinz, 1982, 99–134.

---

6 This passage is not included in the English translation of the book.
7 It seems only logical that Ruth Klüger would also subject her own poems to a reading aimed
at sparking contemplation and counterargument. The collection *Zerreißproben* is an impressive documentation of this – indeed explicitly considering that "we shy away from" the process, and thus, "I want to break this taboo now and set an example with the interpretation of
my own verse." (Klüger 2013, 9)

Klüger, Ruth. *weiter leben: Eine Jugend*. Göttingen: Wallstein, 1992.

Klüger, Ruth. *Katastrophen: Über deutsche Literatur*. Göttingen: Wallstein, 1994.

Klüger, Ruth. *Freuds Ödipus im androgynen Rosenkavalier*. Vienna: Picus, 2012.

Klüger, Ruth. *Still Alive: A Holocaust Girlhood Remembered*. New York: The Feminist Press at the City University of New York, 2001.

Klüger, Ruth. *Gemalte Fensterscheiben: Über Lyrik*. Göttingen: Wallstein, 2007.

Klüger, Ruth. *Was Frauen schreiben*. Vienna: Zsolnay, 2010.

Klüger, Ruth. *Zerreißproben: Kommentierte Gedichte*. Vienna: Zsolnay, 2013.

Klüger, Ruth. *Gegenwind: Gedichte und Interpretationen*. Vienna: Zsolnay, 2018.

Schleiermacher, Friedrich. *Hermeneutics and Criticsm: And Other Writings*. Trans. and Ed. Andrew Bowie. Cambridge: Cambridge University Press, 1998.

Stephan Braese
Speaking with Germans: Ruth Klüger and the "Restitution of Speech between Germans and Jews"

After their liberation from the concentration and death camps, many of the formerly incarcerated saw themselves confronted with an imperative that aided some of them in their struggle to survive, namely, to bear witness and to give testimony to the world about what had occurred in those places. Texts that would later be termed "Holocaust Literature" were subsequently published. They were written in the languages of all of those countries that had been invaded and occupied by Germans, that is in the languages of all of those people whom the Germans had condemned to forced labor and annihilation. Viewed from a *global* perspective provided by the historical gravity of the crimes that had been revealed, literature bearing witness to them in the *German* language initially must have appeared to be somewhat superfluous. This was the language of the perpetrators. A demand on the part of the perpetrators to assess their own deeds seemed paradoxical. The former prisoners had observed too many Germans who were complicit – particularly outside of the camps. As eyewitnesses and as bystanders, they had viewed the degradation and the systematic destruction of the victims, and subsequently there should have been no need among Germans for a literature exposing the crimes. The presumption that the Germans had known nothing about what occurred appeared absurd. In point of fact, however, the persons liberated from the camps as well as the first to repatriate from exile ran into precisely the paradox that Hermann Kesten put into these words in 1947: "A people that wants to pardon itself by claiming it didn't know it had slaughtered six million Jews." (Kesten 1975, 255)

In the immediate aftermath of the war, denial expressed by the perpetrators was not the only sort of reaction to the crimes that could be registered. Looking back from 1959, George Steiner assessed:

> In the three years immediately following the end of the war, many Germans tried to arrive at a realistic insight into the events of the Hitler era. [. . .] Returned soldiers admitted to something of what the occupation of Norway or Poland or France or Yugoslavia had been like – the mass shootings of hostages, the torture, the looting. The churches raised their voice. It was a period of moral scrutiny and grief. Words were spoken that had not been pronounced in twelve years. (Steiner 1979, 148)

(Translation from German: Timothy K. Boyd)

https://doi.org/10.1515/9783110793239-004

Yet, opposing voices which were in contrast to this rather encouraging percep-tion remained undiminished. One example is Alfred Andersch, who declared in the periodical *Der Ruf* in 1946: "The combatants of Stalingrad, El Alamein and Cassino, who were granted respect even by their opponents, are innocent with regard to the crimes of Dachau and Buchenwald." (Andersch 1946a) In that same year, referring to the bombings and stripping of factories, to prisoners of war and displacement, Andersch declared "that the German ledger of guilt [was] gradually beginning to close." (Andersch 1946b) The manner in which such atti-tudes ultimately prevailed over "realistic insight into the event" (Steiner) was ex-perienced with excruciating clarity by Jean Améry and Primo Levi. In 1958, Améry was informed by a southern German salesman during "breakfast in a hotel" (and "not without the prior polite inquiry, whether [he] was an Israelite") that "the German people [. . .] held nothing against the Jewish [people]; as evi-dence [the salesman] mentioned the generous reparation politics of the govern-ment." (Améry 1988, 86) In 1962 Levi was struck by a reader's reaction to the first German edition of "Survival in Auschwitz." In a letter to the editor, "Dr. T.H. of Hamburg" (Levi 1989, 175)[1] wrote: "Germany deservedly counted as the country most friendly to the Jews in the entire world. Never, so far as I know and have read, during the Hitlerian period until its very end, did one ever hear of a single case of spontaneous outrage or aggression against a Jew. Always only (very dan-gerous) attempts to help." (Levi 1989, 177) The reader closed his letter with a phrase that he doubtlessly considered to be reconciliatory: "Dear Dr. Levi (I take the liberty to address you like this, because anyone who has read your book can-not hold you dear), I have no excuses. I have no explanations. The guilt weighs heavily on my poor betrayed and misguided people." (Levi 1989, 177) There is no question that the Germans perceived themselves, as Améry noted, "by all means as a people of victims (Opfervolk)." (Améry 1988, 85)

Manifold strategies of denial and displacement among Germans were not the only things at odds with the possibility of engaging with them in dialogue about their most recent past. The German language itself represented a formi-dable barrier. As the language in which the mass crimes had been conceived and executed it had itself become an idiom of the destruction per se. It became an idiom that lived on as quotes in italics in the written accounts of survivors, for whom understanding it had become a matter of survival from one moment to the next: *"Marschmarsch!"*, *"Oberscharführer"*, *"Rampe"* etc. (Braese 1998, 7)

---

1 In the German edition the reference is to "Dr. H. T. aus Hamburg"; it seems that the initials were mistakenly reversed in the American edition. See Primo Levi, *Die Untergegangenen und die Geretteten*. Trans. From Italian, Moshe Kahn (München: Hanser 1990), 180.

As early as 1945, Dolf Sternberger, Gerhard Storz, and W.E. Süskind brought attention to the extensive contamination of the German language owing to the broadly based language politics of the Nazis in a series of articles for the periodical *Die Wandlung*. These articles were collected and published in 1957 under the title *Aus dem Wörterbuch des Unmenschen* (From the Dictionary of the Inhuman).

Victor Klemperer, who, like Sternberger, Storz, and Süskind had also witnessed these changes of language first-hand over the full twelve years of the Nazi dictatorship in Germany (although under completely different conditions) also determined in 1946 that

> [. . .] Nazism permeated the flesh and blood of the people through single words, idioms and sentence structures which were imposed on them in a million repetitions and taken on board mechanically and unconsciously. [. . .] language does not simply write and think for me, it also increasingly dictates my feelings and governs my entire spiritual being the more unquestioningly and unconsciously I abandon myself to it.
>
> (Klemperer 2008, 14)

He also ascertained, that " [. . .] it appears that the language of the Third Reich [may] survive in the form of certain characteristic expressions; they have lodged themselves so deep below the surface that they appear to be becoming a permanent feature of the German language." (Klemperer 2008, 14)

Perceptive contemporaries quickly recognized that Nazi language politics would also have a far-reaching impact on German literature. In 1947 Heinrich Mann introduced a "German reader" comprised of texts from three centuries with the words: "No deception! Whoever once wrote in German acquired a German reputation and was taken together in the company of all Germans, without exception, to Kiev and to Majdanek." (Mann 1947, 19) Mann – who refers here to the massacre at Babi Yar with the word "Kiev" – was presumably thinking more about the incalculable loss of prestige that the onetime language of the country of poets and thinkers suffered than about the concrete degradation that George Steiner observed in examining the first output of post-war German literature in 1959:

> Languages have great reserves of life. They can absorb masses of hysteria, illiteracy and cheapness. [. . .] But there comes a breaking point. Use a language to conceive, organize, and justify Belsen; use it to make out specifications for gas ovens; use it to dehumanize man during twelve years of calculated bestiality. Something will happen to it. [. . .] Everything forgets. But not a language. When it has been injected with falsehood, only the most drastic truth can cleanse it. Instead, the post-war history of the German language has been one of dissimulation and deliberate forgetting. The remembrance of horrors past has been largely uprooted. But at a high cost. And German literature is paying it right now. (Steiner 1979, 150–151)

All of these circumstances – as extensively as German Studies has attempted to disclose and comprehend them – must be kept in mind, if we want to try to comprehend what "speaking with Germans" actually entails. Ruth Klüger made her first attempt at this in the summer of 1945, when she was yet to turn fourteen years old. She discovered in a southern German newspaper "the first official reports about the liberated concentration camps," (Klüger 2003, 154)[2] and she decided to send two poems about Auschwitz to the newspaper. Weeks later she learned that something of hers seemed to have been printed and she quickly found out "where [she] could get a copy." (Klüger 2003, 154) What Klüger describes in *weiter leben* about what followed accentuates what "speaking with Germans" meant in the summer of 1945:

> Tanned and happy I jumped off my bike at the address he had indicated. House and garden belonged to one of the natives whose faces turned to stone when they saw a Jew. With the joy of a freshly printed author I asked him for the paper. He thrust it at me: "So that's you," he said, with a look as if my appearance and my allegedly horrendous past didn't gel. "You can keep it," he added, not so much giving me a present as removing some seemingly malodorous thing from his home. – Instead of a modest column I found half a page that dealt with me. In the middle was a photo of my cover letter, which had been carefully ripped, so that the jagged edges, together with the awkward handwriting of a girl who hadn't spent much time in school, evoked the impression of an emergency SOS, a kind of message in a bottle. To make matters worse, they had added a drawing of a ragged, terrorized child, who accidentally happened to look a little like me. What I minded most was that they had eviscerated my poetic output without asking, omitting one poem altogether and printing only two stanzas of the other, and these two were embedded in a maudlin, hand-wringing text, in effect asking the public for pity. Now I understood the man's reaction to the girl poet.   (Klüger 2003, 154)

This episode not only illustrates the "inner aversion to unpleasant truths" (*Neue Welt* 1948) that many survivors encountered ubiquitously, but also a widespread reaction among editors with the well-meaning intention of appealing "not primarily to the intellect, but to sentiment and feeling." (*Neue Welt* 1948) The Archimedian point from which such managing of affects was nonchalantly applied was the invocation of unquestionable innocence as embodied in a child, ideally a female child. The success that "The Diary of Anne Frank" achieved soon thereafter – in West Germany primarily by way of theater performances – drew decisively from this factor. (See Loewy 1998, 19–41)

---

2 This essay examines the German reception of *weiter leben*. The American publication *Still Alive* is not identical to *weiter leben*; in some cases they differ by entire passages. *Still Alive* is directly quoted here whenever the text remains very close to the wording of *weiter leben*. All other quotations are translations by Timothy Kyle Boyd.

The first publication of Klüger's poems – only a fragment is extracted, framed by a letter, a drawing and an editorial statement – operates with this disposition of the audience in mind. The rededication along these lines led Klüger to comment: "I wanted to be a young poet who had been in the camps, not a former child prisoner who had written some heart-wrenching verses." (Klüger 2003, 155)[3] In consequence, Klüger's departure from Germany two years later was linked to a decision "to never speak German again."(Klüger/ Radisch 2015, 52)

Klüger did, however, end up attempting to address Germans in a literary fashion about forty-seven years later with her bestseller, *weiter leben,* the "German book" (Klüger 1992, 2) that was dedicated to her "friends in Göttingen." (Klüger 1992, 285) The situation in which *weiter leben* emerged in 1992 was fundamentally different from that of 1945 in a number of respects. Among the substantial shifts were the consequences of the Eichmann trial. As Michael Rothberg emphasized in 2009, those trials contributed decisively "[to bringing] the Nazi genocide of European Jews into the public sphere for the first time as a distinct event on an international scale." (Rothberg 2009, 176) The trial "also helped create a new public identity: the Holocaust survivor." (Rothberg 2009, 177) Later, the Frankfurt Auschwitz trials, the broadcast of the television series "Holocaust" in West Germany, and the so-called "Historikerstreit" (historians' debate) represented additional moments of controversy and pointed to an altered or, more precisely, a considerably heightened responsiveness of Germans in relation to the Nazi past and their connection with it. When Ruth Klüger began to write *weiter leben* in 1989, and certainly by 1992 when it was published, she was by all means determined to attempt to address the Germans in spite of all prior disappointments with them.

In the middle of her book, a question comes to Klüger, allegedly in passing, that appears as an ambush: "For whom am I actually writing this here?" The question is followed by an answer that was often cited in the German reviews: "I wrote it for Germans." (Klüger 1992, 141) This targeted question seems to have the same vanishing point as that of the desire expressed by Primo Levi just a few years earlier in 1986 in a bit more lofty fashion: "'Miteinandersprechen' ("to settle accounts, to put the cards on the table. Above all, the hour of colloquy."), because "[m]y task was to understand them." (Levi 1989, 168)

---

3 See poems "Der Kamin" and "Auschwitz" in Manfred Schlösser (Ed.), *An den Wind geschrieben – Lyrik der Freiheit 1933–1945* (Darmstadt: Agora 1961), 121, 123; the poem "Der Kamin" also in Heinz Seydel (Ed.), *Welch Wort in die Kälte gerufen* (Berlin/DDR: Verlag der Nation 1968), 320.

Klüger's experiences of how Germans reacted whenever their crimes were addressed during the brief period between her liberation and her immigration to the USA most definitely serve as a preface to her renewed attempt at addressing them fifty years later. This is made evident by just how precisely she revisits those experiences in *weiter leben*. In two telling vignettes, she characterizes the aporetic nature of any attempt to talk with Germans about the horrendous crimes and offences. She relates that during her journey from Auschwitz to Christianstadt her train, she

> . . . passed a summer camp for youngsters. I saw a boy in the distance energetically waving a flag. It was a gesture affirming the sunny side of the system that was dragging us along in the blood and excrement of its underside. So much light out there – how could that be? [. . .] I still see myself rushing past him: I see him and he doesn't see me, for I am inside the train. But perhaps he sees the train. Passing trains fit into the image of such a landscape (part photography, part illusion); they convey a pleasant sense of wanderlust, the urge to travel. It was the same train for both of us, the same landscape, too, yet the same for the retina only – for the mind, two irreconcilable sights. (Klüger 2003, 114)

In the second vignette Klüger recalls the march together with her own small group within the stream of displaced persons near the end of the war. She writes:

> It was our luck to be caught up in the general dismemberment of the old Germany, and we followed the train of the newly homeless who were choking on their own misery and hadn't the stomach to ask suspiciously where we came from. They were mourning their losses, the possessions they had had to leave behind, and grieving for the homeland they wouldn't see again, while we were happy to have left our prisons and to have gained so much, that is to say, our naked existence. (Klüger 2003, 137)

And, just a few pages later more pointedly: "I was still carried along by a dizzy sense of happiness, the very opposite of what the genuine German refugees experienced. For they had lost everything, that is, all their property, while we hoped to have gained everything, that is, the rest of our lives." (Klüger 2003, 145) Even when Klüger attempts to emphasize the commonalities of such moments – for example, "the memory of the delicious taste of rutabagas" (Klüger 2003, 137)–, the encounter between the former concentration camp prisoners with the displaced Germans stands for a point of incongruity. Saul Friedländer expressed this incongruity with unsurpassable poignance when characterizing the relationship between Germans and Jews during the Nazi era: "What was traumatic for the one group was obviously not traumatic for the other." (Friedländer 1993, 124) This moment is unerringly captured by Klüger with the detail that it was only the "misery" that those displaced Germans were veritably "choking on" that prevented them from exercising the suspicious manhunt gaze they had practiced for years on persons such as the small group of newcomers.

Klüger describes the mood at war's end in unequivocal terms: "The Germans hadn't lost their hatred and contempt of Jews, but it had become subliminal. It simmered on, as stew in a high-quality saucepan continues to simmer after the gas has been turned off." (Klüger 2003, 151) The reports about the Nuremberg Trials were

> . . . treated with distaste [by our German neighbours], as if the investigators and observers were guilty, and as if turning away from the ugly facts were a proof of innocence. Germans didn't acknowledge or inform themselves of the crimes that were documented there for the first time – crimes that had been committed in their name, by their relatives and by themselves. It was easier to argue that the trials were nothing but a deliberate humiliation of the German people. Sure, the World War hadn't been a picnic, so the argument ran, but war never is. (Kluger 2003, 158)

Twenty years later, at the World Jewish Congress in Brussels, Gershom Scholem provided a very cautious and sceptical interim assessment of both attempted and (mostly) unattempted conversations between "Jews and Germans." He closed his presentation with the statement: "Only in remembrance of the past that shall never be entirely comprehended by us can new hope for restitution of speech between Germans and Jews, for reconciliation of the sundered, germinate." (Scholem 1970, 46) This sentence formulates the condition that had become an essential prerequisite for many Jews after the shutting down of the concentration camps with regard to any (renewed) contact with Germans. How this condition remained chronically unmet is reflected in Klüger's experience of how her poem was disfigured for publication, but also, and more starkly, in her relationship with Christoph. Unlike a publication, that relationship reflects an ongoing process, allowing for continual spontaneous reactions and controversial exchanges.

That the figure of Christoph historically refers to Martin Walser has brought forth a great deal of attention in the German reception of Klüger's book. Michael Ossar, who wrote the entry about Klüger in Lillian Kremer's authoritative encyclopedia on "Holocaust Literature," refers to the figure as a "now [. . .] famous neoconservative German novelist" (Ossar 2003, 675) – a reference both vague and yet fitting. Klüger's own comment about how this person stepped into her field of vision shortly after her liberation is of greatest relevance. He appeared to her as "the epitome of the post-war German intellectual." (Klüger 2003, 114) Emphasizing one aspect of her fascination, she adds that Christoph in a way appeared as the "boy on summer vacation (or was he at Hitler Youth training camp?) who had waved a flag." (Klüger 2003, 165) Although she doesn't explicitly connect the "epitome of the post-war German intellectual" with this "boy" in her imaginings, we may certainly draw this connection in retrospect, since numerous authors and intellectuals who made their voices heard during the post-war period had been members of the Hitler Youth. What is explicit in Klüger's description of Christoph as a prototypical figure is found in the following lines:

> What impressed me the most but irritated me at the same time was that he had his identity. He had his home in Germany, rooted in a certain landscape and became for me the epitome of the German. He knew where he was. Even to this day. [. . .] Generous, likeable, he steps forth to conquer the unknown, not wanting to learn anything more about it than that which will not endanger his autonomy. But is learning without such endangerment genuine learning? (Klüger 1992, 211–212)

Under these circumstances, any "commemoration of the past" on the part of the German post-war intellectual was bound to run up against its own limits rather quickly. This becomes entirely clear to Klüger when she confronts Christoph's refusal to discuss Martin Luther's anti-Judaism with her by accusing him of "being a closet anti-Semite. Not so, he responded. Kafka was one of his models," Klüger continues, "and besides, he had a strong interest in Jewish intellectual life. Could I tell him something about the Kabbala? To my shame I had to admit that I could not." (Klüger 2003, 167) In retrospect, these reactions on Christoph's part appear as appallingly clumsy clichés abounding in uncomprehended affective determination. They can simultaneously be read as evidence of just how utterly unpracticed any – to pick up Levi's term – "Miteinandersprechen" (speaking with one another) was between young Jews and Germans so shortly after the catastrophe. But, of greatest importance is just how early on and to what an obvious degree this aspect became a steadfast attribute of the German post-war intellectual, that is, to engage in learning processes only under the non-negotiable condition that they would not "endanger his autonomy", even (or especially?) when that learning is directed at the most extreme or most egregious of events – the Holocaust, for example. How this attribute leads to Klüger's marginalization and ultimate dismissal both as a conversation partner and as a witness is recounted in *weiter leben*. When an opportunity later arises to talk "about Auschwitz" in West German public discourse, Christoph fails to ask Klüger about her own experiences *in that very place*. At a different encounter:

> Christoph indicates that I was unable to reach a moderate assessment of the catastrophes that threaten us today, because for me everything was innately catastrophic, neither could I understand the principle of hope for biographical reasons. I responded that perhaps the assessment capabilities of the early Hitler Youths was impaired by their upbringing. He considers the remark inappropriate. (Klüger 1992, 217)

The passage underscores yet again to what an extent Christoph is to be read as epitomizing "the post-war German intellectual" and by no means as an individual or isolated case.

About a year after her book was published, Ruth Klüger qualified her statement ("I wrote it for Germans") in a discussion with Sigrid Löffler: "The book is written for Martin Walser. For me, he was the German who didn't listen, but the German who was always friendly, the intellectual with scepticism and sensitivity." (Löffler 1993) The remark shows that Klüger certainly did not fail to notice what attentive readers of her book had been able to recognize about her relationship to Christoph all along: "Miteinandersprechen" with someone "who didn't listen" is impossible.

In the Germany to which Klüger returns about forty years after her first encounter with Christoph, much seems to have changed in comparison with the immediate post-war period, but other things not so much. In addressing a readership that is allegedly very knowledgeable about present-day Germany, Klüger mentions some blind spots. She points out, for example, that by moving to Göttingen, where she will be directing an American academic study center, she "would be living for the first time in a city that practically has no Jews to show, and that up until now [she] had always been, not exclusively, yet for the most part, a Jew among Jews." (Klüger 1992, 269) Among the "new" mannerisms of how Germans deal with the mass crimes is the refusal of two civil service volunteers who had been applying a fresh coat of paint to fences in Auschwitz "to admit the difference between Poles and Jews and to include the Polish anti-Semitism in their meditations on good and evil." (Klüger 2003, 68) For "Germany's hopeful intellectual offspring," as Klüger refers to her students, the fact that a doctoral student from Göttingen encountered a survivor of Auschwitz in Jerusalem who "cursed the Arabs and held them all in contempt" (Klüger 2003, 65) is just as incomprehensible and appalling as a "harmless parody of an absurd poem by Celan" that she had composed. (Klüger 1992, 127) At the same time, Klüger learns that it is best not to talk about her own experiences when horrible, often traumatic experiences with mention of bombings or air raid shelters are being spoken of in social conversational settings:

> [. . .] meanwhile I had this transport to Auschwitz on my mind, but didn't contribute it, because if I had, it would have effectively shut up the rest of the company. They would have been bothered, troubled, sympathetic, and thoroughly uncomfortable.　(Klüger 2003, 93)

For comparable reasons, when Marcel Reich-Ranicki was asked amidst members of the Group 47 about "experiences in Warsaw during the German occupation," he selected "particularly harmless episodes [. . .] so as not to ruin the mood of those present – after all, everyone who was sitting at the table had been a soldier during the war, some of them presumably in Poland." (Reich-Ranicki 1999, 387–388) Klüger assesses the conundrum as follows: "You may and can talk about your wartime experiences, dear friends, not I about mine." (Klüger 1992, 109)

In this setting, little or nothing indicated that the effort to once again attempt to speak with Germans might be worthwhile. In *weiter leben* we read that it was ultimately an accident that triggered the attempt at confrontation or dialogue nonetheless. Klüger describes the collision with a bicyclist in these terms:

> I think he is chasing me, wants to injure me, and despair hits like lightning: I crash into metal and light, like floodlights over barbed wire. I want to push him away with both arms outstretched, but he is on top of me, bike and all. Germany, Deutschland, a moment like hand-to-hand-combat. I am fighting for my life, I am losing. Why this struggle, my life, Deutschland once more, why did I return, or had I never left? (Klüger 2003, 206)

This collision of present and past, of acute perception and memory, a shocking déjà-vu-like narrowing together of "crash" and "Deutschland" seems to have been the decisive impulse for Klüger to write "a German book" – unexpectedly for her, it would seem. Beyond the officially designated recipients, "the Göttingen friends," one may presume that Klüger's book is also directed at readers she cautiously hints at, who not only stood by her during her treatment at the hospital and during her further recuperation, but who also gave her reason to hope that they might – unlike Christoph – be able to listen. The third intended group of recipients is likewise not mentioned in the book's dedication, but is repeatedly evoked in the book: the Germans. Did then any "speaking with Germans" – in the sense of actual attentive encounter – come about by way of the publication of book for the German readership?

Hans Joachim Kreutzer recognizes preliminary signs in the reactions that are already cited in the book:

> They are all inadequate. They are indeed devastating. Relativizations, defensive claims, prejudices, thought clichés abound, there are direct links to today's fears of otherness and xenophobia. No one actually understood, that goes also for the fellow student from Regensburg who was soon a famous author. (Kreutzer 1992)

He finds the final phrase of the greeting that Walser voiced for Klüger on the Bavarian radio station Bayerischer Rundfunk – "welcome back" – to be pertinently symptomatic:

> So there is it retroactively yet again, the small, spurious, the German nuance, in the reactions that the author speaks of, unintentional proof of their truth content. She will never again fully find her way home – a question mark belongs behind Martin Walser's welcome by all means. (Kreutzer 1992)

Hannes Stein views the project with categorical scepticism:

> There are two very different reactions toward the reports from the concentration camps
> that seem to contradict one another, but that are in truth complementary. The first reac-
> tion reads: The horror in the concentration camps was so dreadful that no one can under-
> stand what actually happened there. The second reaction can be summarized in three
> words: I know already. Ruth Klüger's book reveals that the first objection is half banal
> and the other half simply false. Nobody can describe toothache either in such a way that
> the reader suffers it like the person who has it. That applies by analogy to Auschwitz.
> And this analogy proves absolutely nothing. One can comprehend what happened there:
> on the basis of details, the nuances, with the aid of precise recollection. [. . .] The second
> objection is – Ruth Klüger's book shows this as well – more brutal than any neo-Nazi slo-
> gan. It serves exclusively to fend off feelings of guilt. Whoever claims to already know 'all
> of that' in truth knows plain nothing. They will therefore also not be reached by a sen-
> tence like the following: "In Birkenau I stood for inspection and was thirsty and mortally
> frightened. That was all, that was it already." The prose of Ruth Klüger is that brash, that
> sarcastic, that bare of self-pity. [. . .] Who is reached by such quiet screaming, whom is it
> supposed to reach? Like every author, Ruth Klüger also has to ask herself why and for
> whom she actually writes. Her answer is explicit: "I write for Germans . . . [. . .] allow
> yourselves to at least be aggravated . . . Become quarrelsome, seek the dispute." That is a
> favored fantasy that has been spooking through Jewish heads for forty-five years. One
> could enter a dialogue with the non-Jewish Germans and ultimately even understand
> them. The problem is just: Most Germans don't understand themselves.   (Stein 1992)

The early scepticism voiced by these two critics was to be proven appropriate.
About six years later, Irène Heidelberger-Leonard assessed that *weiter leben*,
misunderstood as a "reconciliatory book," had "not been recognized as a concrete challenge to work on today's interaction between Germans and Jews."
(Heidelberger-Leonard 1998, 167) She writes: "The so frequently evoked dialogue remains absent. Talking about the Jew Klüger goes on, but not with her."
(Heidelberger-Leonard 1998, 168)

Such illusionless assessment that is not fooled by the subtle appropriations
and instrumentalizations that the (West-)German culture industry employed
with renewed sophistication, especially after 1989/90, might find a cue in a passage of Klüger's book that is often cited, yet without this segment. The question
"For whom am I actually writing this here?" is followed by a first sentence in
answer that is often skipped over. It reads:

> Well, I'm certainly not writing it for Jews, because I surely wouldn't do that in a language
> that, though it was spoken, read and loved by so many Jews when I was a child that it
> was considered back then by some to be the Jewish language, only very few Jews are in
> good command of today.   (Klüger 1992, 141)

What Klüger is referring to here is "not the German of the Germans," as Aharon
Appelfeld, who is almost the same age as she and was born in the Bukowina

near Czernowitz, once pointed out, "but the German of the Hapsburg Empire, of Vienna, Prague, and Czernowitz, with its special tone, which, by the way, the Jews worked hard to create." (Appelfeld 1994, 63) In many Jewish households the German language was, as Appelfeld comments elsewhere, "more than a language [. . .], more than communication – it was culture, it was religion." (Lang 1988, 285) What is being referred to here is the German language culture of Jews that was widely present throughout Central Europe before the catastrophe and of which German-language literature was just one aspect, albeit an eminently significant one. When Scholem, who was born in 1897, formulates the notion of a "restitution of language between Germans and Jews," we may certainly also understand it as a reference to this specific language culture that was destroyed. No doubt, Scholem, like Klüger, knew that hardly any Jews who had been living witnesses of it were still among the living.

If we concur with the picture that Scholem drew in Brussels regarding the relationship between Jews and Germans, we must then ask ourselves whether and to what extent a one-dimensional restitution would likely carry with it once again all of the problematical components that had not long ago led to a catastrophic end. What remains, notwithstanding, is the renewal of ambitious work on the project of German as a Jewish language by numerous Jewish authors who are formatively impacting contemporary German-language literature and its future.[4] In a German-language-Jewish literature that is making itself heard, a space for encounter between Jews and Germans is being opened that is more complex than the term 'dialogue' describes. Encounters that occur here, in the medium of a language that – depending on the text – is in recurring moments able to be both a German and a Jewish one, are complex, hardly predictable, and it is indeterminable who will learn what here. But, these encounters take place in the spaces of a language whose use is – to once again call on Scholem's pronouncement – tied to commemoration of the past. It is this language that Ruth Klüger worked toward with utterly distinctive force.

Bibliography

Améry, Jean. *Jenseits von Schuld und Sühne*. München: Deutscher Taschenbuch Verlag, 1988.
Andersch, Alfred. „Notwendige Aussage zum Nürnberger Prozeß." *Der Ruf*, Nr. 1, 15.8.1946a.
Andersch, Alfred. „Grundlagen einer deutschen Opposition." *Der Ruf*, Nr. 8, 1.12.1946b.

---

4 For example: Olga Grjasnowa, Lena Gorelik, Katja Petrowskaja, Sasha Marianna Salzmann, and others.

Appelfeld, Aharon. "A Conversation with Philip Roth." In id.: *Beyond Despair. Three Lectures and a Conversation with Philip Roth*. New York: Fromm Int'l, 1994, 59–80.

Braese, Stephan. "Einführung." In id. Ed.: *In der Sprache der Täter – Neue Lektüren deutschsprachiger Nachkriegs- und Gegenwartsliteratur*. Opladen/ Wiesbaden: Westdeutscher Verlag, 1998, 7–11.

Friedlander, Saul. "Trauma and Transference." In id.: *Memory, History, and the Extermination of the Jews of Europe*. Bloomington and Indianapolis: Indiana University Press, 1993, 117–137.

Heidelberger-Leonard, Irene. "Ruth Klüger ‚weiter leben' – ein Grundstein zu einem neuen Auschwitz-Kanon'?" *Deutsche Nachkriegsliteratur und der Holocaust*. Eds. Stephan Braese, Holger Gehle, Doron Kiesel, Hanno Loewy. Frankfurt a. Main/New York: Campus, 1998, 157–169.

Kesten, Hermann. *Deutsche Literatur im Exil – Briefe europäischer Autoren 1933–1949*. Frankfurt am Main: S.Fischer, 1975.

Klemperer, Victor. *The Language of the Third Reich. LTI – Lingua Tertii Imperii. A Philologist's Notebook*. Trans. Martin Brady. London/New York: Continuum, 2008.

Klüger, Ruth/Radisch, Iris. "Der Sinn des Lebens ist das Leben – Die österreichisch-amerikanische Autorin Ruth Klüger zieht Bilanz und spricht über enttäuschte Freundschaften, die Rolle des Zufalls und die befreiende Gelassenheit des Alters." *Die Zeit*, September 24, 2015, 52.

Klüger, Ruth. *weiter leben – Eine Jugend*. Göttingen: Wallstein, 1992.

Kluger, Ruth. *Still Alive – A Holocaust Girlhood Remembered*. New York: The Feminist Press at the City University of New York, 2003.

Kreutzer, Hans Joachim. "Die Auschwitznummer nicht verdecken. Ruth Klügers Erinnerungen – eine Einladung zum Streiten." *Süddeutsche Zeitung*. November 14, 1992.

Lang, Berel (Ed.). *Writing and the Holocaust*. New York/London: Holmes & Meier, 1988.

Levi, Primo. *The Drowned and the Saved*. Trans. Raymond Rosenthal. New York: Vintage International, 1989.

Loewy, Hanno. "Das gerettete Kind – Die ‚Universalisierung' der Anne Frank." *Deutsche Nachkriegsliteratur und der Holocaust*. Eds. Stephan Braese, Holger Gehle, Doron Kiesel, Hanno Loewy. Frankfurt a. Main/New York: Campus, 1998, 19–41.

Löffler, Sigrid. "Davongekommen. Jetzt noch über Auschwitz schreiben? Ruth Klüger ist es mit ‚weiter leben. Eine Jugend' gelungen, ohne Pathos und gefühlsgenau." *Die Zeit*, August 5, 1993.

Mann, Heinrich. "Einführung." *Morgenröte. Ein Lesebuch*. Eds. founders of Aurora Publishing. New York 1947, 19. *Neue Welt – eine Halbmonatsschrift der befreiten Juden*. 3.1.1948.

Ossar, Michael. "Ruth Klüger." *Holocaust Literature – An Encyclopedia of Writers and their Work*. Vol. I. Ed. S. Lillian Kremer. New York/London: Routledge, 2003, 674–679.

Reich-Ranicki, Marcel. *Mein Leben*. Stuttgart: Deutsche Verlagsanstalt, 1999.

Rothberg, Michael. *Multidirectional Memory – Remembering the Holocaust in the Age of Decolonization*. Stanford: Stanford University Press, 2009.

Scholem, Gershom. "Juden und Deutsche." In id.: *Judaica II*. Frankfurt am Main: Suhrkamp, 1970, 20–46.

Stein, Hannes. "Genauigkeit und Skrupel. ‚weiter leben', ein Debüt: Die Lehr- und Wanderjahre der Ruth Klüger." *Frankfurter Allgemeine Zeitung*. October 2, 1992.

Steiner, George. "The Hollow Miracle." In id.: *Language and Silence – Essays 1958–1966*. London: Penguin 1979, 136–151.

Irène Heidelberger-Leonard
Writing Auschwitz: Jean Améry, Imre Kertész, and Ruth Klüger

As we approach the end of the Auschwitz Century with the last survivors disappearing, what will happen to the literature of the Shoah as it passes from memory to history?

Holocaust Studies have changed beyond recognition over the last six decades. In an article for the *New Statesman*,[1] the British historian David Ceserani describes three distinct stages, each foregrounding different players. In the 1950s, after the Nürnberg Trials (1945–1946), the Third Reich was essentially seen as a "criminal regime run by crazed sadists," and it was widely believed that the mass of the German population did not sympathize with the Nazi persecution of the Jews. The Jews themselves, the story goes, had gone to the gas chambers like lambs to the slaughter. The second phase was introduced by the trial of Adolf Eichmann in Jerusalem (1961) and the ensuing Auschwitz trials in Frankfurt (1963–1965). Hannah Arendt exposed Eichmann in his compulsive subordination to Hitler[2] as being the epitome of a totalitarian man; she saw in him the personification of the *banality of evil*. Her claim that the Jewish Councils had colluded in their own destruction provoked more outrage still. This is where the third phase sets in with a much more integrated and nuanced understanding of Holocaust Studies. While German historians were still obsessed with analyzing how the Nazi State functioned, Israeli historians together with Yad Vashem enquired into aspects of Jewish conduct during the Shoah, including varieties of Jewish resistance. In many ways Primo Levi's memoir *If This is a Man* (1959) is the archetypal illustration of the third stage. His was the first Jewish voice. Levi's chronicle was especially compelling, because it was so clear and calm, yet seemingly untouched by bitterness or self-pity.

With Améry, Kertész, and Klüger we enter a fourth stage, which takes the idea of testimony to a much more complex and self-reflexive level, be it in the form of the essay, fiction, or autobiography. Despite being in dialogue with one another, they present Jewish voices in all their diversity. Indeed, their writings are solely driven by the Jewish experience; the perpetrators in Auschwitz and

---

1 David Ceserani, "The Ever-changing Face of Holocaust Studies. The Road to Ruin," *New Statesman*, February 14, 2013.
2 Arendt's claims resonate with Kertész and Klüger far beyond this second phase. See further references in the text.

https://doi.org/10.1515/9783110793239-005

in Buchenwald act mainly as a backdrop. The question that exercises them above all is the question of representation. They are explicit in their warnings about how *not* to write, yet divided about *how* and *what* to write. Jean Améry for instance is wary about using metaphors in his writing, because they mask the rawness of the experience. In his essay on torture, he bans all images and comparisons, because the gulf between reality and imagination simply cannot be bridged. Imre Kertész criticizes all forms of hyperbole, especially when it comes to the depiction of the Nazis. He singles out Jorges Semprun's *The Long Voyage* (1963) and his portrayal of the Lager Commandant Ilse Koch as a sadistic figure. Demonizing her, he claims, falsely reverses the true state of affairs. In his view her evilness was nothing but the norm; indeed, she fulfilled the expectations of the Nazi code to perfection. There was nothing extraordinary about her conduct.

Ruth Klüger tends to agree with Kertész, albeit for very different reasons. It is her fierce feminism that makes her object to male writers always picking on Ilse Koch on the grounds that she is a woman, when there is plenty of evidence that male cruelty by far outweighed female atrocities. Klüger is very explicit in her essay "Missbrauch der Erinnerung,"[3] when Holocaust memory degenerates into sentimentality, into what she calls *KZ-Kitsch*, illustrated for instance by the American TV series called "Holocaust" (1978) or indeed by Steven Spielberg's film *Schindler's List* (1993). The "don'ts" of holocaust literature are much more explicit than are the "do's." Samuel Beckett sums up the dilemma when he writes: "There is nothing to express, nothing with which to express, nothing from which to express, no power to express, no desire to express, together with the obligation to express." (*transition* 49, 1949) In fact, there is a strand of critical reception that thinks that silence is the only respectful response to the Shoah.

Not so Jean Améry, Imre Kertész, and Ruth Klüger. Each one of these survivors battles with this inherent paradox, that is the paradox that entails overcoming the silence and expressing the trauma, because as witnesses it is their "obligation to express." Kertész speaks for all of them when he demands that the writer puts his whole existence on the line, because a writer is someone who has suffered his art. Only art that hurts is worthy of being called art, he proclaims. (Kertész 2016, 33)

For Améry, Kertész, and Klüger "the obligation to express" is an ethical imperative. All three of them stand guard over their inflicted wound – Auschwitz – as their most cherished possession. Contrary to expectations, they embrace it,

---

3 Ruth Klüger, "Missbrauch der Erinnerung: KZ-Kitsch," *Gelesene Wirklichkeit. Fakten und Fiktionen in der Literatur* (Göttingen: Wallstein Verlag 2006), 52–57.

they cultivate and even celebrate it: "Die Erinnerung an das Leiden ist auch eine Art Schatz, ein Besitz, und wer ihn uns entreissen will, macht uns ärmer." (Klüger 2008b, 54) It has become their *raison d'être*, their driving force. In a sense, what had been designed to annihilate them is metamorphosed into a source of unending inspiration.

It is Jean Améry who lays the foundation for the birth of a new literary genre: the art of testimony. He is the architect, who maps out the *terra incognita;* he is the compass. Admittedly, he too is in indirect dialogue with his former fellow prisoner Primo Levi – or should I say monologue, such is his laconic dismissal of the latter's oeuvre. But Levi had preceded Améry's own account; he had gotten his word in first. Améry had taken cognizance of Levi's groundbreaking work *If this is a Man,* published in Italy as early as 1947 and in Germany in 1961. At the time it set the tone for any discussion of Auschwitz. The tense relationship between the two professional Auschwitz inmates, as Jean Améry sarcastically describes the public perception of their role, can be traced back to this unacknowledged rivalry.[4] Primo Levi, to some extent, had stolen the show from him. But Améry was determined to supplant Levi with a version far more in tune with his own predilections, with his crystalline style of writing and razor-sharp thinking. Levi's memoir concentrated on the life *inside* the camp, while Améry's reflections dissect the psyche of the prisoner *after* his incarceration. Levi's masterful report was essentially descriptive, whereas Améry's was substantially analytical. Primo Levi chose to express himself in a continuous narrative, while Améry chose to write his testimony, *At the Mind's Limits* (1966 in German, 1980 in English), in five autonomous essays.

Those essays are to date the most perceptive examination ever written of the condition of victimhood. Read together these seminal texts constitute no less than an ethics of victimhood. The first and second essays are probing explorations into mind versus matter or more precisely, into the powerlessness of the mind when the body is in pain. The third essay concerns the loss of home and language; it is an enquiry into exile. The fourth essay is a demonstration of why harboring resentments towards the Germans is a sign of mental health, even a virtue, and not, as Nietzsche will have it, a psychological deformation. The final and fifth chapter is a treatise, "On the Impossibility and the Necessity of Being a Jew." It is a relentless form of auto-psychoanalysis regarding what it means to a secular, non-Jewish Jew to be designated as a Jew in the post-

---

4 Cf. for a more detailed account of the relationship between Améry and Levi, see Irène Heidelberger-Leonard, *The Philosopher of Auschwitz. Jean Améry and Living with the Holocaust* (London: I.B. Tauris, 2010), 65–72.

Auschwitz era. It is also the key to the other four essays. The contradiction between necessity and impossibility is in fact at the center of all Améry's studies.
He is principally concerned with the necessity and impossibility to live[5] after
Auschwitz and more particularly after having been tortured. There is also necessity and impossibility in his troubled relation to his homeland Austria, not
to mention his guilt-ridden relationship to Germany. It is the country that de-
creed his death, but also the country that anointed him as a writer. It is only
when he defines his own brand of Jewishness that all these necessities and im-
possibilities come together.

Mind versus Body

These four themes – mind versus body, exile and language, resentment, and
Jewish identity – will guide my analysis of the disparate voices of Améry, Kertész, and Klüger. As will be seen, *At the Mind's Limits* supplies both the foundation and the building blocks on which Kertész and Klüger erect their own
testimonial monuments. The part the mind plays when the body is under attack
is a matter of concern to all three writers. Why does the role of the intellectual
in Auschwitz hold Améry's interest? Why does he want to know whether an intellectual, whom he defines as a man of letters, is better or worse equipped to
deal with borderline situations? It is perhaps not irrelevant to know that Améry
came from a modest background and that his erudition was completely self-
taught. He left school at the age of thirteen. Having fought so hard to acquire
this erudition, it is perhaps understandable that he lays so much store by the
power of the intellect, only to have to find out that his literary imagination was
not only useless, but rather it put him at a severe disadvantage compared to a
manual worker for instance, who was physically much stronger than he was.
He recalls a bleak winter evening when dragging himself back to the camp in a
state of total exhaustion, "with the Kapo's unnerving 'left, two, three, four,'
when [. . .] a flag waving in front of a half-finished building caught [his] eye."
(Améry 1999, 7) The waving flag reminds him of a Hölderlin poem which he
murmurs to himself in its entirety, in the hope that the recitation might conjure
up some lofty or comforting memories. But the expected emotional response
does not emerge; the cultural reference does not resonate. "Nothing happened.
The poem no longer transcended reality." (Améry 1999, 7) His response to

---

5 The question of suicide is a constant preoccupation in his work. In October, 1978 he actually
commits suicide.

torture is more extreme still. In his reflections, he comes to the conclusion that in torture "the transformation of the person into flesh becomes complete." (Améry 1999, 33) It is as if the torture victim experienced his own death. Not only has the mind reached its limits; the body has, too. "A slight pressure by the tool-wielding hand is enough to turn the other – along with his head, in which are perhaps Kant and Hegel, and all nine symphonies [. . .], – into a shrilly squealing piglet at slaughter." (Améry 1999, 35) And he concludes: "Whoever has succumbed to torture can no longer feel at home in the world." (Améry 1999, 40) The shame of annihilation, a sense of being a stranger in the world, can never be eradicated. From now on the memory of Auschwitz is engraved in his body. The body for Améry is not instinct, but empiric evidence; it is what is verifiable. The body is the most reliable reservoir for the memory of Auschwitz; it keeps the score. As a bridge between the "I" and the world, it is transformed into the new subject of perception.

The legendary "Weltvertrauen," the trust in the world, that Améry has lost forever is still intact in the unsuspecting adolescent Köves in Kertész' novel *Fateless* (2005), when he, too, a *Muselman* experiences his own death after months of incarceration and forced labor. Whereas Améry is outraged at himself for not having been able to resist mentally the violent onslaught on his body, the fatally ill Köves positively welcomes the fact that his mind has left his body. He contemplates his own decaying flesh almost with serenity: "It had been a long time since I had felt so easy, tranquil, almost lost in reverie," (Kertész 2005, 185) he muses, wallowing in the affection he feels for the other near-cadavers heaped on top of him in the handcart during his transfer from Zeitz to Buchenwald. Being in denial both of his lethal condition and his murderous environment, he is portrayed like a kind of Candide figure, determined to make himself believe that everything is always for the best and even that he lives in the best of all possible worlds. The powers of the mind, let alone literary references, are not Köves' preoccupations.

As for the thirteen-year-old child Klüger, her "Weltvertrauen" is more guarded, more self-aware than that of Köves. She is more knowing, but she holds on to this trust and faith with all her might, not least because she has a mission. Her intellect, the mind, is her most mighty weapon and she will not let the Nazis destroy it, because her literary exploits are her lifeline. They are the one and only element that not only empower her and help her to survive, but they make her want to live on. The poetry she learns by heart during curfew when non-Jewish Austrian children are allowed to play in the street, and the poems she manages to compose herself, even when in the labor camps, help to keep her sane right into adulthood. They are part of her "personal hygiene." In an interview she once joked: "If I have not read any poems for a week, it feels like not having brushed my teeth." But in

Auschwitz the stakes were higher. It was not her teeth, but her whole life that was at stake, and it depended on this cultural exercise: "One may well ask," she writes in the German version of *weiter leben,* "why it is so comforting to recite poetry."(Klüger 1998, 123) She concludes that it is not so much the content that soothes, but the form, the rhyme in particular. In bad times, she writes on, you can do no better than use rhyme to divide up that time and make it go away faster, until each poem turns into a magic spell. (Klüger 1998, 124) Even if Schiller's ballads did not quench her thirst during the endless roll calls in the burning sun, they made it easier for her to endure them, if only because there was always another line of verse to be remembered. And if one had forgotten a line, all of one's attention went into trying to recall it, instead of giving in to one's exhaustion and possibly fainting.

Exile

If literary imagination and culture are matters of survival, the loss of culture must have dire consequences. Where there is loss of culture, there is exile. It is either an exile of choice or as in Améry's and Klüger's case an enforced exile, an exile of necessity. "How much Home does a Person Need?"(Améry 1999, 41–61) asks Améry as a person who is chased out of the Third Reich, as someone who has not only been expelled from his country, but as someone who has also been expelled from his language. Whoever is expelled from language is also expelled from identity. Worse still, one's mother tongue has turned into the language of murderers. All that is left is the writer's eternal exile. Once an emigrant, always an emigrant. Exile is fear, home is security. And Améry finishes his exploration with this very simple, yet convincing paradox: "One must have a home, in order not to need it." (Améry 1999, 46)

Ruth Klüger's exile is less dramatic. Born in Vienna in 1931, she emigrated to the U.S. at the age of sixteen, seemingly young enough to integrate, especially as she was educated largely in America. She was eager to learn English as quickly as possible and chose to complete a degree in English, before she switched to a Ph.D. program in German literature. German was very much looked down upon, especially among the recent immigrants, many of whom strove to write in English. "For me the German language was on the one hand a mobile home, on the other a hunchback, a stain which I could not get rid of, because it had grown a part of me." (Klüger 2013, 15) Most of her academic papers are written in English, which makes it all the more significant that her

memoir *weiter leben*,[6] written shortly before her retirement, was written originally in German. It is a German infused with "Austrianisms" accessible to her
from her childhood. As she said in 2016: "I am more than ever inclined to acknowledge my Austrian patrimony." (Gelber 2021, 113) This is also the time
when she reclaims her Austrian family name and switches from her married
name "Angress" to her father's name "Klüger." Although a proud American
with, as she puts it, a German-accented English, she has never renounced her
origins: I come from Vienna, she used to say, not from Auschwitz. Vienna figures as the first chapter in *Still Alive*. This is the Vienna of her childhood before
the Anschluss; later comes the Vienna from which she is banned and deported
to Theresienstadt. But then there is also the Vienna she visits after the war, and
last, the Vienna where she is welcomed as a celebrated author. Apart from her
very first years, Klüger's relationship to all these Viennas is complex, not to say
conflicted. In her interview in 2016 with Mark Gelber, she explains that Vienna
already became exile when she was six and a half years old. It was "a place,
one wanted to leave," (Gelber 2021, 110) and when she visited it with her
mother briefly after the war, it felt like a graveyard to her and "that the people
living there didn't know it was a graveyard." (Gelber 2021, 110) When she
comes to Vienna in the 1990s, amid never-ending accolades, she is fascinated
by the place: ". . . though I'll probably never love it. You don't love a prison,
even if it's been remodelled as a luxury hotel." (Gelber 2021, 111) There is no
such thing as a real home for her, not Vienna, not New York, not Berkeley, not
Göttingen. Perhaps the academic community of Irvine, where she finished her
career and life, could be called a "virtual home." (Gelber 2021, 112) She always
regretted that her mother did not let her immigrate to Israel when she was a
child.

Kertész, unlike Améry and Klüger, never immigrated, not after his liberation from Buchenwald and not even after the thwarted Hungarian uprising in
1956.[7] And, because he stayed in an enemy land, he perceives himself as an emigrant, an exile inside his own country. He feels that hostile political forces,
first in Auschwitz, then in Budapest, have expropriated his life. An ardent op-
ponent of the Kádár dictatorship, he lives like a recluse for forty years. Being
Hungarian and being a Jew are not compatible, according to him. What is
more, he feels so estranged from his social environment that although he writes
in the language of his country – Hungarian – he considers even his language to

---

6 She translated *weiter leben* into English herself and revised it nine years later. The English
version is in many ways a very different book.
7 He only sets up home in Berlin in 2002, before he returns to Budapest in 2012.

be exiled or rather his language exiles him. That is one of the reasons why he resorts to creating a new language for his novel *Fateless,* an *atonal* language modelled on Schönberg's atonal music. It is a language beyond tradition, beyond all established morality. Whereas the moralist Améry is an heir to, and a passionate defender of, the Enlightenment, Kertész denounces the failure of the Enlightenment's humanist values. They are both strangers in their respective languages. The Austrian Améry lives after the Shoah in Brussels, where he remains unknown, because he writes in German. The Hungarian Kertész writes in Hungarian, but his idiosyncratic language, not to mention his subject matter, finds no favor with his compatriots.

Resentments

It is only natural that being an outsider, a "pariah"[8] to use an Arendtian term, creates resentment. For Jean Améry the problem of resentment is far more acute than it is for Kertész or Klüger. Perhaps this is the case, one may speculate, because they were younger and more resilient when they were incarcerated. But perhaps it is because they live at a greater distance from Germany. For Améry, maintaining his resentments towards the Germans is a *sine qua non* on the way to redemption, if there is redemption. Forgiveness erases the past, while resentment preserves the past. Resentment is resistance against the erosion of time. It is a virtue, because it keeps the wound open before the healing process can set in. In fact, if you read the "Resentment" chapter in *At the Mind's Limits* against the grain, it is not a declaration of hate; rather, it is a declaration of love. It is essentially a fervent plea to the Germans to acknowledge their guilt, and by so doing – freely – reversing the course of history to clear the way for a conciliatory future. Nowhere else does the rationalist Améry indulge in such a utopian vision as here. If the perpetrator confesses to his crime, his argument goes, and if the resentment of the victim is recognized as legitimate, "the overpowered and those who overpowered them would be joined in the desire that time be turned back, and with it, that history become moral. If this demand were raised by the German people [. . .] it would have tremendous weight, enough so that by this alone it would already be fulfilled. The German revolution would be made good, Hitler disowned. And in the end, Germans would really achieve what the people once did not have the might or the will to do [. . .] the eradication of the ignominy." (Améry 1999,78)

---

8 Cf. Hannah Arendt, "The Jew as Pariah." In: *Jewish Social Studies*, Vol. 6, No. 2 (1944), 99–122.

The East European Kertész has no bone to pick with the Germans. While Améry talks of resentments, Kertész talks of revenge: "Perhaps I started to write," the Old Man in *Fiasco* explains, "to take revenge on the world." In fact, his protagonist wants to take revenge on the *whole world*. Kertész, who is seventeen years younger than Améry, looks at the genocide of the Jews from his unique perspective. Améry is deeply rooted in German culture, and it is that culture that has betrayed him. Kertész, socialized in Hungary, has never considered the Shoah to be the result of an unbridgeable chasm between Germans and Jews. On the contrary, it is in Germany that he found his first recognition as a writer. It is paradoxically by means of German culture that he tries to come to grips with the horror that Germany brought to the world. When he wrote *Fateless*, he remembers, "[hatten] daran die deutsche Kultur, die deutsche Philosophie, die deutsche Musik einen Anteil [. . .]; vielleicht kann man sagen, dass ich in gewisser Weise das Grauen, das Deutschland über die Welt gebracht hat, mit den Mitteln der deutschen Kultur gestaltet und den Deutschen fünfzig Jahre später als Kultur zurückgegeben habe." (Kertész 2004, 219) He wants to take revenge *on the whole world*, because he knows that he was not only robbed of his freedom in Auschwitz and Buchenwald, but also during the Stalinist dictatorships of Rákosi and Kádár in the postwar era. This is the reason why he insists that his novel *Fateless* is not primarily a book about the Holocaust, but rather the critique of a totalitarian state. For Améry, Auschwitz and the extermination of the Jews are essentially German crimes. For Kertész, National Socialism is part of European history, of a European Culture which National Socialism did everything to destroy.

Contrary to Kertész, resentment is a familiar concept to Klüger. She is in no mood to forgive the Germans; nor does she feel entitled to do so. In her view only the dead can forgive. But rather than harboring resentment, she is eager to enter into a dialogue with the Germans. The first version of *Still Alive – weiter leben*[9] – is explicitly dedicated to her "friends in Göttingen." And, she calls *weiter leben* "ein deutsches Buch." But just how fragile this dialogue is, is illustrated by her long friendship with Martin Walser which abruptly comes to an end after he publishes an anti-Semitic novel.[10] Her friendships are definitely not unconditional, for it is in the "Göttingen" chapter that we read: "I can only recognize myself in my inability to forgive; to this I will always hold on." (Klüger 1992, 279) Or more violently still: "I can't forget. Forgiving makes me sick." (Klüger 1992, 279)

---

9 In *Still Alive* (her own translation and a revision of *weiter leben*) the original epilogue entitled "Göttingen" has been replaced by an epilogue dedicated to her mother.
10 Martin Walser, *Tod eines Kritikers*. Martin Walser is the epitome of a German to her, the German who will not listen to the account of her experiences in Auschwitz.

Jewishness / Victimhood

Exile. Resentment. Strangeness. Kertész speaks of all three when he designates his own state of alienation: "The true name of my 'alienation' is called Jewishness." (Kertész 2002, 85) He echoes Améry's state of mind: "Without trust in the world I face my surroundings as a Jew who is alien and alone." (Améry 1999, 95) On reflection, though, it is precisely this state of alienation from their surroundings, and even from their language, which is their biggest capital, when it comes to their writing.

Like Kertész and Klüger, Améry is a secular Jew who adheres neither to Jewish tradition nor to the Jewish faith. It is solely Hitler's decree that turned him into a Jew. Already in his very first novel, *Die Schiffbrüchigen* (1933), written even before the Nürnberg Laws (1935), he feels the urge to join forces with the "hunted," precisely because they are hunted. After Auschwitz he calls himself a "catastrophe Jew," whose Auschwitz number has become the most visible manifestation of his Jewishness. But in rebelling against being the victimized Jew, Améry transforms the self that had been imposed on him through an act of self-determination into a self that he has freely chosen. His answer is not denial, but wholehearted affirmation of his Jewishness and of the historical experience integral to Jewishness. Thus, the "non-non-Jew," as he coins the term for himself, pleads for dis-similation, not assimilation. If you are attacked as a Jew, you have to defend yourself as a Jew. And yet, the self-confident acceptance cannot mask the fact that you remain – politically speaking – a victim. That is why Améry sums up his book as being "a phenomenological description of the existence of the victim."[11]

In Améry's mind there is a red line between the Nazi perpetrator and the Jewish victim; it is a red line never to be crossed. "To be a Jew" after the Nürnberg Laws, he remembers, "that meant for me to be a dead man on leave, someone to be murdered, who only by chance was not yet where he properly belonged; and so it has remained, in many variations [. . .] until today." (Améry 1999, 86) For him it was the "degradation of the Jews," the "denial of human dignity" that sealed his fate as a victim. Although the status of victimhood was not negotiable, he manages to develop strategies to regain what he calls his dignity. To illustrate his point he relates the following scene: "Before me I see the prisoner foreman Juszek, a Polish professional criminal of horrifying vigor. In Auschwitz he once hit me in the face because of a trifle; that is how he was used to dealing with all the Jews under his command. [. . .] In open revolt I struck Juszek in the face in

---

11 ATML Preface 1966.

turn. My human dignity lay in this punch to his jaw – and that it was in the end I, the physically much weaker man, who succumbed and was woefully thrashed, meant nothing to me. Painfully beaten, I was satisfied with myself. [. . .] My body, when it tensed to strike, was my physical and metaphysical dignity." (Améry 1999, 90–91) Given the social reality of the camp, for Améry the victim remains a victim. But, by physically rebelling against his victimhood, he turns the victim as object into a victim as subject; thus, he scores a moral victory.

Although Kertész will only discover Améry's work twenty years after the publication of his first novel *Fateless,* he fully shares Améry's premises when it comes to his self understanding as a "non-non-Jew." But, when it comes to victimhood, he reverses Améry's insights. Far from aligning himself with Améry's heroic rebellion, he chooses to show the moral fallibility of the victim. To him there is no such thing as an innocent victim. Being a "mere" victim is so abhorrent to the inmate Köves returning to Budapest after his liberation from Buchenwald, that there is only one way of recuperating some sort of agency. Namely, he turns himself into someone who was complicit in his own destruction, by presenting himself as a collaborator with the Nazis. The fifteen-year old Köves wills himself a part of the evil system, as an accessory to crime. Victim and perpetrator have become interchangeable. In Kertész' view there is no greater ignominy than the shame of being reduced to a victim. Every victim, he claims, is also a virtual malefactor. It is therefore not surprising that Kertész in his very first attempt at bearing witness goes as far as slipping into the skin of a tormentor. He gives it the inflammatory title "I, the Henchman." No Auschwitz survivor has ever held himself to account as mercilessly as Kertész. Much later he will confess that it is not the fact that he endured Auschwitz that drove him to writing, but that it was the "situation of the henchman, the perpetrator." (Kertész 2013, 69) The frightening realization that the victim can also turn into a henchman is a sort of "flexibility" which Kertész denounces as "'fateless." He singles it out as characteristic not only of the Nazi camps, but more widely of any totalitarian structure, like the Rákosi and then the Kádár regime in Hungary. Being "fateless," he laments, is the *novum*, the signature of our epoch. Kertész knows only too well how this type of "functional" man, "this man without properties," is manipulated by the authority in power, until he complies unquestioningly with any regime or ideology.

Klüger positions herself somewhere between Améry and Kertész. On the one hand, she would agree with Améry that there is a distinction to be drawn between victim and perpetrator. But what distinguishes Klüger above all from her male colleagues is that she complements their view with another dimension: namely, that being Jewish is exacerbated by being a Jew-*ess*. In *unterwegs verloren* (2008), the second volume of her autobiography, she conflates the two in the abbreviation: "der Jude als Frau," the Jew as a woman.[12] This expression exposes how being both a woman and a Jew constitutes a double victimization. In an interview in *Der Spiegel* she maintains that being a woman and being a Jewess are comparable. Prejudices against both are still extant. "You never know whether you are being patronized [because] you are a woman or a Jew," she complains. (*Spiegel* 33/2008) In her experience the two victimizations are intimately linked. Antisemitism and misogyny are two sides of the same coin.

On the other hand, like Kertész she too has nothing but contempt for those who glory in their victimhood. Her stance in *Still Alive* is more optimistic than those in *Fateless* or *At the Mind's Limits*. More forward looking than both Kertész and Améry, she concentrates on how, even as a child of eight and later of thirteen, there is always a fissure in the tight web of determinations open to the one who cares to see it. When the eight-year-old is told she has to wear a Star of David, she does not only comply; she is resolved to wear it with pride. And because she despises those who are in denial of their Jewishness, she demonstratively changes her name Susi to Ruth to exhibit her Jewish origins. More sensationally still: in the camp the thirteen-year-old revolts against having been selected for the gas chamber by joining another queue and pretending to be older in order to be selected for forced labor instead. This form of rebellion in the camp against the Nazi edicts is unheard of. Who says the Jews went to the gas chambers like lambs to the slaughter?

But she had some help and Klüger makes the anonymous helper, a Jewish clerk – an endangered prisoner like herself – the centerpiece of her account: "I was saved by a young woman who was in as helpless a situation as the rest of us, and who nonetheless wanted nothing other than to help me." (Klüger 2001, 106) Until the end Klüger marvels at this person, and the fact that she is a woman is anything but a coincidence to her. In an act of free will "in a place which promoted the instinct of self preservation to the point of crime," (Klüger 2001, 107) she puts her own life on the line to save another.

In fact, the narrative "I" of Klüger's memoirs *Still Alive,* which she insists is identical with her own persona, is the exact antithesis of the fictional character Köves in *Fateless*. While Köves's is solely intent on decoding the logic of the Nazi mentality and eager to obey its rules to the letter, the Klüger-"I" is on the lookout for cracks in the hermetically closed order. Even the tattooing of the Auschwitz number on her left arm arouses feelings in her that almost

---

12 We find the same constellation in Hélène Cixous, who talks about 'juifemme.' See "Sorties," in *La jeune née*. Paris: 1975. In English: Hélène Cixous and Catherine Clément, *The Newly Born Woman*, Trans. Betsy Wing (London: I. B. Tauris, 1996), 101.

approximate joy: "Thanks to the dog tag under my skin, I was suddenly so aware of the enormity, the monstrosity [. . .] of my situation that I felt a kind of glee about it. I was living through something that was worth witnessing. Perhaps I would write a book with a title like *A Hundred Days in a Concentration Camp.*" (Klüger 2001, 98) Being Jewish then is not only a source of suffering; being Jewish is a source of indomitable strength, even jubilation.

Klüger's narrative seems to set in, where Köves' account ends. Only on his return does the teenager come to the realization that he foregoes all agency in the camp. He indicts himself as being a "guilty" victim. The child Klüger on the other hand uses every opportunity to rebel against the system, so much so that together with her mother she manages to liberate herself prior to the liberation by the allies. It is as if Améry had first to establish the legitimacy of victimhood, so that Kertész and Klüger could reject victimhood, albeit in antithetical ways: Kertész by making Köves accuse himself of having been a collaborator and Klüger by celebrating the free will for good.[13] Even in the perverse environment of Auschwitz, Klüger declares solemnly: "goodness was a possibility."(Klüger 2001, 109)

Who Owns Auschwitz?

At the Mind's Limits, Fateless, and *Still Alive* are three foundational texts implicitly and explicitly in dialogue with one another. All three constitute "Bildungsromane" (novels of education) in reverse. The progress towards growth and integration into society is rewound backwards from growth to near death and then back to growth again. These texts are stories of unlearning and relearning human possibilities. They represent three literary genres: one in the form of the essay, the second as fiction, the third as autobiography. It is tempting to say that the medium is the message. "The essay," Adorno writes, "allows for the consciousness of non-identity." Améry's concept of the "non-non-Jew" illustrates his point. And Adorno continues: It is "radical in its non-radicalism." What could be more radical in thought and yet non-radical in its conclusion than Améry's experience-based demonstration that a tortured man is reduced to flesh, to meat? Other criteria he singles out are the "fragmentary" and the "subjective" nature of the essay, and Adorno sums up: "Hence the essay's innermost formal law is heresy." (Adorno 1991, 23)

---

13 There is also one figure in *Fateless* – "der Herr Lehrer" – whom Kertész depicts as being self sacrificing, ein "Heiliger des Holocaust," like Améry in "Der Holocaust als Kultur."

Heresy is not the reserve of the essay alone, for the word "heretic" could equally be applied to Kertész' fiction. Throughout the novel Köves' attitude, if taken at its face value, is truly shocking to the reader. Instead of showing indignation, one hears him say how "'natural" all the monstrosities are which he has to endure. Also, he talks about his nostalgia for the "beautiful concentration camp." These are deliberate provocations. More than anything they externalize the double bind that the teenager finds himself in. On the one hand, there is his total ignorance of things to come; on the other, there is the necessity to justify Nazi conduct to himself, if he wants to survive. Kertész maintains that the concentration camp is imaginable only and exclusively in literature, never as reality. It can only be evoked through the distance that fiction allows, through testimony as fiction. And Köves, contrary to the autobiographical narrator "I" in *weiter leben*, is definitely not identical with his creator Kertész. Köves, insofar as he is a character at all,[14] is in every respect a fictional construction. The facts, Kertész maintains, tell you nothing. Truth can only be distilled and communicated through what the individual witness *adds* to the facts. Klüger disagrees. She insists that autobiography is "history written in the first person," and it is the most subjective form of historiography. Although the genre can be akin to the novel, it should not be confounded with the fictional character of the novel. To her the facts are the pillars. They should be respected and they set limits to our imagination.

These survivor-authors present three landmark testimonies, three paradigms, each one of them engendering a new form of discourse on Auschwitz. Kertész pays tribute to Améry in his manifesto: "Holocaust as Culture." (*Die exilierte Sprache* 2004, 76–90) Klüger pays tribute to Kertész in her review of *Fateless*. (*Die Weltwoche* 17/25. April 1996)

Is this really the end of the Auschwitz Century? With Ruth Klüger's death in 2020, one may well ask who will take over the mantle now that the survivors and first-hand witnesses are dying out. Klüger herself points the way forward by entrusting her memory to the next generation and engaging in a dialogue with young Germans in *weiter leben*. In *Still Alive* she addresses herself to her American children and grandchildren, preparing the way for a transgenerational memory. However possessive she may be about her very own testimony, she knows that nobody "owns" Auschwitz, not even the first-hand witness, not even the Jewish survivor. When asked specifically about W. G. Sebald as a

---

14 In *Galeerentagebuch* Kertész explains that he is not really an individual, but what he calls a 'functional' man, a man who foregoes all agency. In this sense he is not an autonomous character.

Holocaust writer, she singles out his novel *Austerlitz* as being the only valuable present-day book dealing with the Holocaust coming from "the other side." This means, in her view, that even non-Jewish Germans can write Holocaust books, as long as they know how to do it.[15]

"The Holocaust is not a private property," warns the Polish sociologist and philosopher Zygmunt Baumann, "not of its perpetrators, to be punished for; not of its direct victims, to ask for special sympathy [. . .]; and not of its witnesses, to seek redemption or certificates of innocence. The present-day significance of the Holocaust is the lesson it contains for the whole of humanity." (Baumann 1989, 206)

Bibliography

Adorno, Theodor W. *Notes to Literature*, Vol. 1, Ed. Rolf Tiedemann. Trans. Shierry Weber Nicholsen. New York: Columbia University Press 1991.

Améry, Jean. *At the Mind's Limits*. Trans. Sidney Rosenfeld and Stella P. Rosenfeld, London: Granta Books, 1999.

Améry, Jean. *Werke*, Band 1–9. Ed. Irène Heidelberger-Leonard, Stuttgart: Klett-Cotta, 2002–2008.

Arendt, Hannah. *Wir Juden. Schriften 1932–1966*. Ed. Marie Luise Knott and Ursula Ludz, München: Piper, 2019.

Arendt, Hannah. *Eichmann in Jerusalem. A Report on the Banality of Evil*. London: Penguin Books, 2006.

Arendt, Hannah. *Elemente und Ursprünge totaler Herrschaft*. München: Piper, 1986.

Baumann, Zygmunt. *Modernity and the Holocaust*. Cambridge: Polity Press, 1989.

Gelber, Mark H. "Ruth Klüger on Vienna and Austria: An Interview." *Journal of Austrian Studies*, 54, 3 (2021): 109–114.

Heidelberger-Leonard, Irène. *The Philosopher of Auschwitz. Jean Améry and Living with the Holocaust*. Trans. Anthea Bell, London: I. B. Tauris, 2010.

Heidelberger-Leonard, Irène. *Imre Kertész. Leben und Werk*. Göttingen: Wallstein Verlag, 2015.

Heidelberger-Leonard, Irène. *weiter leben. Eine Jugend*. Oldenburg Interpretationen, Band 81, München: Oldenburg Verlag, 1996.

Kertész, Imre. *Der Betrachter. Aufzeichnungen 1991–2001*. Reinbek bei Hamburg: Rowohlt Verlag, 2016.

Kertész, Imre. *Fateless*. Trans. Tim Wilkinson, London: Vintage Books, 2005.

Kertész, Imre. *Fiasco*. Trans. Tim Wilkinson, London: Melville House, 2011.

Kertész, Imre. *Die exilierte Sprache*. Trans. Kristin Schwamm, György Buda, Géza Déreky, Krisztina Koenen, Laslo Kornitzer, Christian Polzin, Ilma Rakusa, Irene Rübberdt, Christina Viragh und Ernö Zeltner. Frankfurt: suhrkamp taschenbuch, 2004.

---

15 Thomas Honickel, *Curriculum Vitae. Die W.G. Sebald-Interviews*, Ed. U. Schütte und Kay Wolfinger (Würzburg: Königshausen & Neumann 2021), 225–226.

Kertész, Imre. *Ich—ein anderer*. Reinbek bei Hamburg: Rowohlt Verlag, 2002.

Kertész, Imre. *Letzte Einkehr*. Reinbek bei Hamburg: Rowohlt Verlag, 2013.

Klüger, Ruth. *Still Alive. A Holocaust Girlhood Remembered*. New York: The Feminist Press at the City University of New York, 2001.

Klüger, Ruth. *weiter leben. Eine Jugend*. München: dtv 1998.

Klüger, Ruth. *weiter leben. Eine Jugend*. Göttingen: Wallstein Verlag, 1992.

Klüger, Ruth. *unterwegs verloren. Erinnerungen*. Wien: Paul Zsolnay Verlag, 2008a.

Klüger, Ruth. *Gelesene Wirklichkeit. Fakten und Fiktionen in der Literatur*. Göttingen: Wallstein Verlag, 2008b.

Klüger, Ruth. *Zerreißproben. Kommentierte Gedichte*. Wien: Paul Zsolnay, 2013.

Klüger, Ruth. *"Wer rechnet schon mit Lesern?" Aufsätze zur Literatur*. Ed. Gesa Dane, Göttingen: Wallstein Verlag, 2021.

Klüger, Ruth. *Katastrophen. Über deutsche Literatur*. Göttingen: Wallstein Verlag, 1994.

Levi, Primo. *If This is a Man*. London: Abacus, 1991.

Semprun, Jorge. *The Long Voyage*. New York: Harry N. Abrams, 2005.

Ulrike Offenberg
"... but the dead set us certain tasks, don't they?" Ruth Klüger and the Jewish Tradition on Women Saying Kaddish

Ruth Klüger on Kaddish[1]

"Yitgadal veyitkadash shmeh raba . . . ." The opening words of the Kaddish prayer may cause many Jews to shiver. Next to the creed "Shema Yisrael" it is very likely the best known text of Jewish prayer, and it is widely understood as the most important expression of Jewish mourning. Though the Aramaic words are barely comprehensible for contemporary Jews, reciting the Kaddish is seen as the genuinely Jewish expression of mourning, while at the same time this act is perceived as an obligation of the children for their deceased parents. It is often an emotional moment, for the mourner as well as for the congregation, when a congregant stands during the prayer service and utters these words. Normally, the entire congregation answers the mourner with the prescribed responses. For the duration of the Kaddish prayer recited by a congregant, the congregation turns away from the prayer leader and focuses on one of its members, in an attempt to comfort a mourner by acknowledging his or her loss. It is a ritual that evokes the sympathy of the congregation and offers the mourner comfort, or at least a language, when it is impossible to describe in one's own words what exactly happened and what the loss means.

In *weiter leben*, Ruth Klüger gives bitter testimony regarding her estrangement from the Jewish religion. Having been persecuted from early childhood on for being a Jew and barely surviving deportation, starvation, death camp, forced labor, a death march, escape, and hiding, she found herself being denied access to essential Jewish rites, the traditional expressions of mourning for her father and her brother. Despite her personal and the general Jewish experience of suffering, death, and loss beyond comprehension, Ruth Klüger felt compelled to refuse to say Kaddish, owing to the reason of her gender. A ritual that had evolved in Judaism to comfort mourners – that is, by and large to comfort Jewish men – and to give them a space and status within the Jewish community

---

1 Ruth Klüger, *Still Alive. A Holocaust Girlhood Remembered* (New York: The Feminist Press at the City University of New York, 2001), 31; Cf. "Ja, aber die Toten stellen uns Aufgaben, oder?" In: Ruth Klüger, *weiter leben. Eine Jugend* (Göttingen: Wallstein, 1992), 23.

https://doi.org/10.1515/9783110793239-006

was denied to her, as she understood it, only because she was a woman. The text *weiter leben* bears witness to her wrestling with her memories and her wish to find a language of mourning and remembrance, because as a woman she felt she was not permitted to use the traditional Jewish language for doing so.

Ruth Klüger was the only child of her father and she saw him for the last time when she was eight years old, not having had the chance to say good-bye to him properly and not being able to process that this leave taking would be a farewell forever. Only after the Nürnberg Trials did she begin to understand fully that her father, as well as her half-brother, probably did not survive, that they died and she would never see them again. In her search for an appropriate expression of her mourning, she lamented the lack of the possibility to fulfill her obligation as her father's child to recite Kaddish for him. Here follow both the German and the English versions, which provide her reasoning:

> Bei uns Juden sagen nur die Männer den Kaddisch, das Totengebet. Mein immer freundlicher Großvater, den ich mir nur mit ausgestreckten Armen und Taschen voller Geschenke denken kann, soll mit gespielter Trauermiene zu seinem Hund gesagt haben: „Du bist der einzige hier, der Kaddisch für mich sagen kann." Vor seinen Töchtern hat er so mit seinem Hund gesprochen, und meine Mutter hat mir das unkritisch erzählt, hat die Herabsetzung hingenommen, wie es sich für jüdische Töchter schickte. Es war ja humorvoll gemeint. Wär's anders und ich könnte sozusagen offiziell um meine Gespenster trauern, zum Beispiel für meinen Vater Kaddisch sagen kann, könnte ich mich eventuell mit dieser Religion anfreunden, die die Gottesliebe ihrer Töchter zur Hilfsfunktion der Männer erniedrigt und ihre geistlichen Bedürfnisse im häuslichen eindämmt, sie zum Beispiel mit Kochrezepten für gefilte fish abspeist.
>
> Du unterschätzt die Rolle der Frau im Judentum, sagen mir die Leute. Sie darf die Sabbatkerzen anzünden am gedeckten Tisch, eine wichtige Funktion. Ich will keine Tische decken und Sabbatkerzen anzünden, Kaddisch möchte ich sagen. Sonst bleib ich bei meinen Gedichten.
>
> Und warum willst du Kaddisch sagen? fragen mich dann die Leute erstaunt. Bist doch sonst nicht aufs Beten versessen und raufst dir auch die Haare nicht in der Öffentlichkeit. Ja, aber die Toten stellen uns Aufgaben, oder? Wollen gefeiert und bewältigt sein. . . .
>
> Also wie soll ich ihn feiern? (Klüger 1992, 23–24)

In the Jewish tradition only men say the kaddish, the prayer for the dead. (Who is keeping you from saying any prayer you please? my friends ask. But it wouldn't count, couldn't be part of a prescribed communal ritual, so what would be the point?) My much beloved grandfather, who always had a welcome smile and his pockets full of presents for me, used to say with playful somberness to his (male) dog: "You are the only one around who'll be able to say kaddish for me." That's how he talked to his dog in front of his two daughters, because he had no sons, and my mother, who adored him, told me the story without the slightest criticism, accepting the humiliation like a good Jewish girl, for after all, it had been only a joke. If it were different, if I could mourn my ghosts in some accepted public way, like saying kaddish for my father, I'd have a friendlier attitude towards this religion, which reduces its daughters to helpmeets of men and circumscribes their spiritual life within the confines of domestic functions. Recipes for gefilte fish are no recipe for coping with the Holocaust.

Yet I am often told that I underestimate the role of woman in Judaism. She may light the Sabbath candles after having set the table, an important function. I don't want to set the Sabbath table or light candles; I don't live with tablecloths and silverware. And why do you want to say kaddish? the same people, who know me, ask in astonishment. We haven't seen you pray a lot, nor do you wear sackcloth and ashes in public. True, true, but the dead set us certain tasks, don't they? They want to be remembered and revered, they want to be resurrected and buried at the same time. . . . So how shall I celebrate?   (Klüger 2001, 30–31)

The Origins of Reciting the Mourner's Kaddish

The famous Kaddish prayer is actually not a petitionary prayer or supplication but a praise of God, a sanctification of God's name. It starts with: "May His great name be magnified and sanctified in the world that He created according to His will." The following lines continue to bless, laud, glorify, extol, raise, honor, and exalt the Holy One and His kingdom in eternity, in heaven, and on earth. And the final line reads: "May He who makes peace in His heights, bring peace upon us, and upon all Israel. Now respond: Amen." The Kaddish does not contain a request on behalf of the soul of the dead person nor a single word of comfort for the mourners or any reminder or contemplation of death. Its origins are not the cemetery or the house of mourning but rather the study hall. After a rabbi gave a lesson, a lecture, or a sermon, the students used to praise God's name. This practice probably dates back to the Second Temple period, some 2000 years ago, but the designation "Kaddish" for this specific text appears much later in post-Talmudic times.

The wording and the function of this prayer have varied over time. The oldest textual proof of it so far is to be found in the Seder Rav Amram Gaon from the nineth century in Babylonia. He was the head of the Jewish Talmud Academy in Sura. At least five versions of the Kaddish evolved with specific additions or omissions, and they are recited on different occasions. The Kaddish Shalem (the so-called Full Kaddish) and an abbreviated version of it, the Hatzi Kaddish (Half Kaddish), serve as markers or dividers between different parts of the communal prayer service. Thus, they designate the structure of a prayer service. Neither of these versions has been understood as an expression of mourning, and usually they are recited by the cantor or prayer leader, and not by a bereaved person. Only the "Burial Kaddish," recited after laying someone to rest in the cemetery or after completion of studying a Talmudic tractate, has a line added which mentions the resurrection of the dead. But usually, when the Kaddish is mentioned or referenced – and also Ruth Klüger had this in mind –, it refers to the version which is said by children, siblings, spouses, or parents of a dead person. Seven categories of relations (son, daughter, brother, sister, father, mother, spouse) are required halakhically (according to Jewish law) following a death to recite Kaddish, and they are obliged to adopt the most intense mourning rituals which last for varying amounts of time over one year. Children of the deceased recite Kaddish for eleven months, while those in the other bereaved categories recite it for thirty days. The obligation is most demanding for the children of the dead, since it continues for almost an entire year. Accordingly, the Kaddish prayer has always been regarded among Jewry as the most famous expression of Jewish mourning. Also, it is perhaps the most public sign of it. In fact, though, it may only be said when a "minyan" is present, that is, a quorum of ten Jews. Traditionally, this has meant ten Jewish males over the age of thirteen. But still, this so-called Kaddish Yatom (orphan's Kaddish) is the newest of all the Kaddish versions in terms of their evolution over time. The Kaddish prayer is related to mourning for the first time in Tractate Sofrim 19, which was written sometime after the eleventh century. (Marx 2014, 137, note 2.)

The historical background of this development helps clarify this particular role of the prayer in Jewish communal life. It was a catastrophe of heretofore unthinkable dimensions that established the Kaddish Yatom as a widespread liturgical practice in order to express mourning in public. During the First Crusade (1096–99), the blossoming Jewish communities in Central Europe and along the Rhine, which were well-known centers of Jewish scholarship and trade, exhibiting a rich communal tapestry, for example Mainz, Speyer, and Worms were almost extinguished. Marauding mobs killed thousands of Jews, slaughtering men, women, and children brutally. Confronted with the alternative of "death or baptism," many Jews chose to kill their families and to commit suicide immediately afterwards in order to resist the forced conversion to Christianity. Survivors fled to communities in France, bringing with them horrifying memories and emotional shock. The need to find liturgical and theological expressions for this traumatic experience is documented by the great number of "piyyutim" (poems), "kinot" prayers (lamentations), and liturgical insertions, which originate during this time. One well-known for example is the "Av Harachaman," which asks for Divine retribution. The Kaddish Yatom answered this need because it served the religious framing of the murdered Jews as martyrs, that is, their having died "al Kiddush Hashem," for the sanctification of the Divine name. This theological interpretation gave the cruel death of the martyrs meaning and elevated in a spiritual sense their cutoff lives.

The Kaddish Yatom, which is recited by mourners, is found in Siddur Rashi, a compilation of prayer customs from the twelfth century. An orphan or another mourner would lead a prayer service or step forward at its conclusion in order to recite the words of Kaddish out loud, to which the congregation would answer with "Amen" and other words of affirmation. The survivors of the catastrophic attacks drew comfort, perhaps, from the fact that they could express their mourning within the congregation during the prayer service. Their loss and pain were thus acknowledged publicly. Additionally, this practice is connected to the medieval, mystical idea that the souls of the dead first have to descend into Gehenna, a sort of hell, from where they would be raised step by step by each Kaddish that their children said for them. This way the dead would benefit from deeds of the living, which also gave some comfort to the living as well. This thought established responsibility and a strong bonding of the children to their deceased parents and to the community as well. Two Aggadic stories served as the basis for Kaddish Yatom. The Babylonian Talmud, Tractate Shabbat 152a–b, tells of Rav Yehudah, who ordered that when a person without offspring died, ten men should sit at his place for receiving condolences and performing mourning rites vicariously. One time, when Rav Yehudah did that – that is, he gathered ten men to sit daily to receive condolences and perform mourning rites – after seven days the deceased appeared to him in a dream, saying: "Put your mind to rest, because you have put my mind to rest." This story conveys a sense of the ongoing mutual relationship between the dead and the living, and it furthermore suggests that the soul cannot find rest until a public mourning of the dead had taken place.

Another story gained popularity as a reason for reciting Kaddish Yatom. Once, Rabbi Akiva encountered the tormented soul of a man which could not find rest until his son would lead the congregation in prayer and say Kaddish. Rabbi Akiva sought and found the lost son of this man, taught him Torah and prayers, and only after the son recited the Kaddish prayer for his deceased father, was his soul released from its punishment in the afterlife. Although this tale concerns the famous tannaitic Rabbi Akiva who lived end of the first and early second century CE, the story itself appears for the first time in *Or Zarua*, a commentary and collection of ritual laws and customs compiled by Moses of Vienna from the mid-thirteenth century. (Golinkin, 2012, 232, n.1) There are many different versions of this story, but all are documented first in Germany and France after the First Crusade. In this example, the case and rationale for reciting Kaddish apparently came to justify an already existing custom, namely mourners saying Kaddish and thus doing something good for the dead, while contributing to put the mourners' mind to rest.

Should Women Also Say Kaddish?

In the following centuries, the custom of saying Kaddish during the mourning period and on the "Yahrzeit," that is every subsequent year on the anniversary of the death, became widespread apparently because it answered many different needs. Despite the inclusion of Aramaic words in the Kaddish – a language which became unintelligible to most Jews as time went on – efforts to say the prayer in Hebrew or even in a vernacular met with heavy resistance. Beyond their literal meaning, the words of the Kaddish assumed the status of an almost magic formula and as the authentic Jewish expression of mourning. Perhaps it is the very sound itself of the Aramaic words that helps explain why Jews who are not familiar with liturgical texts insist on reading it aloud in transliteration, for example either into Latin or Cyrillic script. The halakhic requirement that it be recited in the presence of a "minyan" gives the prayer a special place within the community, usually in the synagogue, and thereby public acknowledgement for the mourner. Although many Jews today would reject the idea that reciting a prayer could have repercussions on the condition or state of the soul of the deceased, there is a common understanding that saying Kaddish creates an intimate relationship, a posthumous interaction between the dead and the living, and perhaps a way for the survivor to reassure the dead that they are not forgotten. Therefore, saying Kaddish can be a deep emotional moment; it can help evoke memories, express the loss, and aim towards a reconnection with the dead relatives.

Owing to the rich symbolism and the emotional impact of saying Kaddish, the prayer has been a frequent topic of discussion and rabbinical assessments regarding the question of whether also women could or should practice this ritual. There are no occurrences documented until the seventeenth century that mourning women were reciting Kaddish. The oldest halakhic responsum that deals with this question was written by Rabbi Yair Chayim Bacharach (1638–1702), who referred to a specific incident in Amsterdam. A man had passed away, leaving no son, and in his last will he gave the instruction that for one year after his death, ten men should be paid to study in his house daily and upon finishing their daily lesson, his daughter should recite Kaddish. In a way, this request combined the stories of Rav Yehuda about ten men "sitting in his place" and of Rabbi Akiva's suggestion for solving the problem of the tormented soul. "And the scholars and the leaders of the community did not protest against this," Rabbi Bacharach noted in astonishment. (Golinkin 2012, 231) He even stated that: "There is logic, for a daughter also gives contentment to the soul because she is his offspring." But he strongly discouraged such a practice in general because the power of customs would be weakened if any given person changed them to his heart's content.

(Golinkin 2012, 234) Another incident from the Crimea is reported questioning the reciting of Kaddish exclusively by a son. A man who had no sons wanted his daughter to recite Kaddish for him after his death. The halakhic work *Sdei Chemed* by Rabbi Chayim Chizkiah Medini (1832–1904) likewise condemned this practice, as it appeared to deviate from the established custom.

Each of these responsa reacted to the cases of fathers with solely female off-spring, who before their death requested that the daughter fulfill the duty of re-deeming his soul by reciting Kaddish. In Judaism, the responsa make clear that the last will and requests of a dying person have to be treated with utmost re-spect, and the pain of having no one who would recite Kaddish was taken into consideration. However, customs ("minhagim") should always be respected in Judaism and, if possible, one should prevent any change in their practice.

Arguments against daughters saying Kaddish for their deceased parents fo-cused on the question whether this practice would allow them to be counted in the "minyan," that is the quorum of ten Jewish men required for public prayer. According to traditional "halakha," women are exempt from this obligation. And owing to their not being obliged to do so, they are exempt from reciting the prayer and are not able to fulfill the obligation for others vicariously by leading the prayer service. A congregant who sees a woman reciting Kaddish might as-sume that she is a regular member of the "minyan." And thus, the issue of impro-priety or "lewdness" was brought up. The presence of a girl or a woman in the prayer space reserved for men, or simply having men listen to her voice, even if she recited the Kaddish out loud from behind the "mechitzah" (divider) in the women's section of the synagogue, might distract men from their praying. At least that is a common claim. However, women and girls are also obliged to sanc-tify God's name and to honor their parents; both of these are commandments which are fulfilled by their reciting Kaddish. Taking all these arguments into ac-count, there were several attempts to harmonize the wish of the deceased or their bereaved to recite Kaddish and to avoid any doubts about the status of customs or of women in public prayer. Some rabbis argued that the story about Rabbi Akiva is just accidently about a son, and that the wording actually means off-spring and would include daughters, too. (Golinkin, 2012, 243). But then the question remained: where and how could a daughter recite Kaddish which re-quires the presence of a "minyan?"

Since it is the custom to hold religious services in the house of the deceased, many rabbis appeared to be more lenient when daughters would say Kaddish at home in the presence of the "minyan" there. For women to say Kaddish in the home with a "minyan" present would constitute a clear distinction in contrast to synagogue guidelines, because obviously the home is a personal space where the family practice could be allowed to deviate from the synagogue custom. And, comforting the mourners is the main goal of holding prayer services at home any-way. There are also reports of congregations affirming the custom of having daughters recite Kaddish in the vestibule or in the courtyard of the synagogue, rather than in the main sanctuary. Rabbi El'azar Fleckeles (1754–1826) shared his observations in this regard concerning the Jewish community of Prague:

> But I saw in the holy congregation of Prague a nice custom of our ancestors in the vestibule of the Klausen synagogue where elderly men and women, the blind and the lame, sat from *Shakharit* [the morning prayer service] until the afternoon and recited every day the entire book of Psalms. And it is the custom that [for] all those who left no sons, only daughters aged five and six, [might] recite Kaddish there, but inside a synagogue designated specifi-cally for prayers, I have never seen this. And it is wrong for any woman, young or old, to come into the men's section of the synagogue . . . . (Golinkin 2012, 244).

Beyond the issue of the specific space (that is, outside the synagogue or outside the sanctuary proper) also the specific age of the daughter was a topic of con-troversy. Some rabbis would allow daughters up to the age of Bat Mitzvah (twelve years) to recite Kaddish; others would only allow it for younger girls who were four to six years old. Most arguments are based less on discussions of traditional "halakhic" sources, but are rather mostly concerned with the danger of crossing established gender boundaries. One common claim is that the sight or the voice of a mourning daughter reciting Kaddish for her parents might be perceived as immodest and actually lead to lewdness! Among the more lenient positions are those which make clear that it would be better for a daughter in mourning to fulfill this commemorative duty than some other male representa-tive, for instance a grandson or son-in-law of the deceased, or a stranger who would be paid to say Kaddish. That is the opinion of Rabbi Eliezer Grayevsky (1843–1899), who as a rule permitted daughters to recite Kaddish Yatom.

The acceptance of this practice by communities depended also on local cus-toms. Apparently, the custom of women reciting Kaddish was unknown in Poland, while in Lithuania at the end of the nineteenth century there were occurrences of girls and also women reciting Kaddish from behind the "mechitzah," that is in the women's section of the synagogue. The renowned "halakhic" authority, Rabbi Moshe Feinstein (1895–1986) confirmed: "In all generations they were accustomed that occasionally a poor woman would enter the Bet Midrash to receive "tzedakah" [alms] or a female mourner to recite Kaddish." (Golinkin, 2012, 249)

Also, in several synagogues in Jerusalem it was not a rare occurence to hear Kaddish being recited from the women's side of the sanctuary. But, in Orthodox synagogues worldwide up until today there is no consensual position on whether girls and women are allowed to say Kaddish in the public space of the synagogue, or in the cemetery or at a minyan in the house of the mourning family. In ultra-Orthodox communities this practice is usually rejected, and in Israel it depends on the respective burial society, whether or not female mourners are whooshed and silenced when they start to recite Kaddish in public. For many Israeli TV viewers, it was a startling sight in 2014 when Racheli Frenkel, the Orthodox mother of a murdered terror victim, recited Kaddish for her son in public during the burial ceremony. Her respectable reputation and the widespread consideration for this mother's pain initiated a new public discussion about reviewing traditional mourning customs. In most Modern Orthodox circles, the practice of women reciting Kaddish in public has been widely accepted. It has been acknowledged that performing this duty helps the mourner immensely to process the experienced loss, and it also provides certain comfort.

After the Shoah, many non-Orthodox synagogues in the UK and in the U. S. developed a specific approach to Kaddish Yatom. Without taking the gender aspect into account at all, many congregations started to recite together a collective mourners' Kaddish at the end of each service for those who perished in the Shoah and had no descendants who could perform this ritual for them. Given the unimaginable number of victims it was assumed that every day would be the Yahrzeit of perished Jews in this category. The practice of an individual mourner reciting Kaddish continued apace, but in view of the communal obligation to remember and to mourn the countless number of murdered victims of the Shoah, gender issues lost their importance. Additionally, the Liberal streams of Judaism reacted to the changes in the societal position of women in Western countries during the twentieth century by renegotiating their participation in liturgical settings. In egalitarian synagogues which have evolved since the 1970s, and in which the partition between the different genders disappeared, men and women have the same religious rights and obligations. Both men and women function as prayer leaders, Torah readers, and rabbis. In these congregations, no one would perceive a woman reciting Kaddish as immodest or as transgressing gender roles. Rather, it has been understood that giving women an equal space in the public life of congregations enhances their bond with Judaism and enables their practicing Jewish life and rituals actively. When women recite Kaddish in the presence of the community, they take part in the same meaningful and comforting experience that this ritual has had for male mourners during a thousand years.

Poems Instead of Prayer

As a woman and feminist, Ruth Klüger felt excluded from partaking in aspects of Jewish religious life and its rituals. The traditional Jewish division of the gender roles was in her eyes outdated and was tantamount to nothing less than the denigration of women. She lamented the discrimination which led to measuring men and women with different standards and allowing men a broader and dominant space in society and religion. It gave her sufficient reason to break with Judaism as a religion. Her understanding of the gender-specific persecution of women during the Shoah and her need to be included as a woman in public commemoration ceremonies, both Jewish and non-Jewish, led to her alienation from the established patriarchal forms of remembrance:

> Ich hörte nur die Verachtung für Frauen, die in dieser Unterscheidung und in der Anmaßung der Männer lag, eine Art Vormundschaft über mich ausüben zu wollen. Erst hatte es die Verachtung der arischen Kinder für die jüdischen in Wien, danach die der tschechischen Kinder für die deutschen in Theresienstadt gegeben, jetzt die der Männer für Frauen. Diese drei Arten der Verachtung sind inkommensurabel, werdet ihr sagen, ich aber erlebte sie an mir selber, in der angegebenen Reihenfolge. Ich war das *tertium comparationis*, das Versuchskarnickel dieses Vergleichs, und darum stimmt er für mich.
>
> (Klüger 1992, 214.)

> (I was insufficiently socialized in the nuances of gender roles and heard only contempt for women in their words and the arrogance of an authority which they didn't have, but presumed to have because they were male. First, in my childhood, there had been the contempt of Aryan children for Jewish children in Vienna, then the condescension of Czech children for German-speakers in Theresienstadt, and now the arrogance of men towards women. These three types of contempt may be considered incommensurable, but I experienced them within a few years in my own person, in the order mentioned. I am, so to speak, the guinea pig of the comparison, and so it has validity for me.)
>
> (Klüger 2001, 166)

Why didn't Ruth Klüger later take advantage of reciting Kaddish in a Liberal (or Reform or other) synagogue where men **and** women have equal access to religious functions, rituals, and their public performance? Perhaps, this egalitarian approach came a few decades too late for her. Also, Reform/Liberal Judaism takes an affirmative stance towards the existence of God and of religious truth. But Ruth Klüger could not agree anymore to the doxology of the Kaddish, the praise of God's eternal reign. The persecution she experienced as a child, the witnessing of the suffering and dying around her, led her give up belief, religion, and ritual. After referring at first to a friend, she speaks of herself:

> . . . obwohl sie mit dem Herrgott so wenig anfangen kann wie ich. Ich hab erstens kein Talent zur Transzendenz. Zwar kann ich ein paar Kunststücke, die das Bewusstsein heben, senken, zumindest auf eine andere Platte schieben, aber sie sind gehaltlos und hauptsächlich gut als Mittel gegen Schlaflosigkeit und Nervosität. Zweitens kommt der christlich-jüdische Gott aus einer Gesellschaftsstruktur, die mir wenig behagt, denn der Sprung über Adams Rippe hinweg zu diesem Patriarchen ist mir zu weit, und ich schaffe

ihn nicht. Weder zum Mann mit dem Bart noch zu seiner logozentrischen Abstraktion. Ich seh mich im Spiegel und bin nicht sein Ebenbild. Und drittens war ich zu früh in gottverlassenen Räumen. (Klüger 1992, 252)

(. . . although she can deal with [the idea of an] Almighty God as little as I can. First of all, I have no talent for transcendence. To be sure, I can do a few tricks, which raise or lower consciousness, [or] at least push it to another place, but they are without content and mostly good as a pill against sleeplessness and nervousness. Second, the Christian-Jewish God derives from a social structure, which gives me little comfort, because the leap from Adam's rib to this patriarch is too far for me, and I cannot manage it. Neither the man with the beard, nor his logocentric abstraction. I look at myself in the mirror and I am not [made] in his image. And third, I [found myself] too early in godforsaken spaces.)

(Trans. Mark H. Gelber)

Meanwhile she had developed her own means and rituals, which replaced the Jewish custom of saying Kaddish. Nevertheless, it is a sad coincidence that it is the work of a rabbi from Vienna in the thirteenth century, the *Or Zarua*, that first mentions Kaddish as a mourning rite, while seven hundred years later the Viennese Jewess Ruth Klüger stated full of bitterness that as a woman she was denied reciting Kaddish. It left her with a void and the need to find her own rituals of mourning for her father:

Nicht los werde ich den Impuls, ihn zu feiern, eine Zeremonie, eine Totenfeier für ihn zu finden oder zu erfinden. Doch Feierlichkeiten sind mir suspekt, lächerlich, und ich wüsste auch nicht, wie ich es anstellen sollte. (Klüger 1992, 23)

(I keep wanting to celebrate him in some way, to find or invent an appropriate way of mourning, some ceremony for him. And yet celebrations and ceremonies are not my thing. I suspect them of mendacity, and often they strike me as ridiculous. Nor would I know where to start. (Klüger 2001, 30)

By lighting the "Yahrzeit" candle she still resorted to a traditional mourning ritual:

Ich zündete Jahrzeitlichter, wie sie auf Jiddisch heißen, für ihn an. (Klüger 1992, 34)

(I lit yahrzeit candles – as they are called in Yiddish – for him.) (Trans. Mark H. Gelber)

But she described it as a false and cheap gesture, because it used a ready-made candle from the supermarket with only a special label in Hebrew. She perceived it as an almost meaningless ceremony, as a way of summoning her father: "Meine Kerze will dich einmal noch beschwören." (Klüger 1992, 35) (My candle will conjure you once more.) She attempts to process what remained incomprehensible to her and beyond her emotional grasp:

> Zeremonien, mit denen man sich behilft, wenn das Ausmaß des verschwendeten Lebens die Mitleidsfähigkeit übersteigt und sogar das Grauen in die Defensive treibt.
> (Klüger 1992, 260)

> (Ceremonies, which one turns to for help, when the extent of a squandered life goes beyond the ability to feel pity and drives even the horror into the defensive.)
> (Trans. Mark H. Gelber)

The lack of the traditional verbal expression of mourning, that is reciting Kaddish, contributed to her attempts of emotional denial, of refusing to accept the definitiveness of the loss and to acknowledge the cruel way her father died:

> Darum habe ich auch jahrelang, nein, jahrzehntelang nicht glauben wollen und können, dass er wirklich vergast worden ist. (Klüger 1992, 33)

> (That's why for years, no, for decades, I did not want and could not believe, that he had really been gassed.) (Trans. Mark H. Gelber)

For years she was looking for a ritual or ceremony that would convey the bitter truth but also guide her despite unbearable thoughts and in face of her feelings of rage and loss. Her search and her attempts to preserve the father's (and her half-brother's) name and memory were reflected in poems she composed:

> Ich schrieb ihm Gedichte, deutsche und englische, eine Art Exorzismus, oder vielmehr, ich schrieb sie nicht nur, ich verfasste sie im Kopf, gedächtnisfreundliche Verse, mit denen ich wie mit leichtem Gepäck herumlaufen konnte, die einzelnen Strophen sozusagen auf der Zunge zergehen ließ und immer wieder ein Wort daran verbesserte.
> (Klüger 1992, 33–34)

> (I wrote him poems, in German and English, a kind of exorcism, or even more, I did not only write them, I composed them in my head, memory-friendly verse, with which I could walk around as if with light baggage. The individual strophes melted on my tongue, so to speak, and over and over again, a word improved.) (Trans. Mark H. Gelber)

Apparently, the most important thing about those poems was not writing down the text, not to have the words in a written and publishable form, but rather the act of moving the words around in her head, repeating them, working on them, from time to time changing a bit of the wording but keeping the form intact. She repeated the lines in her mind time and again. The words and their rhythm formed an inner recital that created a ritual, as she calls it:

> . . . diesen hausbackenen Kaddisch der Tochter, hausbacken im wörtlichen Sinne, das heißt in keinem Tempel gelernt und gesprochen. (Klüger 1992, 36)

> (this home-baked Kaddish of the daughter, home-baked in the literal sense, which means not learned or spoken in any temple.) (Trans. Mark H. Gelber)

I do not know whether Ruth Klüger was aware of it, but this technique connects her with a deeply rooted way in which Judaism attempted to cope with loss. In fact, in Judaism memory or commemoration is not a matter of recalling incidents, people, and loss occasionally in memorial speeches; rather it is about literally memorializing them by repeating the formulations word for word, learning them by heart and transmitting them to other students/recipients, that is, to the next generation. Thus, the perished world would be preserved in the form of texts and images which actually only existed in the mind. This oral tradition, the studying and transmission of teachings by learning them by heart, allowed for an elasticity, both preservation and adaptation to change at the same time. The hesitation and even prohibition to write down this Oral Torah were rooted in the fear that by committing the words to ink on parchment, they would lose their dynamics and relevance. Historically, this already long established practice proved to be useful after 70 CE when it became necessary to confront the catastrophe of the destruction of the Second Temple in Jerusalem by the Romans. Rabbinic Judaism evolved, and its main characteristic was the endeavor to preserve the memory of what had been destroyed and simultaneously to find new forms for Jewish life in face of the destruction. New forms of religious expression were developed which enabled the survivors to remain faithful to what had been lost and at the same time to move on and find new ways to continue the religion and the Jewish way of life. In effect, they sought to remind themselves of their ancestors' practices even though they could no longer follow them. The Temple rituals and what they symbolized – the permanent presence of God – were reconstructed in words, in an immaterial form which allowed for adapting them to the new reality where other forms of prayer, rituals, and of the transformation of religious values into civil life had to be created.

For this difficult transition the rabbis were able draw on the oral tradition already in place. In fact, it became a decisive tool. The intensity of the oral tradition and its method are hardly accessible to us today, because we live in a text-based culture – rapidly becoming a screen-based culture – and we have been used to writing things down in order not to forget them. The memory skills of the students in ancient times should fill us with awe. We must conclude that it was simply necessary to transform the oral tradition of Judaism into a written one in order to preserve it. This is what eventually happened regarding the creation of the Mishnah and other works of Rabbinical literature decades and centuries later. What we often do not take into account is the intense nature of this encounter which is created in the mind of the learner beyond simple memorizing. In order to be able to recall an inordinate amount of text by heart, one must repeat it again and again, while putting all other thoughts about the text aside, until the text begins to speak from inside of oneself. From that moment, the text accompanies the self wherever one goes. It is always present, and it is hard to discern which one prevails: the individual or the text. I see a parallel between this dynamic, living encounter and devotion to words, spoken or recited in the mind, and not frozen on a written piece of any kind of material, which formed the foundations of Judaism two thousand years ago, and the way or manner of remembering and memorializing the dead that Ruth Klüger practiced. Working on a poem, repeating it, exchanging a few words, and revising it were part of this intense process. Being denied to say Kaddish and herself refusing to be part of a religious tradition that does not encompass the fullness of her person and her biographical experiences, she developed expressions which are nonetheless deeply embedded in Jewish tradition. The poems that she composed as a daughter for her deceased father became her own form of Kaddish.

Also, in another way her own poetical expressions have a deep affinity to the Kaddish and its mystical dimensions. The legend of Rabbi Akiva and the tormented soul described above depicts a connection between the dead parent and the surviving child. By reciting prayers and Kaddish, the son influences the well-being of the deceased father, raising his soul from Gehenna and alleviating his suffering. During the eleven months of this ritual the two – one alive and one deceased – remain bound to each other in a dynamic relationship. The souls are elevated through a verbal act (reciting the Kaddish) and the commitment of the surviving child, an obligation that could not be fulfilled by anyone else. Ruth Klüger was able to relate to and pick up on this mystical idea. Commemoration of the dead is actually a form of interaction with them; she called her attempt to approach and to get close to them "incantation" or conjuring:

> Erinnerung ist Beschwörung, und wirksame Beschwörung ist Hexerei. Ich bin ja nicht gläubig, nur abergläubisch. Ich sag manchmal als Scherz, doch es stimmt, dass ich nicht an Gott glaub, aber an Gespenster schon. Um mit Gespenstern umzugehen, muss man sie ködern mit Fleisch der Gegenwart. Ihnen Reibflächen hinhalten, um sie aus ihrem Ruhezustand herauszureizen und sie in Bewegung zu bringen.　　　　(Klüger 1992, 79)

> (Remembering is a branch of witchcraft; its tool is incantation. I often say, as if it were a joke – but it's true – that instead of God I believe in ghosts. To conjure up the dead you have to dangle the bait of the present before them, the flesh of the living, to coax them out of their inertia. You have to grate and scrape the old roots with tools from the shelves of ancient kitchens.)　　　　(Klüger 2001, 69)

Communication with the souls of the dead is by no means absurd for her. Her father and her half-brother are present in her life as "nackte, frierende Gespenster am gedeckten Tisch." (Klüger 1992, 97) (naked, freezing ghosts at the banquet. Klüger 2001, 83) But compared to the Kaddish, the relation is reversed: the survivor is reaching out for a connection, while the dead withdraw and distance themselves from the living. After learning with certainty about the murder of her half-brother Schorschi and grasping the circumstances of his death, she dreamed:

> . . . von einer öden Landschaft, wo ein paar Menschen aus großer Entfernung einander winken oder bedrohen. Unübersteigbarer Stacheldraht zwischen uns und den Toten. Ich hatte schon früher versucht, sie in Bilder und Worte zu bannen. „Mit erfrorenen roten / Händen schaufelt mein Bruder sein eigenes Grab." Sie ließen sich nicht bannen. Wie sie uns hassen müssen. Wir gehen ihnen entgegen, sie ziehen sich zurück.   (Klüger 1992, 97)

> (. . . of a barren landscape, where several people are winking at, or threatening, each other from a great distance. Insurmountable barbed wire between us and the dead. I had tried much earlier to captivate them in images and words: "with frozen red/ hands my brother digs his own grave." They were not to be captivated. How they must hate us. We approach them, they pull back.)

Also, in her poem "Yom Kippur" Ruth Klüger describes her attempt in vain to get close to the dead, but they turn away from her and the survivors in disdain:

> Und ihr helft uns nicht und bleibt uns entzogen,
> Ihr verweigert Versöhnung zur Jahreswende,
> Und ihr stoßt von euch unsre Münder und Hände,
> Wie unreine Tiere aus Synagogen.
>
> Ich war doch vor Jahren dir Jahr um Jahr Schwester,
> Der du dich abkehrst, starrsinnig erstarrt,
> Wo dein Sterben dich einschließt wie Stacheldraht.
> Sind wir Lebenden denn den Toten Gespenster?
> > (Klüger 1992, 98)

> (And you do not help us and remain detached from us,
> You refuse reconciliation at the turn of the year,
> And you push away from yourselves our mouths and hands,
> Like impure animals from synagogues.
>
> I was still your sister years ago and year after year,
> From whom you turned away, stubbornly frozen,
> Where your dying closed in around you like barbed wire.
> Are we living just the ghosts of the dead?)
> > (Trans. Mark H. Gelber)

It is in actuality the soul of the survivor which remains tormented and unredeemed from pain. Despite intense encounters, the dead refuse to grant the living alleviation, closure, and peace. Writing poems is Ruth Klüger's coping strategy. Already as a child in Auschwitz and also later in life she composed verse in a therapeutical attempt to process her experiences and as an act of resistance against the barbaric, horrible reality. She criticized Adorno and other intellectuals who demanded that one should not compose poems after and about Auschwitz. Apparently, they never needed poetic language to survive mentally, while she emphasizes:

> Gedichte sind eine bestimmte Art von Kritik am Leben und könnten . . . beim Verstehen helfen.
> (Klüger 1992, 126)

> (Poems are a certain kind of critique of life and they can . . . by understanding [them] help.)
> (Trans. Mark H. Gelber)

For her, only poetic language is able to capture reality without claiming to be ordinary communication. For Ruth Klüger poems functioned similarly to prayers, by attempting to get closer and to establish a relationship to another dimension. She had found a substitute mourning ritual for the Kaddish, but the bitter sting remained because her life and her losses went largely unacknowledged since she was a woman.

Bibliography

Golinkin, David. "Women and the Mourner's Kaddish." Tshuva on Yoreh De'ah 376: 4. In: Golinkin, *The Status of Women in Jewish Law: Responsa*, Jerusalem: 2012.

Klüger, Ruth. *Still Alive. A Holocaust Girlhood Remembered*. New York: Feminist Press at the City University of New York, 2001.

Klüger, Ruth. *weiter leben. Eine Jugend*. Göttingen: Wallstein, 1992.

Marx, Dalia. "Kaddish: From the Rhine Valley to Jezreel Valley. Innovative Versions of the Mourners' Kaddish in the Kibbutz Movement." In: Michael Meyer and David A. Myers (Eds.). *Between Tradition and Modernity. Rethinking Old Oppositions. Essays in Honor of David Ellenson*. Detroit: Wayne State University Press, 2014, 123–141.

Mark H. Gelber

Ruth Klüger, Judaism, and Zionism: An American Perspective

> "I regard my book as a kind of Kaddish prayer, or perhaps a grave, for my family that was murdered in the Shoah."
>
> Anne Berest, in an interview about her new novel, *The Postcard*[1]

> "Instead of God, I believe in ghosts."
>
> Ruth Klüger, *Still Alive. A Holocaust Girlhood Remembered*

The following analysis of Ruth Klüger's relationship to Judaism and Zionism opens with the presentation of a passage from the novel *Zuckerman Unbound* (1981), written by the popular American-Jewish writer, Philip Roth (1933–2018), who was a contemporary of hers. Admittedly, inclusion of references to Philip Roth in a discussion about Ruth Klüger is somewhat problematical, because it may appear to some to be an instance of comparing apples with oranges, as the saying goes. In addition, she almost certainly did not consider him to be a worthy or compelling writer. More likely, she would have found some or most of his writing to be trash or pornography, and she probably would have dismissed his fiction peremptorily. Although Roth famously rejected for himself the label of "American-Jewish writer," many observers consider him to be one. (Roth 2017, 46–47) In any case, he certainly viewed himself as an American writer.[2] While a convincing case could be made in favor of Ruth Klüger being categorized as a Jewish writer, that is not the purpose of this essay. However, she may be fairly categorized and understood to a degree as an American Jew, who engaged seriously with Judaism and Zionism.

Toward the end of Roth's novel, the protagonist Nathan Zuckerman attends the funeral of his father in Florida. The fictional text is, characteristically for Roth, outrageous in several ways, but nonetheless the typical Jewish respect for the dead is mentioned. (Roth 1981, 136) At the interment, Nathan recites the

---

1 Quoted in Gaby Levin, "The word Jewish was never mentioned at home," *Ha'aretz* (English edition), November 25, 2021, 8.

2 Philip Roth, "I have fallen in love with American names," *The New Yorker*, June 5, June 12, 2017, 46–47. Roth consistently admitted to being a "Newark Jew," but viewed labels such as "American Jewish writer" or "Jewish American writer" to be self-limiting: "I have never considered myself for the length of a single sentence as an American Jewish or Jewish American writer, any more than I can imagine Dreiser and Hemingway and Cheever thought of themselves while at work as American Christian or Christian American or just plain Christian writers." (47)

https://doi.org/10.1515/9783110793239-007

Jewish prayer for the dead, the Kaddish, as is traditional: "He recited the Mourner's Kaddish. Over a sinking coffin, even a nonbeliever needs some words to chant, and '*Yisgadal v'yiskadash . . .*' made more sense to him than . . . . If ever there was a man to bury as a Jew, it was his father. Nathan would probably wind up letting them bury him as one too. Better as that than as a bohemian." (Roth 1981, 136) This passage is pertinent to the following discussion of Ruth Klüger for a few reasons: the first has to do with death itself and the second with the Kaddish prayer, which she took quite seriously. The third has to do with the American or American-Jewish context which informs both Roth and Klüger. Her parallel texts, *weiter leben* and *Still Alive,* both open with the topic of death, labelling it as the secret subject in family discussions when she was a child in Vienna. Death is a recurrent topos in her writing, and for good reason given her background as a child survivor of the Shoah, many of whose relatives – including her father and half-brother – were murdered by the Nazis. The other two reasons for citing this passage in Roth's novel which mentions the Kaddish prayer have to do with Jewish burial in general and with the actual burials of Roth and Klüger in the U.S., in particular.

First, it is important to state that the issue of burial is by no means neutral or a purely pragmatic act in Judaism. Over centuries Jewish law and custom have stipulated for living Judaism the proper guidelines for preparation of the corpse for interment, as well as a host of other issues related to the "what, when, and how" of the ceremony, such as what may be said, and what not or when not. Like most matters in Judaism, it is a complicated issue. The same is true for the prolonged period of traditional Jewish mourning, which unfolds in stages after the death of a member of the family. In Judaism these rituals are sacred to the faithful and the Jewish cemetery is deemed sacred property. The guiding principle behind the Jewish laws concerning burial, which are rather strict or rigid in orthodox or traditional Judaism, is a basic, uncompromising, and irrevocable respect for the dead, or in Hebrew: honoring the deceased. Nevertheless, in modern times rabbis affiliated with more liberal varieties of Judaism, for example Reform Judaism, have been exceedingly flexible and accepting of congregants who wished to choose what had been viewed for centuries as non-Jewish burial customs or even cremation. Some rabbis will agree reluctantly to officiate at non-traditional end-of-life events, if they have been asked to do so, and others regularly support such practices by their congregants or others. When Roth wrote his novel, he may have intended to be buried in the historic Gomel Hesed Jewish cemetery in Newark, New Jersey, where his parents were buried. Incidentally, Allen Ginsberg (1926–1997), the well-known Amerian poet of the beat generation, is buried in Gomel Hesed. Related perhaps is that Roth was widely associated with Newark, since it was a setting and reference point for so much of his fiction over decades. However, he changed his mind at some point and decided in the end to be buried at the non-denominational cemetery at Bard College in Annandale-on-Hudson in New York State, where one of his friends, the Romanian(-Jewish) writer Norman Manea (b. 1936), who was teaching at Bard, wished to be buried. Incidentally, Hannah Arendt (1906–1975), the well-known German-Jewish political philosopher who sought refuge in the U.S. during the Nazi period, is also buried in the Bard College cemetery. Roth had previously received an honorary doctorate from Bard College and he knew Leon Botstein, the president of the college. In fact Roth had been friendly or even close to him, and Botstein would have been able to facilitate and implement Roth's final decision. Evidently, Roth forbade any religious rituals at his funeral, Jewish or otherwise.

The burial of Ruth Klüger represents a contrasting example to that of Roth. She, resident in Irvine, California towards the end of her life, had at first decided to be cremated after her death. But, sometime following her mother's funeral in 2000, she changed her mind and subsequently expressed a wish to be buried in the same Jewish cemetery where her mother was buried, the Mount Sinai Memorial Park in Los Angeles. This decision evidently followed her belated realization and perhaps new belief that it was important to bury the dead. That is, her change of mind indicates that for her the act of burial itself had become potentially significant in its own right, especially given the fact that so many of those who were murdered during the Nazi genocide and also during World War II altogether were never given a proper burial or they were dumped indiscriminately in mass graves or cremated in the death camps. Another reason for her change of mind pertained possibly to a realization concerning her feelings about family. After attending her own mother's funeral, with whom she survived the Shoah – but with whom she had had a very complicated and difficult relationship – she felt that she would prefer to be buried close to her mother, to be buried close to her family. Ruth Klüger wrote repeatedly in a positive manner about family and family feelings in general, and it sometimes appears that her family feelings are related to her sense of Jewishness, that is to her Jewish sensibility. Strong family feelings and family solidarity have often been cited as characteristics common to Jews. Ruth once compared visiting a memorial center or museum dedicated to remembrance of those killed during the Shoah to attending a funeral in a cemetery, attributing priority to visiting in a cemetery, since it – the act of visiting itself – could help one to come to terms with the death and the loss of a loved person.[3]

---

3 This discussion took place following her address concerning forced labor at the Bundestag in Berlin on January 27, 2016. Cf. "The German Bundestag: Young people spoke with writer Ruth Klüger." (YouTube)

It was important to Ruth Klüger, as a feminist, that a female rabbi would officiate at her interment ceremony. This stipulation of hers had been made clear in advance. It is of interest because she had in principle avoided seeking rabbinical advice or services during her adulthood, although she did agree to undergo the formalities of a religious Jewish divorce from her husband, when he requested one. Rabbi Carla Howard, the founder and executive director of the Jewish Healing and Hospice Center of Los Angeles, presided over the service and gave a traditional Jewish eulogy preceding the interment. The rabbi mentioned how important the commandment to bury the dead is in the Jewish religion, and she also discussed the significance of the fact that the day of Ruth Klüger's burial coincided on the Jewish calendar with the holiday of Simchat Torah, with its symbolic commemoration of ending and beginning. She chanted the "Malei Rachamim" (God, full of mercy) prayer, a traditional prayer normally recited at Jewish burials, bidding farewell to the soul and beseeching God to give the soul of the deceased infinite rest. But, her eulogy, in my view, missed the mark completely, because almost everything she said did not pertain to the person Ruth Klüger was and Ruth certainly would not have appreciated her remarks. Whereas as a young child in Vienna she celebrated Jewish holidays with her family, for example the Passover seder, and she recalls Rosh Hashanah and Yom Kippur in Vienna as well, she never reported about Jewish holiday celebrations in her family after the war. She was mostly alienated from them and they did not signify much for her in her adult life; she never or rarely incorporated rituals or other acts regarding the Jewish holidays or Jewish calendar into her adult life – also not as a mother. Her Jewish allegiances as an adult are to be found elsewhere.

Nevertheless, when one contrasts Ruth Klüger with Philip Roth in the matter of end of life and choice of a final resting place, one may sum up as follows: whereas Roth appeared to care deeply about his Jewish identity throughout his life and concomitantly integrated an inordinate amount of Jewish-related material into his fiction, which serves to a degree as evidence of this aspect of his understanding of self, he nevertheless chose in the end not to be buried in a Jewish cemetery, stipulating that no specific Jewish rituals should be practiced at his burial. The non-religious son in his novel recites the Kaddish prayer in the cemetery as a matter of course. However, Ruth Klüger, who consistently distanced herself from religious ritual and traditional Jewish practice in her adult life, and has been embraced, as well as appropriated to a degree, by her European – specifically Austrian and German – readerships, did in the end decide in favor of a Jewish burial in an American Jewish cemetery.

A good indication of her view late in life of burial can be found in the chapter "Sterben im Exil" (dying in exile) in *unterwegs verloren* (2008), because she writes there in detail about the burial of her cousin Heinz, who lived after the war in Chicago. She made a major effort to travel from California to attend this funeral of her cousin, to whom she was not especially close after the war, and she also spoke afterwards at a reception hosted by his friends. The fact that Ruth and Heinz were family members who shared much as children in Europe, and afterwards as survivors as well, seems to have been decisive in terms of her deciding to be present. What complicates to a degree her discussion of Heinz's burial is that he had converted to Christianity some time before; also, to a lesser degree, that he was a homosexual needed to be taken into account. Despite his conversion, Klüger insisted on his basic, ineradicable Jewish identity. It was an inexpungable fact of his existence, just as it was an irrefutable fact of her own existence. For her, being Jewish was something that transcended religion. She referred to Heinz as "this dead Jew." (Klüger 2008, 42) What seemed to strike Klüger as especially sorrowful was that this burial was for her the epitome of Jewish diaspora existence, something she disdained owing to its ineluctably negative impact on individual identity and the stability of the self: ". . . [die] Zerstreuung an Orte wo man nicht hingehört, die Fremdheit, die er irgendwie zu überwinden gesucht hatte, in dem er sich einer Kirchengemeinde anschloß." (Klüger 2008, 49) (. . . the dispersion to places, in which one did not belong, the foreignness, which he had somehow sought to overcome, by joining a Christian community.) She recognized that her own basic, larger family situation after the war was one of diaspora, characterized by dislocations, alienation, disorientation, and distance from any specific place but also from any surviving family members. In this section of her report about the funeral, she quotes some poignant lines from a poem by the Austrian poet and politician Guido Zernatto (1903–1943), which he himself wrote in American exile:

> Dieser Wind der fremden Kontinente
> Hat den Atem einer andern Zeit.
> Andere Menschen, einer andern Welt geboren,
> Mag's erfrischen. Ich bin hier verloren
> Wie ein Waldtier, das in Winternächten schreit. (Klüger 2008, 49)

> (This wind of foreign continents
> Has the breath of a different time
> Different people, born to a different world,
> May it refresh. I am lost here
> Like a wild animal in the forest, which screams in the winter nights.)

The negative condition of exile and its connection to death and burial as described by Ruth Klüger are common aspects of Jewish sensibility and consciousness, which appear repeatedly in Jewish literature. The Jewish cemetery and the

Kaddish prayer, given the background of persecution and genocide, provide frameworks for numerous Jewish writers to express the agony of life in face of, and after, the Shoah. Considering the German (language)-Jewish literary corpus, one may think of Franz Werfel's poem "Der gute Ort zu Wien," (The good place [i.e. the cemetery] in Vienna) which was written after Jews were forbidden to enter all public parks and gardens in June, 1938. It was tantamount to a kind of exile in their own homeland. However, they were still permitted to visit in the Jewish cemetery. The first stanza reads:

> Volksgarten, Stadt/ und Rathauspark,
> Ihr Frühling war noch nie so stark.
> Den Juden Wiens ist er verboten.
> Ihr einziges Grün wächst bei den Toten. (Kaznelson 1959, 50)

> (People's park/garden, Municipal Park and City Hall Park
> Your spring has never been so strong
> The Jews of Vienna have been forbidden [to enter].
> Their only green grows near the dead.)

Ruth Klüger reported in retrospect on this development sardonically, noting that as a child she was not allowed to enter a public park or sit on a park bench in Vienna, while consoling herself with the thought that at least she belonged to the chosen people. And, at the time it was still possible for children to romp and play in the Jewish cemetery. (Klüger 2001, 122)

Another example is the poem "Kaddisch 1943," written by the Austrian writer and poet, Friedrich Torberg (1908–1979), who went into exile during the Nazi period in France and in the U.S., before returning to Vienna after the war. His poem attempted to give expression to the futility of commemorating the mass murder and the concomitant human suffering by traditional formulas of Jewish prayer. The third stanza reads:

> Trieb es dich, den Vater zu beweinen?
> Stehst du um der Mutter willen hier?
> Aber tausend Väter sind die deinen.
> Aber tausend Mütter starben dir. (Kaznelson 1959, 368)

> (Were you moved, to cry for your father?
> Are you standing here on account of your mother?
> But a thousand fathers are yours.
> But a thousand mothers are dead to you.)

Torberg's verse laments the situation in which no son remains alive to say Kaddish and no family members are alive who might light Yahrzeit candles: "Und da ist kein Sohn zum Kaddisch-Sagen/ und da brennt kein Licht zur Jahrzeit mehr."

(Kaznelson 1959, 368) (And there is no son to say Kaddish/ and no light burns anymore for Yahrzeit.) The last line of this German-language poem consists of the transliterated first line of the Hebrew-Aramaic Kaddish prayer: "Jisgadal wejiskadasch schameh rabbo." It is not glossed in any way. Related perhaps to these poetic expressions is the poem "Kaddisch" (1945) by Mascha Kaleko (1907–1975), who was born in Austro-Hungarian Galicia, immigrated to the U.S. in face of Nazism, and eventually came to live in Israel. Her poem specifically laments and memorializes "/den Hunderttausend, die kein Grabstein nennt,/" (Röttger 1966, 55), (the hundred thousand, which no gravestone names).

Ruth Klüger eventually came to believe that it was important **to bury** the dead, since burial in a cemetery would provide a locus – a fixed memorial site and a place to visit, which had in itself the potential to help family, friends, and others come to terms with the loss of a loved person. It is not necessary to understand her decision as a religious act *per se*, but it may be viewed certainly as an act which expressed her Jewish sensibility. In the same way, she dedicated *Still Alive* in 2001 to the memory of her mother –Alma Hirschel (1903–2000) – with whom she had had a painfully complicated relationship for most of her life; she came to acknowledge in the end the ultimate significance of family as part of Jewish life. Ruth also relished the Jewish custom of placing a small stone on the headstone or at the gravesite upon visiting the deceased. For example, in 1988 when she paid a visit to the grave of the celebrated German-Jewish poet Else Lasker-Schüler (1869–1945), who was buried in the Jewish cemetery on the Mount of Olives in Jerusalem, she placed a small stone on the gravesite, and she asked her original German publisher, Thedel von Wallmoden, who accompanied her, if he would place a stone on her own grave after she died. Ruth certainly would have known Else Lasker-Schüler's memorial poem "Meine Mutter" (1942), which refers to lighting a candle in memory of her deceased mother: "Es brennt die Kerze auf meiner Tisch/ Für meine Mutter die ganze Nacht./" (Schlösser 1960, 55) (The candle on my table burns/ for my mother the entire night./) Ruth also discussed the Jewish custom of placing a stone at burial sites with the journalist and filmmaker Renate Schmidtkunz during a visit to Bergen-Belsen in a documentary film that was made about Ruth's life.

The late decision to be buried in a Jewish cemetery must be understood within the context of her discussion of the Kaddish prayer in her memoirs.[4] As much as she desired to say Kaddish for her father, she emphatically dismissed

---

4 For a detailed discussion of the Kaddish prayer, see the chapter in this book written by Rabbi Ulrike Offenberg, 73–88.

the possibility of doing it, because the traditional orthodox practice stipulated that only men – that is, primarily, the sons of the deceased, but also the fathers and siblings of the deceased– were enjoined to recite Kaddish. Furthermore, it needed to be recited in the presence of a *minyan*, that is, ten men, whether at the funeral, during the Shiva (the traditional seven days of mourning following the burial), and then daily during the year of mourning, but also afterwards on the annual recurring day of death. The orthodox rabbinate relieves women of this commandment; Ruth Klüger understood this aspect of Judaism to be part and parcel of a discriminatory, anti-feminist patriarchal system, which characterized traditional Jewish life. In *Still Alive* she wrote that she wished to recite the Kaddish for her father for the sake of the dead: ". . . but the dead set us certain tasks, don't they? They want to be remembered and revered, they want to be resurrected and buried at the same time. I want to say kaddish because I live with the dead. If I can't do it, forget about religion." (Klüger 2001, 31) That Reform Judaism and other more liberal varieties of the Jewish religion have consistently rejected limiting this practice to men, while encouraging women to recite the Kaddish, if they so wished, made little impression on her. The position of these more liberal varieties of organized Jewish religion exerted no immediate impact, even though she was well aware that it was becoming more and more common during her lifetime for women in almost all of the various branches of organized Judaism, including modern orthodoxy (but not in ultra-orthodox and Hassidic varieties), to recite the Kaddish prayer for the deceased. As opposed to her rejection of reciting the Kaddish in her own case, she nevertheless lit Yahrzeit candles in memory of her father, a traditional Jewish practice. Like many human beings, Ruth Klüger was not always one hundred percent consistent. She also penned a moving poem entitled "Mit einem Jahrzeitlicht für den Vater." (With a yahrzeit candle for the father) In her own commentary on the genesis of this poem, she referred to an evening in California, when she walked to a local playground. Memories from her childhood in Vienna, in which her father played a role before he attempted to escape from the Nazis, ineluctably intermingled with her American experience and her desire to light the memorial candle. (Klüger 1992, 34–35)

The background and point of departure in the following part of this chapter are related to my wish to correct or qualify what I deem to be mistaken understandings of Ruth Klüger's relationships to Judaism and to Zionism, as well as to refute some erroneous general claims, like the one proffered by Janine Pohle, namely that "she felt that she did not belong to any specific identity." (Pohle, e-book) However she repeatedly embraced her Jewish ethnicity and regularly expressed pride in her belonging to the Jewish people. (Klüger 2008, 58) Regarding

Judaism, Michael Ossar claimed that Ruth Klüger's autobiographical *weiter leben-Still Alive* is a Bildungsroman that "describes the sense in which a basically non-religious person became a Jew (a process Klüger has in common with a great many survivors." (Ossar 2003, 677) However, her first poems or those stanzas of poetry she composed as a teenager during the Shoah and which were published in German soon after liberation refer to God and question faith in God in face of the genocide. For example, in the third stanza of her early poem "Auschwitz," the poetic persona (or the young Ruth, if she may be identified as the poetic voice) addresses God directly, maybe even piously, while bitterly lamenting the endless murder taking place in front of her (or the poetic persona's) very eyes, an act which is scornful of God's law:

> Gott, du allein darft's doch nur geben,
> das große, heilige Menschenleben,
> du gibst das Dasein und du gibst den Tod.
> Und du siehst dieses endlose Morden,
> du siehst diese blutigen, grausamen Horden,
> und Menschen verachten dein höchstes Gebot! (Klüger 2008, 45)

> (God, you alone may only give
> the great, holy human life
> you give existence and you give death.
> And you see this endless murdering,
> you see these bloodly, gruesome hordes,
> and people scorn your highest commandment.)

Later in life, she referred on several occasions to her loss of faith or her agnosticism. In *Still Alive* she wrote that ". . . what little [she] had been taught of a Jewish faith in a Jewish God crumbled in the course of the years that ensued"; furthermore, ". . . with the passing years many fervent convictions and certainly all manner of faith, has drained out of [her]." (Klüger 2008, 18, 45) And, in *unterwegs verloren*, she specified the evolution of her loss of faith:

> Damals glaubte ich noch an einen sozusagen unverbindlichen Gott, einen, den man zwar weder für die natürlichen noch die menschlichen Übel in der Welt verwantwortlich machen kann, der aber doch eine höhere Instanz darstellt, ein universeller Geist, der existiert, weil es etwas Umfassenderes geben muß als das, was ich bin. Auch dieser Glaube ist mit der Zeit verschwunden . . . .   (Klüger 2008, 127)

> (At that time I still believed in a non-binding God, so-to-speak, one who could not be held responsible for the natural or the human evil in the world, but rather one who represented a higher authority, a universal spirit, which exists, because there must be something more comprehensive than what I am. But, this belief too disappeared over time . . . .)

Therefore, the process described by Ossar cannot be close to the truth.

And, while Heidelberger-Leonard has analyzed many Jewish aspects of Klüger's writing trenchantly – she understands Klüger to have been a very consciously Jewish women ("eine sehr bewußte Jüdin"), (Heidelberger-Leonard 1996, 50) – she has misjudged, I believe, Ruth Klüger's relationship to Zionism, because she claimed that Klüger never considered seriously immigrating to Israel. (Heidelberger-Leonard 1996, 58) Heidelberger-Leonard is correct, though, when she labels Zionism as an item of "unfinished business" ("zum Unerledigten" [Heidelberger-Leonard 1996, 74]) in Klüger's life. Moreover, it was an open wound ("eine Wunde"). She rejected out of hand the idea and term "assimilation" in her case. As she insisted: her family was emancipated, not assimilated. (Klüger 2001, 43) Although she by and large rejected organized Jewish religion, and usually decided not to follow established Jewish customs, her decision to be buried in a Jewish cemetery close to her mother may be understood as one aspect of her Jewish sensibility.

I have written at length on the topic of Jewish sensibility in Austrian-Jewish literature in general (Gelber 2018, 11–12) and regarding Ruth Klüger specifically. (Gelber 2014, Gelber 2022) Aspects of her Jewish sensibility are sometimes related to Jewish religion, but more often they are directly related to Jewish culture, history, and values. Here follow a few examples which are pertinent to Ruth Klüger:

– Her repeated use of vocabulary derived from specifically Jewish languages in her German-language or American English-language texts. The most obvious examples in this category pertain to Yiddish and Hebrew lexical items, sometimes glossed in the fabric of the German or English language text. Ruth knew Yiddish terms from her childhood in Vienna, but her Yiddish improved greatly during the Shoah, when she came into contact with Yiddish-speaking Eastern European Jewish women in the camps. Terms or expressions like "risches," "Naches," and "Rachmones" from Yiddish or "Maneschtane," "Hatikvah," or "Zaddik" from Hebrew are good examples. These terms differ to a degree from "Mischpoche" or "Goj," which she also employs, because these Yiddish terms, derived from the Hebrew, are perhaps somewhat recognizable or known among non-Jewish readerships, especially American and German readers. However, "risches," "Rachmones," or "Maneschtane" would not normally be comprehensible for the wider American or German readerships.

– Her references to, or quotations from, Jewish prayer, Jewish learning, traditional Jewish texts (the Hebrew Bible, for example), and to Jewish rituals. Examples include her citing the "Shema Yisroel" prayer. Her report in *weiter leben* on the lesson taught by Rabbi Leo Baeck in Theresienstadt concerning a possible interpretation of the Biblical tale of creation (Klüger 1992, 101) pertains here as well, especially because she views his teaching as a means of restoring or recovering the Jewish heritage in cogent modern terms. She refers repeatedly to stories from the Bible or utilizes similes which refer to the Hebrew Bible, that is, the Old Testament.

– Her references to Jewish holidays, synagogue attendance, and Jewish customs.

Examples in this category include her descriptions of her family Seder on Passover eve in Vienna, eating "matzoh," unleavened bread, attending synagogue services on Rosh Hashanah, the Jewish New Year, or fasting on Yom Kippur, the annual day of atonement on the Jewish calendar. She decided to fast on Yom Kippur in a labor camp in solidarity with other religious women inmates who were fasting. Yet, in *Still Alive* she wrote that her "Jewishness [was] really nothing to be proud of." [. . .] "[she] cannot remember a single religious celebration, that [she] honestly enjoyed." (Klüger 2001, 44) Her characterization of herself as "a bad Jew"– by which she meant her laxness regarding Jewish observance –or her alienation from, rejection of, or ambivalence about the Jewish holidays and her feminist critique of patriarchal aspects of them do not in fact compromise or diminish significantly a Jewish sensibility which came to expression in her writings and work.

– Her many references to topics of special Jewish interest, sometimes hidden references to specifically Jewish concepts, precepts, or common admonitions.

Much of her writing, especially her poetry, centers on Jewish-related topics, like diaspora, exile, and Jewish holidays. Her use of the expression: "Leuchtturm für die übrige Menschheit" (Klüger 1992, 90) is worthy of special mention. Although not glossed or explicated in *weiter leben*, it is in fact a translation from the Hebrew, or in English: "a light unto the nations." This phrase is a common Jewish designation and understanding of the purpose of Jewish existence in the world altogether, that is, to serve as a paradigmatic beacon of morality and justice for all nations. Another example is the notion that Jews should not marry non-Jews; it comes up repeatedly in her writing as a normative although quite problematical Jewish injunction.

– Her spatial orientation towards specifically Jewish space or spaces, most often the land of Israel, and references to and discussions of Zionism, its ideologues and its ideology, as far as it promulgated a return to Zion from the diaspora and the establishment of a Jewish State. The Jewish ghettos, points of deportation, and even the concentration camps – or most of them – may be viewed in this same context, that is as Jewish spaces as well.

Ruth Klüger uses the very positive Hebrew term "Eretz Israel" (the land of Israel) to refer to Zion and reports how Zionism dominated discussions and her thinking during her incarceration in Theresienstadt. She came to consider Zionism the most reasonable solution to pernicious anti-Semitism and the problems facing Jewry. She reports in a matter of fact way that her father had been a member of a Zionist youth group in Vienna. Also, Theodor Herzl, the well-known Viennese *homme de lettres*, is referred to in *weiter leben* as a hero, (Klüger 1992, 84) and he is sometimes quoted in the text without a direct reference to him. For example, she cited Herzl's phrase: "Aus Judenjungen junge Juden machen." (Klüger 1992, 89) (To make young Jews out of young 'yidn.') Herzl's play *Das neue Ghetto* (The New Ghetto, 1894), a turning point in his conversion to Jewish nationalism and Zionism, is referenced in *weiter leben* as well. She expressed her deep dismay regarding her mother's refusal to consider sending her from Vienna to Palestine within the framework of a "Kindertransport," in order to try to save her life at the last moment. (Klüger 1992, 63) For years, she harbored the desire to immigrate to Israel, to make "Aliyah," in order to help build a just, socialist Jewish State. Furthermore, as a work in progress, *weiter leben* was tentatively entitled "Stationen," and descriptions of experiences in three concentration/labor camps, – which she understood as kinds of Jewish spaces –as well as responses to her experiences in them, as she reflected about them over the years, form the bulk of several chapters.

– Her emphatic reliance on, and reference to, Jewish writers and the Jewish literary tradition in Jewish or non-Jewish literatures. Also, her particular interest in Jewish literary characters in literature written by non-Jews.

In her autobiographical writing, Ruth Klüger referred repeatedly to a wide range of Jewish writers, many or most of whom were Austrian-Jewish writers. Sometimes the references are not explicit, for example her depiction of a later stage in her life as an American, when she explains that she now had a profession in "ein weites Land" and she enjoyed "ein freies Leben." These terms very likely derive from Arthur Schnitzler's play *Das weite Land* (1911), (The Distant Land) and perhaps also his novel *Der Weg ins Freie* (1908), (The Road to the Open). Ruth Klüger regularly tended to focus on Jewish writers in her scholarly lectures and essays, but by no means did she limit herself exclusively to Jewish writers. In this respect, one could name German-language Jewish writers, many of whom were Austrian Jews, such as Schnitzler (again), Theodor Herzl, Stefan Zweig, Joseph Roth, Franz Werfel, Friedrich Torberg, Theodor Kramer, and Heinrich Heine (who was, of course, not Austrian). She tended to include Ilse Aichinger and Hermann Broch in this group, although they are not always or not usually categorized as specifically Jewish writers. Also, she edited a collection of stories by the once popular, but mostly forgotten nineteenth-century Austrian-Jewish writer Salomon Hermann Mosenthal (1821–1877), and she wrote a long and

engaging afterwards for the volume as well. Regarding Jewish characters in literature, she showed sustained interest, for example, in G.E. Lessing's Nathan the
Wise and in Shakespeare's Shylock and his daughter Jessica, among others. In her
well-known poem, "Jessica lässt sich scheiden," (Jessica gets divorced) she presented an image of the poetic persona, perhaps a version of herself, as a "counter-
image" to Shakespeare's Jessica in *The Merchant of Venice*. (Klüger 1992, 261–263)[5]
An additional example in this regard is her essay: "A Jewish Problem in German
Postwar Fiction"(1985).

– Her sensitivity and critical concern regarding anti-Semitism in general.

Given the victimization she suffered during the Nazi period owing to her Jewishness, it appears obvious that her engagement with, and detailed analysis of,
the phenomenon of anti-Semitism and its impact on her and her life would be
central to her autobiographical writings. Beyond that, though, she analyzed aspects of anti-Semitism in her scholarship. One example especially worthy of mention is her essay: "The Theme of Anti-Semitism in the Work of Austrian Jews." In
her talk at the International Association of Germanists (IVG) in 1985, which
turned out to be pivotal for the later part of her career, she spoke about depic-
tions of Jewish characters in the German literature of the nineteenth century,
with an eye towards revealing and analyzing the tradition of anti-Semitism
which informed the background of those negatively depicted characters.

– Her repeated use of the inclusive first-person plural form "we" to mean "we
Jews" and to express Jewish belonging and solidarity, and her concomitant defiant
or assertive exclamations regarding her Jewish self or Jewish achievement.

In *weiter leben* she wrote about her determination to be proud of her Jewishness in face of Nazism: "aufs selbstbewusste gesetzt." (Klüger 1992, 17) Since Na-
zified Austria rejected her, she defiantly embraced her Jewishness in self-defense.
In the section concerning Rabbi Leo Baeck in Theresienstadt, the text refers to
"unser Erbe," (Klüger 1992, 101) meaning "our [shared Jewish] tradition" inherited from one generation to the next over centuries. Although the autobiographical voice repeats how nothing good ever came from the concentration camps, in
weiter leben the reflecting autobiographical "I" expresses pride at how the Jewish
inmates managed to maintain humane social values, to create culture, and to
transmit knowledge. Later, when describing the years she spent in Princeton as a
professor and head of the German department, she refers to typical topics, specifically those concerning Jewish victims of the Shoah, which tended to come up in

---

5 Cf. Irène Heidelberger-Leonard 1996, 59. Heidelberger-Leonard reads Klüger's Jessica as a
counter-figure to herself, at least as far as the Jewish issue is concerned.

discussions, whenever several Jews, including herself, sat around a table. In *unterwegs verloren*, Ruth Klüger cited proudly "[die] grossen geistigen Leistungen der Juden auf allen Gebieten." (Klüger 2008, 11) ("the great spiritual-cultural achievements of Jews in every area") Elsewhere, she expressed the view that Vienna owed half of its innovative thought and culture to Jews. (Klüger 2001, 21) On this point, she seemed to be following the lead of the acclaimed Austrian-Jewish writer, Stefan Zweig (1881–1942), who committed suicide in exile; he wrote in his highly regarded, posthumously published memoirs, *The World of Yesterday,* that "nine-tenths of what the world celebrated as Viennese culture in the nineteenth century was promoted, nourished, or even created by Viennese Jewry." (Stefan Zweig 1964, 22)

Whereas the issue of Ruth Klüger's relationship to Judaism has been considered by several observers to be quite complex, perhaps owing to her changing understanding of a few Jewish-related issues over time, as well as to her contradictory statements concerning some Jewish issues and related factors – some of which have been discussed above – her relationship to Zionism is fairly straightforward. In her biographical writing she relates how she became a Zionist early on, namely in Theresienstadt, and she remained a Zionist and a supporter of the State of Israel for her entire life. As already mentioned, she idealized Theodor Herzl (1860–1904), the Viennese journalist and *homme de lettres*, who at the end of the nineteenth century became the leader of the modern Zionist movement and head of the World Zionist Organization, which he established. Later on in life, as an academic, she happily participated in Theodor Herzl conferences in Vienna. On several occasions she referred in her writing to "the ideal community like the Eretz Israel of our dreams, which was still the goal of all [her] wishful thinking." (Klüger 2001, 121) Her long term desire was to immigrate to Palestine/ Israel, to "help build a country inspired by socialist ideals, where justice and humanity would prevail." (Klüger 2001, 160) She yearned to "live in a kibbutz, the goal of all [her] dreams." (Klüger 2001 152) She pondered late in life what kind of an existence she might have endured, had she immigrated to Israel. (Klüger 2008, 96) At one point she was also willing to accept the idea that she might have to compromise and be prepared to reside in a city in Israel, rather than in a collective, agricultural community, in order to realize her Zionist dream. But, it would be worth it. Klüger also wrote about the decision of one of her closest friends during her years in New York, who decided idealistically to immigrate to Israel, only to return eventually with her enthusiasm partially diminished by the harsh reality of life in a country surrounded by enemies and regularly under siege, a place always prepared for war. Klüger reported vaguely in *Still Alive* about her own "abortive attempts" to immigrate to Israel in order to realize her Zionist dream, but as she explained: ". . . life interfered." (Klüger 2001, 195) These attempts and efforts alone would suffice to contradict or at least qualify the statement made by Irène Heidelberger-Leonard that Ruth Klüger never took her Zionism seriously. Although a Jew like Ruth Klüger, capable and intelligent, with a strong personality and no particularly deep roots in any one place for an extended period of time, may appear in retrospect perhaps to have been a suitable candidate for immigration within a Zionist context, timing and other factors, which she called "life," evidently interceded. Her successful "Americanization" is certainly a related factor. (Klüger 2008, 159) At least that is how she came to understand her failure to realize her Zionist aspirations. In any case, a would-be immigrant's success – especially financial and professional success – in the diaspora often tends to impinge on the realization of Zionist ideology, unless there are very strong motivations and passion or fanaticism or possibly pernicious anti-Semitism, which are involved. Certainly, the young Holocaust survivor and immigrant to New York, Ruth Klüger, integrated well into American society, eventually achieving outstanding success and becoming highly respected professionally in American academe, despite her having to overcome certain obstacles to her advancement owing to discrimination against Jews and women in her specific field.

One complicating aspect regarding the issue of Ruth Klüger and Zionism is that the meaning or possible meanings of the term "Zionist" have changed over the years. Another one might be that the State of Israel – as the realization of political Zionist ideology – came into existence shortly after the Shoah while Ruth was still a teenager, and the political fortunes of the State, the numerous wars and threats to its existence, the various and radically different governments and leaderships, have exerted a certain impact on Zionists and those sympathetic to Israel living in the diaspora. This phenomenon continues until the present day. Of course, it is important to remember that David Ben-Gurion (1886–1973), the staunch Zionist ideologue, political activist, and socialist labor leader who became Israel's first prime minister, announced boldly – and he maintained his position for years – that no Jewish individuals living in the diaspora had the right call themselves Zionists unless their living in the State of Israel was part and parcel of their life plan for the immediate future. He played a decisive role in the political process which led to the establishment of a Jewish State at the end of the British Mandate period in Palestine after the departure of British soldiers from the land and in the formative years of the state's existence; his worldwide impact on perceptions of Zionism and Israel was fundamental and extensive. However, over time supporters of the idea of Zionism – that is of the importance and viability of the existence of a Jewish State in the land of Israel – have come to label themselves Zionists rather comfortably and without controversy, solely on the basis of supporting the idea itself and without the necessity of embracing or implementing a plan to relocate and immigrate to Israel. Also, as it turns out, many vocal supporters of Zionism and the continued existence of Israel as a Jewish State disagree with, or oppose vociferously, actions and specific policies of Israeli governments. Normally, these oppositional voices cite kindred oppositional opinions in the Israeli government, society, and media. Thus, the continued characterization of Ruth Klüger as a Zionist and her self-understanding as a Zionist up until her death are non-controversial in the context of contemporary understandings of modern Zionism. While it is almost definite that Ruth Klüger would have expressed dismay about, and opposition to, many political and military policies initiated by various Israeli governments, especially after the Labor Party lost its hegemony in Israeli political life, she never wavered in her support of the continued existence of the Jewish State. As a rule, she followed closely political developments and election results in Israel, and she visited the country happily on numerous occasions. She understood and supported the necessity for the State of Israel to maintain a qualitatively superior army and large reserve contingents, and she delighted in seeing young Israeli men and especially young women in uniform – – and often carrying weapons in public – during her visits. She expressed her conviction that had the State of Israel existed before the Shoah, and had it been able to demonstrate at that time diplomatic strength and military power, the genocide would have never taken place. Thus, her childhood and her subsequent life would have been considerably different. This view is in fact widespread among Zionists, although its veracity cannot be corroborated in any way. In general, her support of Zionism and the State of Israel is congruent to the general and basic American and especially American-Jewish support of the Jewish State. In fact, it is more ardent and enthusiastic than the norm in these groups. It is but one more aspect of her life that is characteristic of a large portion of American Jewry.

In order to buttress and contextualize my claim about Ruth Klüger fitting neatly into the category of American Jew, I would like to cite some data culled from a well-respected survey conducted every few years in the United States. In 2020, following a previous study a few years earlier, the Pew Research Center in Washington, D.C., which is a nonpartisan American think tank providing information on social issues, public opinion, and demographic trends in the U.S. and the world for a wide audience, issued the results of a survey, the purpose of which was to try to convey a sense of Jewish-Americans' self-identities, religious and cultural practices, and political attitudes. Regarding the Shoah, more than seven decades after it took place, roughly three quarters of American Jews (76%) stated that "remembering the Holocaust" is essential to what being Jewish means to them personally. No other option listed on the survey about what is important for American Jews in terms of their being Jewish – their Jewish identity– was more important to those surveyed. Another option that came close among those surveyed was "leading an ethical and moral life"; 72% of those surveyed said this aspect was essential to their Jewish identity. Both of these attitudes shared by a large segment of American Jewry were very important or essential for Ruth Klüger too during her lifetime, and she expressed them repeatedly in her writings and speeches. According to the Pew Report, more than half of those American Jews surveyed stated that working for justice and equality in society (59%) and being intellectually curious (56%) were essential to their being Jewish. Again, these characteristics resonate strongly with Ruth Klüger's life experience as an adult in the U.S. Close to half (45%) of the American Jews who participated in the survey claimed that caring about Israel was essential to what it means to be Jewish. Again, Ruth's Zionist sympathies correspond well to this category. And, on the other end of the spectrum, only 15% of those surveyed felt that observing Jewish (religious) law was an essential aspect of their Jewishness. Two-thirds of American Jews surveyed say that one can be Jewish even if one does not believe in God. For only 15% of American Jews is being Jewish a matter of religion. Also, most American Jews do not really care if their children marry Jews. But, sharing and expressing common political convictions with children and grandchildren appeared to be much more important attributes for a majority of Jews surveyed. Surprisingly, perhaps, spending time with friends or pets and having a job, career, and education were all more important to those surveyed than religious faith in terms of their specifically Jewish identities. Not surprisingly though, spending time with family scored very high (74%) among the priorities of American Jews concerning what it means to them to be Jewish. All of these aspects or attitudes and behaviors match to a degree or resonate strongly with Ruth Klüger's views and practices as an American Jewish woman.

To summarize then, according to the Pew Report, American Jews tend to understand being Jewish as a matter of ancestry, culture, ethinicity, and values, rather than of religious observance. And, an overwhelming majority (75%) expressed a strong sense of belonging to the Jewish people – a response that was common to religious and to non-religious Jews alike. American Jews are staunchly liberal (71%) and they vote democratic in impressive numbers. As it turns out, only orthodox and ultra-orthodox Jews tend, statistically, to vote republican. A very high percentage of those surveyed (94%) expressed pride in their being Jewish. Although as a child survivor of the Shoah and a young immigrant to the U.S., her specific experience pertains to a delimited category of American Jewry, she certainly fits well the typology of attitudes expressed by the sample in this survey compiled for the Pew Report. But, beyond that, as an American Jewish women born before the second World War in Europe, she seems to have anticipated other characteristics and trends which by the end of the twentieth century came to be identified widely as characteristic of a relatively large percentage of American Jewish women, namely their attainment of a very high level of education, their pronounced feminism, and their mobility, which often went hand in hand with their impressive professional successes.

It is pertinent to add that the Kaddish prayer, discussed at the beginning of this chapter, is also part of the American-Jewish poetic landscape – a literary landscape quite familiar to Ruth Klüger. David Biale wrote that "American Jewish writers and artists in particular have frequently made use of the Kaddish and its ritualized recitation in memory of the dead, in an attempt [. . .] to cope with the absence of adequate secular resources for dealing with death." (Biale 2010, 189) Hanna Wirth-Nesher has even written of "the eruption of the Kaddish into so many American works of literature," and perhaps its functioning as a signifier of communal identity. (Wirth-Nesher 2006, 166) Ruth Klüger would have almost certainly been familiar with literary texts in this category, since she was well versed in modern American poetry. For example, in *Still Alive* she repeatedly quoted American poetry written by Emily Dickinson, W.H. Auden, Adrienne Rich, Maya Angelou, and others. She was especially drawn to the poetry of American women poets, just as she was very familiar with poetry written by German (language)-Jewish poets, already mentioned above. For instance, she would have undoubtedly known the famous poem by Allen Ginsberg, "Kaddish," published in 1961, which includes partially translated phrases – and also paraphrases in English – of the Hebrew-Aramaic prayer. In section II, part of the Kaddish prayer is transliterated into Latin letters: "Yisborach, v'yistabach, v'yispoar, v'yisromam, v'yisnaseh, v'yishador, v'yishalleh, v'yishallal, sh'meh d'kudsho, b'rich hu." (Ginsberg 1984, 219). What he hoped to achieve by doing so remains open to interpretation. Given the fact that Philip Roth's *Zuckerman Unbound* or Friedrich Torberg's "Kaddisch 1943," both cited above, and many other texts which reference the prayer incorporate transliterated parts of it – usually the first lines –it may be that a special quality of the sounds themselves militates in favor of including a transliteration of the original Hebrew-Aramaic prayer into texts written in other languages. Perhaps the poets and authors who use this strategy hope to strike an empathetic chord in a receptive audience that possibly matches the emotional response on the part of the mourner who recites this prayer in its original language. However, Ruth Klüger, who also includes transliterated Hebrew and Yiddish lexical items into her writings – and these may be considered as aspects of her multilingualism and Jewish sensibility – would have scarcely appreciated much of the stream-of-consciousness and vulgar poetic language of Ginsberg's "Kaddish." This is my guess, even though he does refer to Buchenwald (as well as to Emily Dickinson) in the poem.

Also, she may have known some of the poetry of the highly respected and influential American-Jewish poet, Charles Reznikoff (1894–1976), particularly his poem "Kaddish," and possibly his posthumously published collection, *Holocaust*, as well as his poem about "The Socialists of Vienna." (Reznikoff 1976, 175–177) No doubt she would have responded more positively to his "Kaddish" than to Ginsberg's poem. Joseph Ballen wrote about Reznikoff's "Kaddish" as follows: "In declaring, finally, the superfluity or disposability of 'prayers and words and lights' before the presence or memory of a dead loved one, [his] Kaddish exemplifies a break with the traditional Kaddish, and appears to mediate a self-consciously secular memorialization, ... it labors to articulate an uncertain yet recognizably Jewish sensibility of the secular." (Ballan 2017, 71) Ruth Klüger would have found a kindred poetic spirit in Reznikoff.[6] Some lines from his Kaddish poem in memory of his mother resonate with Klüger's writing in this regard. For example:

> I know you do not mind
> if you mind at all
> that I do not pray for you
> or burn a light
> on the day of your death:
> but we do not need these trifles
> between us –
> prayers and words and lights.
>   (Ballen 2017, https://doi.org/
>   10.5325/studamerjewilite.36.
>   1.0071)

Stephen Fredman went so far as to call this poem in his book on Reznikoff a "counter-kaddish." (Fredman 2001, 26) Ruth Klüger's related views, as expressed in her writings, correlate positively to the idea of a "counter-kaddish" and to these secular Jewish sentiments.

Similarly, one might imagine her having responded approvingly to the first stanza of Heinrich Heine's well-known poem, "Gedächtnisfeier" (Commemoration

---

6 Charles Reznikoff (1894–1976), an American-Jewish poet usually associated with Objectivism, was resident in New York City for most of his life. He has been called by the Virtual Jewish Library project "one of the most important Jewish poets of the 20th century." His poetry (or poetic documentary) collections, *Holocaust* (1975) and *Testimony* (1965), are perhaps his best known book publications. See Milton Hindus, "Of History, Literature, and Charles Reznikoff (1894–1976)," in Mark H. Gelber (Ed.) *Identity and Ethos. A Festschrift for Sol Liptzin on the Occasion of his 85th Birthday* (New York, Berne, Frankfurt am Main: Peter Lang, 1986), 305–310; Cf. Milton Hindus (Ed.), *Charles Reznikoff: Man and Poet* (Orono, ME: National Poetry Foundation, 1984).

Service), which appeared in the second part of his late poetry collection, *Romanzero* (1848):

> Keine Messe wird man singen,
> Keinen Kadosch wird man sagen,
> Nichts gesagt und nichts gesungen
> Wird an meinen Sterbetagen.

> (No Mass will be sung,
> No Kaddish will be said,
> Nothing said, and nothing sung,
> On the day when I die.)[7]

For a certain period of time, Ruth Klüger would have naturally assumed that no one would recite the Kaddish prayer at her own funeral or in the years afterwards on her "yahrzeit," her annual day of death. But, as a matter of fact, the Kaddish was recited at her funeral, and the traditional stones placed on the graves and gravestone by visitors in Jewish cemeteries will almost certainly be placed on her grave, when family, friends, and admirers come to visit it in the future.

At the time of the writing of this essay, more than a year after Ruth Klüger's burial, no gravestone has yet been erected in the cemetery for her. Evidently, this delay has to do with technical reasons. However, a draft version of the wording that will appear on the headstone has been approved by the family. (See Fig. 1).[8]

Under Ruth Klüger's name and the dates of her birth and death, the short poem "To make a prairie," appears. It was written by one of her favorite American poets, Emily Dickinson. The poem reads as follows:

> To make a prairie it takes a clover and one bee,
> One clover, and a bee.
> And revery.
> The revery alone will do,
> If bees are few.

---

7 Hal Draper translated these lines as follows: "/Not a mass will be sung for me,/Not a Kaddish will be said,/None will say or sing a service/On the day that I lie dead." Cf. *The Complete Poems of Heinrich Heine. A Modern English Version* by Hal Draper (Boston: Suhrkamp/Insel Publishers Boston, Inc. 1982), 643.
8 I would like to thank Ruth Klüger's son, Dan Angress, for providing me with this draft version of the headstone and for additional assistance and information.

Mount Sinai Memorial Parks
Ruth Kluger 1st Proof

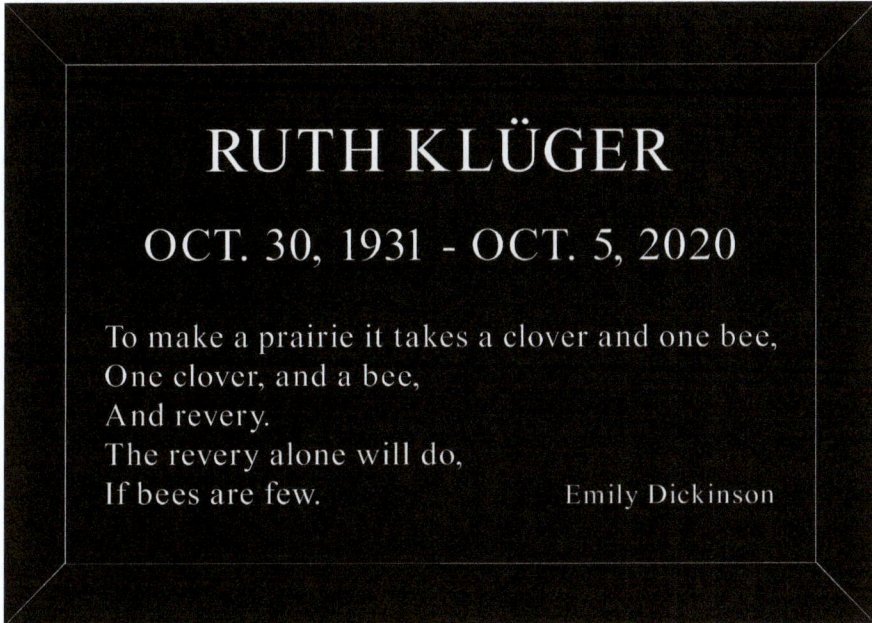

> # RUTH KLÜGER
>
> ## OCT. 30, 1931 - OCT. 5, 2020
>
> To make a prairie it takes a clover and one bee,
> One clover, and a bee,
> And revery.
> The revery alone will do,
> If bees are few.   Emily Dickinson

Fig. 1: Draft version for Ruth Klüger's gravestone.

In the context of the material presented in this chapter, it is important to emphasize that the headstone at her grave – at her final or "eternal" resting place, as the rabbi put it at her funeral – will be devoid of Jewish markers or specifically Jewish significance; rather, it is her American and poetic sensibilities, first and foremost, that come to expression here in an American-Jewish cemetery. It is only the *Umlaut* in her name, as it will appear on the headstone – Klüger – that serves to remind visitors of her Central European origin. However, all of these aspects have their rightful place in understanding the person, the work, and the legacy of Ruth Klüger.

Bibliography

Ballan, Joseph. "Poetry of Secular Memorialization: Charles Reznikoff's 'Kaddish' and George Oppen's 'In Memoriam Charles Reznikoff.'" *Studies in American Jewish Literature*, 36, 1 (2017): 71–83.

Biale, David. *Not in the Heavens. The Tradition of Jewish Secular Thought*. Princeton: Princeton University Press, 2010.

Bos, Pascale R. *German-Jewish Literature in Wake of the Holocaust. Grete Weil. Ruth Klüger, and the Politics of Address*. New York: Palgrave Macmillan, 2005.

Drucker, Reuven. *The Mourner's Companion*. 2nd ed. Highland Park, NJ: Ramat Gan Publications, 2012.

Michael A. Meyer and Navid N. Myers (Eds.). *Between Jewish Tradition and Modernity. Rethinking an Old Opposition. Essays in Honor of David Ellenson*. Detroit: Wayne State University Press, 2014.

Fredman, Stephen. *A Menorah for Athena: Charles Reznikoff and the Jewish Dilemmas of Objectivist Poetry*. Chicago: University of Chicago Press, 2001.

Gelber, Mark H. "Mehrsprachigkeit und Stationen des Exils in der Literatur des Überlebens. Stefan Zweig, Fanya Gottesfeld Heller, Ruth Klüger. In *Sprache(n) im Exil*. Ed. Doerte Bischoff, Christoph Gabriel and Esther Kilchmann. *Exilforschung. Ein internationales Jahrbuch*. 32/2014: 231–242.

Gelber, Mark H. "Jüdische Sensibilitäten in der österreichisch-jüdischen Literatur." In: Liu Wei, Urs Luger, Alexandra Wagner (Eds.) *Jüdisches Österreich – Jüdisches China. Geschichte und Geschichten aus dem 20. Jahrhundert*. Vienna: Praesens Verlag, 2018, 11–24.

Gelber, Mark H. "Ruth Klüger on Vienna and Austria: An Interview." *Journal of Austrian Studies*, 54, 3 (2021): 109–114.

Gelber, Mark H. "Ruth Klüger's Jewish Sensibility and her Jewish Poetry." In: Gesa Dane and Gail Hart (Eds.), *Ich kann eigentlich nichts anders als Lesen und Schreiben. Neue Perspektiven auf das Werk von Ruth Klüger*. Göttingen: Wallstein, 2022. In press.

Gelber, Mark H. "Stefan Zweigs jüdisches Manifest und seine jüdische Sensibilitäten." In: Mark H. Gelber (Ed.). *Stefan Zweig, Judentum und Zionismus*. Innsbruck, Vienna, Bozen: Studien Verlag, 2014, 11–31.

Ginsberg, Allen. "Kaddish." *Collected Poems. 1947–1980*. New York: Harper & Row, 1984, 219.

Hartman, Geoffrey H. *Scars of the Spirit. The Struggle Against Inauthenticity*. New York: Palgrave Macmillan, 2002.

Heidelberger-Leonard, Irène. *Ruth Klüger. weiter leben. Eine Jugend*. München: R. Oldenbourg Verlag, 1996.

Heine, Heinrich. *The Complete Poems of Heinrich Heine. A Modern English Version* Ed. And Trans. Hal Draper. Boston: Suhrkamp/Insel Publishers Boston, Inc. 1982.

Kaznelson, Siegmund. (Ed.) *Jüdisches Schicksal in Deutschen Gedichten. Eine abschließende Anthologie*. Berlin: Jüdischer Verlag, 1959.

Klüger, Ruth. *Still Alive. A Holocaust Girlhood Remembered*. New York: Feminist Press at the City University of New York, 2001.

Klüger, Ruth. *unterwegs verloren. Erinnerungen*. Vienna: Zsolnay Verlag, 2008.

Klüger, Ruth. *weiter leben. Eine Jugend*. Göttingen: Wallstein Verlag, 1992.

Maltz, Judy. "10 Surprising Facts about U.S. Jews from the Pew Report." *Ha'aretz*, May 12, 2021, 7.

Ossar, Michael. "Ruth Klüger (1931-)." *Holocaust Literature. An Encyclopedia of Writers and their Work*. Ed. S.Lillian Kremer. New York & London: Routledge, 2003.Vol 1, 674–679.

Pohle, Janine. *Ruth Klüger "weiter leben. Eine Jugend"* (eBook epub), https://hugendubel.de

Reznikoff, Charles. *By the Well of Living & Seeing. New & Selected Poems 1918–1973*. Los Angeles: Black Sparrow Press, 1974.

Reznikoff, Charles. *Poems. 1918–1936*. Vol. I of The Complete Poems. Ed. Seamus Cooney. Santa Barbara: Black Sparrow Press, 1976.

Röttger, Thilo (Ed.). *Die Stimme Israels. Deutsch-jüdische Lyrik nach 1933*. München: Kösel Verlag 1966.

Roth, Philip. "I have fallen in love with American names." *The New Yorker*, June 5 & June 12, 2017, 46–47.

Roth, Philip. *Zuckerman Unbound*. London: Penguin, 1981.

Schlant, Ernestine. *The Language of Silence. West German Literature and the Holocaust*. New York, London: Routledge, 1999.

Schlösser, Manfred (Ed.) *An den Wind Geschrieben. Lyrik der Freiheit. Gedichte der Jahre 1933–1945*. Darmstadt: Agora Verlag, 1960.

Wirth-Nesher, Hana. *Call it English. The Languages of Jewish American Literature*. Princeton: Princeton University Press, 2006.

Zweig, Stefan. *The World of Yesterday. Memories of a European*. Trans. Harry Zohn. Lincoln and London: University of Nebraska Press, 1964.

Monica Tempian

"Ver zenen mir?" Children's Voices in the Poetry of the Shoah

Beyond Comprehension

[. . .] the number of Jews killed was a top secret of the Reich, but Eichmann said that it was close to 6 million, 4 million of which killed in camps, the rest in shootings of special operations groups and other things. (Hoettl 1961, n.p.)

The above line originates with Dr. Wilhelm Hoettl, Austrian-born SS Sturmbann-führer and chief advisor on Southeastern Europe in Amt VI (foreign intelligence), who first testified at the Nuremberg Tribunal in 1946, and repeated his testimony in the 1961 trial of Adolf Eichmann in Israel. The number six million has been part of public consciousness for over seven decades; yet it is still beyond comprehension. The magnitude of destruction and death in its numeric expression simply escapes the powers of the human imagination. Behind such numbers, however, there are individuals with personal stories, dreams, feelings, and hopes. In her memoir *Still Alive: A Holocaust Girlhood Remembered*, Ruth Klüger reminds us: "Though the Shoah involved millions of people, it was a unique experience for each of them." (Klüger 2001, 66) We may never comprehend what the Shoah *was* for the millions affected by Nazi persecution, but we can build up knowledge and understanding of *what* has been written about it, of *how* the authors have chosen to write about their experience and *why* they have chosen to write at all. Journals and diaries, riddles and plays, stories and poems – each of these writings gives access to the unique voice of its author, to the specificity of the events that took place and the individuality of those who died, those who suffered, and those who mourned, and collectively they form part of the narrative history of the Shoah. Elie Wiesel does not shy away from pointing out the "compulsory nature" of these writings, not only for the authors but for the readers themselves: "If they had the courage and the desperate faith, if they had the strength to write such words, then we must have the strength to read them." (Wiesel 1980, 11) The question, then, that foregrounds any enquiry by those of us who cannot provide personal insights but must learn about the Shoah through texts, is "how words help us to imagine what reason rejects – a reality that makes the frail spirit cringe." (Langer 1995, 4)

Well acquainted with the power of words, rhythms, and meter, which she relied on during the painful hours on the *Appellplatz* in Auschwitz and later on in the concentration camp Groß–Rosen, where she composed poems to shield herself from the ultimate terror of death, Ruth Klüger invites the reader of her

https://doi.org/10.1515/9783110793239-008

memoir to engage with her in an interactive process of countering forgetting, warning in playful words that the results may numb and leave one challenged by the twisted features of the unfamiliar rather than soothed and consoled:

> Remembering is a branch of witchcraft; its tool is incantation. To conjure up the dead you have to dangle the bait of the present before them, the flesh of the living, to coax them out of their inertia. [. . .] If I succeed, together with my readers [. . .] we could exchange magic formulas like favorite recipes and season to taste the marinade which the old stories and histories offer us, in as much comfort as our witches' kitchen provides. It won't get too cosy, don't worry: where we stir our cauldron, there will be cold and hot currents from half-open windows, unhinged doors, and earthquake-prone walls. (Klüger 2001, 69)

This essay takes its cue from Klüger's invitation to enter the world of the literature of the Shoah, in particular that of the figurative discourse of children, and to reflect on the variety and complexity in their responses to the atrocities they endured. Since children used figurative language in poetry and diary form alike, and sometimes also included poems framed by reflections in their diaries, this essay will interweave these two literary forms in its argument, in order to address in comprehensive, authentic detail questions about the children's motivations for writing, their artistic inclinations, and their concerns. The texts chosen were written by boys and girls of diverse cultural backgrounds, aged twelve to eighteen, who devoted a great portion of their time to writing about the Shoah. Though lesser known than Anne Frank's *The Diary of a Young Girl* or Pavel Friedman's poem "The Butterfly," they all suggest that children's writings, and particularly their poems, personalize the events of the Shoah in unique vividness and authenticity. As Young argues in reference to the broader literature of the Shoah:

> Once we take into account the eye-witnesses' voices, their apprehension or misapprehension of events, their reflexive interpretations of experience, we understand more deeply why and how the victims responded to unfolding events as they did. [. . .] By recognizing the role their own narratives may have played in their lives, we acknowledge that their ongoing narrative grasp of events was very much a part of the historical reality itself.
> (Young 1990, 51–55)

Speaking the Unspeakable

Jewish children suffered both physically and psychologically from the atrocities of the Shoah. The sense of a violently disrupted life course, disorientation, confusion, and the uncertainty about their identity never left many of the survivors. The diary entries by the unknown youth in the Łódź Ghetto and by Eva Heyman, a teenager in the Nagyvárad Ghetto, murdered in Auschwitz in 1944, illustrate how children experienced the passage from a heavily regulated life – yet still possessing some vestiges of normality – in a city under Nazi occupation to their segregated existence in ghettos, and in labor and concentration camps.

May 1944

After my fantasy of writing in various languages, I return to my own tongue, to Yiddish, to mammelushen, because only in Yiddish am I able to give clear expression, directly and without artificiality, to my innermost thoughts. I am ashamed that I have for so long not valued Yiddish properly. Yet, even if I could rob Homer, Shakespeare, Goethe, and Dante of their muses, would I be capable of describing what we suffer, what we sense, what we experience, what we are living through? Is it humanly possible? . . . It is as possible to describe our suffering as to drink up the ocean or to embrace the earth.

(unknown youth, in Holliday 1995, 398)

5 May 1944

Dear Diary, I'm still too little a girl to write down what I felt while we waited to be taken into the Ghetto. (Heyman, in Marton 1974, 84)

18 May 1944

Dear Diary, Agi [her mother] also told other things, like what the gendarmes do to the women, because woman are also taken there, things that it would be better if I didn't write them down in you. Things that I am incapable of putting into words, even though you know, dear diary, that I haven't kept any secrets from you till now.

(Heyman 1974, 122)

The forced move into the ghetto marked a major rupture in the youngsters' lives. Segregation, forced labor, as well as the National Socialist notion of "racially worthless youngsters" were concepts utterly foreign to children old enough to grasp the radical changes in their lives. As Stargardt notes: "The pre-ghetto world and the ghetto world stood, in reality, in sharp contrast to each other. The transition from the one to the other was in practice abrupt and brutal." (1998, 224) At no point, however, did the children's young age or their vulnerability in the face of the sudden and massive change of their immediate reality preclude them from participating in events as they unfolded: observing their surroundings, having their own memories and feelings, formulating their own interpretations of events, and even trying to respond to the conditions imposed on them through writing. In March 1942, two months before her execution by the Nazis in Camp Dwortz, eighteen-year-old Sarah Fishkin from Rubzewitz reiterates what it means to her to be alive in the camp:

What is the significance of one day of life? To see the brightness of day, even so it is dark for us? If to live means to suffer, we are already suffering greatly. In that case, my years have been fulfilled. And if to live is to experience at least some sense of joy, I have not yet been born. [. . .] I am still alive, still can think. I see everything, understand all and am

> still capable of contemplation. I still live and, so far, have not taken leave from you, my
> dear diary [. . .].
> (Fishkin n.p., 18, 25)

The reader of children's writings from the time of the Shoah may be equally astounded by the fact *that* children and youth wrote to tell about the dehumanizing
world they were cast into, and by *how* they wrote. One of the first truths we learn
upon engaging with their writing is that they were acutely aware of and tormented by the challenge of representing the landscape of disaster as they experienced it. As language is a human enterprise, the inhuman, in the form of radical
evil, poses a specific challenge to the potential of human conceptualization and
hence to language. This profound philosophical dilemma is emphasized over
and over again by young adolescents in their diary notes and poetry alike.

When the unknown youth notes in his 1944 Łódź Ghetto diary that what
the Nazis are doing to the Jews is unspeakable, he is implicitly identifying this
action as inhuman and hence as inaccessible to human understanding, and as
alien to the language communities that form human cultures. The linguistic
sovereignty revealed in his note astonishes in many ways: firstly, the use of the
rhetorical device of the adynaton, a form of hyperbole in which exaggeration is
taken to such an extreme that it emphatically refers to impossibility, denotes
an incontestable talent for language; secondly, the expressivity and immediacy
of his writing paradoxically counters and resists its content, that is the inability
to find adequate words to express the suffering of the persecuted Jews. While
the thirteen-year-old Eva Heyman recognizes with a maturity beyond her age how
challenging it is for a young girl to measure up through her writing to the morass
of moral confusion she is cast into and hold her ground within this unfamiliar, uncertain terrain, the unknown boy from Łódź, painfully aware of the limitations of
words, conjures the great masters of language and literature to convey the thought
that it is the reality itself in its unprecedented vastness and violence beyond any
conceivable framework of meaning, which now poses an irresolvable problem to
experience, imagination, conceptualization, and, finally, representation in writing.
In a later, undated entry he achieves clarity of this thought as he writes:

> Thank heavens that I'm no realist for to be a realist is to realise and realising the whole
> horror of our situation would have been more than any human being could endure. I go
> on dreaming.
> (unknown youth 1995, 400)

His subsequent diary entries spanning four languages – Polish, Yiddish, Hebrew,
and English – reveal his desperate struggle with the reality of the ghetto and his
groping search for language. But even as he concedes the futility of his writing and
his decision to surrender to "dreaming," he goes on writing, leaving behind an account of the events that nothing *but* language could have captured for the future.

In the face of an incomprehensible reality which only leaves the alternative of speech or silence, some children turned to poetry, plunging into a desperate search for potent metaphors to forge analogies with their incomparable fate. In his poem "Five", 1929-born Hanuš Hachenburg, editor of the Theresienstadt children's paper *Vedem*, who died in Auschwitz in 1943, elaborates with remarkable eloquence and philosophical depth on the paradoxical connection between the loss of words and the desperate need for dialogue.

Five

This morning at seven, so bright and so early
Five novels lay there, sewn up in a sack
Sewn up in a sack, like all of our lives,
They lay there, so silent, so silent all five.

Five books that flung back the curtain of silence,
Calling for freedom, and not for the world,
They're somebody's novels, someone who loves them . . .
They called out, they cried, they shed tears, and they pleaded
That they hadn't been finished, the pitiful five.

They declared to the world that the state trades in bodies
Then slowly they vanished and went out of sight.

They kept their eyes open, they looked for the world
But nothing they found. They were silent, all five.
(Hachenburg, in Křížková et al. 1995, 31. Trans. from the
Czech, R. Elizabeth Novak)

In the opening lines of his poem, Hanuš conjures up the ghastly image of five novels sewn up in a sack, and uses rhetorical devices such as simile, chiasmus and repetition to emphasize the significance of the "novel"-metaphor: "Five novels [. . .] Sewn up in a sack, like all of our lives." The text, he suggests in his poetic evocation, is not just a medium of communication between the speaker and the world, but speaker and text share a symbiotic existence, as if the lives of the confined "Us" have turned into books which remarkably stand out for their attributes of aliveness. Hanuš pushes forward in stanzas two to five, describing the books as having flung back the "curtain of silence" calling for freedom, being in a loving relationship, expressing feelings, and finding many emotionally nuanced tones to communicate with the world – all that under the premise of futility ("slowly they vanished," "nothing they found") which is sealed in the last stanza with the repetition of the sobering observation that they were five. The intensely sought dialogue thus ends without a chance for self-fulfillment which the speaker pleaded for with heightened emotionality in stanza three. Both the strong connection created by Hanuš between life and the written word and the poem's abrupt ending compel us to concede that it is the reader who is called upon to make meaning of his poetic legacy. Indeed, while Hanuš performatively enacts in his poem the failure of a dialogue with the world, he ardently keeps writing because: "For me, poems are what friends are to other people. They are what I cannot tell anyone, because they would laugh at me." (Hachenburg 1995, 177) Not only does poetry allow all these inner emotions and anxieties that cannot be spoken or made sense of aloud to find rest and clarity within the openness of its lines, it also offers the chance to leave a memory behind for the generations to come. Hanuš own words testify to this, when in his poem "The Heart" he takes up the challenge to bridge his isolating present into the future by imagining – at the young age of thirteen – a dialogue with no other than his own child:

The Heart

In every heart, in a nameless corner
There's probably a tiny room
Where a man cherishes his "I"
Like a ring on his little finger.

A terrible burden I cherish there,
So many feelings without a name
And I cannot express them.
I am an echo in the wind.
My child, when he is born,
Eager to live, will be a man
May he never live through
What I have seen and suffered.

I do not know what name to give
To my small room with its small door,
Perhaps a bird will whisper a message
In my ear like an echo.

Perhaps my child will say:
"Dad, I know how you are."
My heart is so cruel to me
It will not let me dream,
But always says:
"My good man –
How would you put me into words?"
Today I said: the heart is a fire,
I have no strength to put it out.
    (Hachenburg 1995, 147. Trans. from
        the Czech, R. Elizabeth Novak)

The plight of the speaker carrying the "terrible burden" whilst trapped in a three-fold lockdown "(i)n . . . heart," "in a nameless corner," and "a tiny room" is so immense, his hope to find a way out of a helpless existence so small, that he appeals to the next generation as a last resort for comfort: "Perhaps my child will say:/ Dad, I know how you are."

Similar thoughts about having to relay what happened for future generations to understand are voiced by Ruthka Lieblich, a fifteen-year-old adolescent from Andrychow, who perished in Auschwitz in 1942: "When writing, I sometimes feel . . ., that one day a reliable, loving person will read, feel, and understand my childish scribblings. I feel that some eyes, eyes of the future, look and command me . . . and I have to write . . .." (Lieblich, in Eibeshitz 1993, 82)

Seven decades later, we realize that little else could so poignantly capture the sufferings of a people targeted for genocide by the Nazis than the "wounded metaphors" (Langer 1995, 558) of the children. The aura "surrounding the new arrival at Auschwitz or Treblinka – disoriented, hesitant, fearful, hoping for the best – until he or she grew acquainted with the worst, and then had to find a vacant chamber in the imagination for the unthinkable," (Langer 1995, 7) can still be sensed today in children's writings of the Shoah. It becomes apparent in the reservation and timidity we feel when picking up their texts.

"there is silence everywhere"

In his essay, "What Philosophy Can and Cannot Say about Evil," Kenneth Seeskin argues that the philosophical, rather than historical, incomprehensibility of the Shoah is not meant to lead to silence:

> The understanding I speak of is philosophical. To say that the enactment of the Final Solution is incomprehensible is not to deny that historians can keep accurate records or that jurists can find cause for assessing blame. We have much to learn about the events that led from traditional hatred of Jews to the construction of gas chambers. What I am denying is that we still have a general theory to answer the question we most want to ask. How could people with outward signs of rationality drive the trains or drop the crystals into the gas chambers? How could millions of the other people look on as they did so?   (1988, 117)

Among the many motivations for writing, as the dreadful events increased the persecuted youngsters' suffering and anguish, were the desire to challenge and defy the incomprehensible, to chronicle the devastation surrounding them, and to assert their identity and humanity, for "(w)e knew, silence is forbidden, talk, impossible." (Wiesel 2001, n.p.) At a time when the Nazis sought to stifle Jewish individuality, when they attempted to confiscate everything the Jews owned, pen and paper – if left in the possession of youngsters – may have seemed rather brittle tools to oppose the concentration camp guard, and yet:

Poems, litanies, plays: to write them, Jews went without sleep, bartered their food for pencils and paper. They gambled with their fate. They risked their lives. No matter. They went on fitting together words and symbols. [. . .] They did not write them for me, for us, but for the others, those on the outside and those yet unborn.   (Wiesel, in Schwencke 1988, 41)

Sarah Fishkin illustrates with great sensibility the act of resistance through writing, as she strives to express her feelings in universal terms and without losing sight of the larger framework of collective loss:

The Jew's glance is downcast; not upon people does it fall but as though to penetrate into earth. . . . No human heart can remain untouched and unpained by all this. It is beyond human endurance to see so much trouble and so much suffering experienced. It is painful to see people tortured by people until life is ended. Where is human conscience, to demand the truth, to cry out? . . . The oppressors are being helped to make them touch bottom – I am impelled to write. I see no help underway; there is silence everywhere.   (Fishkin n.p., 25)

Once the decision to pick up the pen was made, writing required the young authors to find form for chaos, to select, omit, emphasize or circumscribe the elements of their disparate immediate reality – a challenge for the poetic imagination and a condition for the internal dynamics of the text itself. Hanuš Hachenburg, in his programmatic poem "The Picture," outlines with unmatched abstracting sympathetic understanding the young artists' concerns:

The Picture

You painters of Terezín,
Letting a little bluish water
Float in a small jasper dish,
You creatures – be human.
You who mix the yellow of hunch-back barracks
Silently and smoothly
With the bright red of the roofs
On sunny days,
This is not a flamboyant event
You are painting.
These are only small clouds, and dreaming,
And cursed dead walls.

This is not the world. They are only walls,
A carnival of colours, a world of sun and precious stones.
It is the great sun, light in the universe
And bitter beauty, bitter terrifying illusions.

You painters of Terezín, who let wide windows
Open to the world, float against
A backdrop of clouds in your silent idylls:
One day you will tumble into mouths open in agony.

Get rid of ellipses that lead to the abyss,
And live, create in darkness!
(Hachenburg 1995, 158. Trans. from the Czech,
R. Elizabeth Novak)

The paintings mentioned by Hanuš in the first stanza may well fit into the category Milton describes as "whitewashed pictures," that is, pictures that represent a world free of fear and terror. (1989, 32) The painters seem to be mixing colors in a carefree way, while avoiding the dark colors and details that may truthfully reflect their reality. Hanuš uses the word "ellipses" to refer to this strategy of avoidance. Of great significance for his poetological program is his assessment of the elliptic images: "Get rid of ellipses that lead to the abyss." The abyss he alludes to may be a moral rather than an artistic abyss, since already in verse four he urges the artists: "You creatures – be human." In what follows, Hanuš states with unerring clarity that whatever "beauty" art within the ghetto walls may achieve, it will be soiled by the misery of its theme. The reality perceived through the window is that of the oxymoronic "bitter beauty, bitter terrifying illusions." The poem ends with the speaker's urge to avoid the temptation to force artistic creation into the mold of familiar themes and conventional style, and instead to gaze into the depth of darkness and destruction without flinching, accepting that: "One day you will tumble into mouths open in agony."

Rikla Glazer, a young teenager who eventually escaped from the Vilna Ghetto and survived the war fighting together with partisans in the woods, wrote verse that seems to resonate with Hanuš's poetological program, when she evokes life in the ghetto, established in 1941:

This grey and dark in the ghetto

Grey and dark in the ghetto is life;
Our wills blocked, our aspirations strangled,
Not a single sun's ray of freedom and rest
Comes through the wooden gates.

We were confined behind heavy gates,
From the outside world, no sound penetrates,
Sealed, locked away like the greatest criminals,
And the heart trembles and is full of anguish.

. . . Step after step go I and think.
My lips parched, my heart is faint;
A day without having eaten, there is no more bread,
My mother does the wash and in the house starvation reigns.

I forget the way; of freedom I dream,
I gaze upon a post and I think a tree blooms,
I forget everything, my delight is enormous,

I already touch freedom, but alas! It's the gate. . . .
(Glazer, in Berkowitz/Edelman 1979, 32–34. Trans. from the
Yiddish, Judith Berkowitz and Eve Edelman)

"... more than bread we need poetry ..."

In the face of hardship and a daily ration of 184 calories a day, Warsaw Ghetto diarist Chaim Kaplan declared: "More than bread we need poetry." (Kaplan 1990, 9) As we have seen, the use of the figurative discourse in poems and diaries becomes one modality to give expression to the alienating experience of the Nazi concentration camp and ghetto, as well as to bridge between past, present, and sometimes an imagined future. Metaphors, similes, metonymies, and oxymorons "that might serve as workable [. . .] analogues" and "organizing categories" for their experience (Howe 1988, 187–188) and also the use of the literary devices of Greek tragedy – irony and paradox – play a vital role in the young authors' survival ordeal and in their attempts to wrest some understanding from the jarring incongruities they perceive.

In an attempt to overcome the paralyzing feeling of powerlessness upon his deportation to Theresienstadt, fourteen-year-old Petr Ginz, murdered at age sixteen in Auschwitz, skillfully employs sharp wit and irony to evoke what children perceive as a "topsy-turvy world" (Heyman, in Marton 1974, 75):

The Madman

I walk the streets alone and alone
Pondering the evil in the world.
And thoughts about it fill my mind,
As I walk the dark streets
Alone and alone,
I remember. Long, long ago,
A madman wished to change the world,
Turn it upside down and inside out,
Fill people and youth with one ideal:
Take nothing on trust, let nothing stand,
Fight for every inch of land.
If something is down, then lift it up,
If others stay silent, you must speak up.
And so this madman years ago
Tried turning the world upside down
And walked his cat instead of his dog.
(Ginz, in Křížková et al. 1995, 145. Trans.
from the Czech, R. Elizabeth Novak)

Poetic forms, as Klüger points out, also function as a means to oppose and contain chaos through clarity of thought set into formally fixed language. (Klüger 2005, 124) In her discussion of poetry as a phenotype of language held together by meter, cadence, rhythm, and form, she explains that poetry offered children like herself a refuge from the crazed logic of genocide and a means of investing time with a perceptible measure in the process of reciting rhythmical, rhyming stanzas:

> Es sind Kindergedichte, die in ihrer Regelmäßigkeit ein Gegengewicht zum Chaos stiften wollten, ein poetischer und therapeutischer Versuch, diesem sinnlosen und destruktiven Zirkus, in dem wir untergingen, ein sprachlich Ganzes, Gereimtes entgegenzuhalten; also eigentlich das älteste ästhetische Anliegen.　　　　　　　　　　　　 (Klüger 2005, 126–127)

> (These are poems of a child who made use of regular patterns to create a counterpoint against chaos – a poetical and therapeutic attempt to confront the abyss of the destructive circus we were exposed to through rhyme and structure – which is perhaps the most archaic function of art.)　　　　　　　　　　　　 (Trans. Monica Tempian)

The children's concern for finding form in chaos is reflected in a wide range of poetic expressions from simple rhymes and riddles to elaborate compositions, which altogether represent a tribute to the artistic imagination "to meet a chaotic challenge and change it with inventive skill into durable, if often difficult and unfamiliar, poetic forms." (Langer 1995, 559) In her poem "Barracks Song," twelve-year-old Esther Shtub, assumed to have perished in 1944 in Bergen-Belsen, demonstrates her sensibility for the relationship of content and form and its articulation at the semantic level:

Barracks Song

One, two, three
When will we be free!
Hungry, barefoot, ragged
Of fathers and mothers we know nothing
God! O how it hurts.

One, two, three
The day doesn't want to pass
Lugging bricks, boards, stones
And dead people's bones,
God! O how it hurts.

One, two, three
Listen to my plea –
From unknown mass graves,
Little children from their cheders
No mothers are with them.
One, two, three

We believe faithfully
We wait and hope
As you have promised us,
Am Yisroel chai!
    (Stub, in Berkowitz/Edelman 1979, 56.
    Trans. from Yiddish, Judith Berkowitz
           and Eve Edelman)

Esther represents the harshness of life in the forced labor camp and her Zionist hopes in four similarly constructed, (in the Yiddish original) rhyming stanzas, all with an identical first line that further accentuates the unity of her poetic composition. Quite tellingly, the initial contrast between the military tone of the first line and the emphatic expression of the prisoners' vulnerability – "God! O how it hurts" – is semantically inverted in the last stanza to reflect the victorious tone of the faithful, believing Jewish people. Such skillful poetic construction could be said to reflect the children's ingenuity in capping their trauma with a poem's verse and turning despair into hope. Langer justly points out: As the writers themselves "shift between hope and despair, seizing on the tiniest rumor to verify their yearning for rescue," the readers "are given glimpses of the dual world of promise and doom that nurtured Holocaust victims then and continues to haunt its survivors today." (1995, 8)

In the face of an evil that defies imagination, two major themes emerge as the crux of the young authors' writing, which allow them to cope with the detrimental effects of the chaos within their lives and achieve a new sense of orientation: the relationship to nature and the dreamlike crossing of borders. Nature seems to offer the only continuity in the children's violently disrupted existence. A cloud, wind, or a butterfly can sometimes create a sense of constancy and a brief moment of relief from the struggle with incessant change, confusion, and the fear of being alone. In his poem "The Thaw," survivor-author Zdeněk Ornest (Ohrenstein), born in 1929, the same year as Hanuš Hachenburg and a good friend of his in Theresienstadt, evokes in powerful metaphors the comfort offered by nature and its regular cycle of seasons:

The Thaw

Silently, lightly, slowly it drifts down
Onto the black and bleeding earth,
From somewhere up high, steadily descending
Whirling in the air on a tender breeze.

Covering all and glittering strangely,
As if to envelop this aged rot
And as in a dream, suddenly everything
Becomes once again what it once used to be.

Hidden is the filth that blankets the world,
Hidden the darkness that blinds us all,
Hidden the hunger that makes us retch,
Hidden the pain that breaks our backs.

Just for a while we breathe again freely
Drugged by the glitter, by the world all in white.
I look out the window, the steady snow falling
And suddenly everything's water again.
    (Ornest, in Křížková et al. 1995, 91. Trans. from
                the Czech, R. Elizabeth Novak)

The dream of the restored purity of the earth, evoked in the image of "the steady snow" falling and covering the world like a protective blanket, instills a comforting feeling of continuity between past and present, intensely enjoyed by the speaker, who looks "out the window" despite being acutely aware of its fleeting nature and the inevitable, sobering awakening to the reality of the concentration camp.

Seventeen-year-old Sarah Fishkin takes the same step to reconnect with nature and her own individuality in her poetic evocation of a walk through the woods on a Shabbat evening of the year 1941:

Untitled

Of the woods' denseness . . .
Of the secrets of the forest
Concealed in its surroundings . . .
Gentle softness caressing my face,
Recounting legends of the distant greyness
And the sun rosy in early morning,
Unfolding the rosy bloom . . .
Colouring the trees.
Let it beckon me to lose my way,
To bathe and be refreshed
In its rosy stream!
I would, if I could, wander in an ancient forest,
Its venerable oaks veiled in a net of hidden secrets!!
Over narrow footpaths
Overgrown with flowers
That sparkle like brilliants
In the morning pearliness,
In the gentle rosiness,
Without knowing wither . . .
    (Fishkin n.d., 5–6. Trans. from Yiddish, Eva Zeitlin
                    Dobkin)

The five lines in central position (nine to thirteen), which stand out for their emphatic gesturing and the engaged presence of the speaker despite a sense of the unreal implied by the subjunctive form of the verbs, express a strong determination to cross the border into another world, to "lose my way" in an "ancient forest" invested with the attributes of the venerable and the mysterious. Here, the communion with nature carries the promise of a safe distancing from the harsh reality of the Rubzewitz Ghetto, and the wandering itself becomes a metaphor for freedom and self-assertion, conveying a re-discovered sense of dignity and worth as the poetic persona finds solace in a world of rites and rituals known to her from the past.

The theme of the imaginary border crossing re-surfaces with magical power in the poetry of the adolescent Selma Meerbaum-Eisinger from Czernowitz, who perished at the age of eighteen in the labor camp of Mikhailovka:

My Number is 434

In Marie Theresa's fortress, captive behind the wall,
I dream I am wearing an organdie dress,
for I'm sixteen, at my first ball.
In my hair is a poppy, in my heart a thrill,
in my dream I float on a parquet floor;
then I wake from that dream and I'm still a captive!
My number is four thirty-four.
  (Meerbaum-Eisinger, in Kingsley 2001, n.p. Trans.
     from German, Rabbi Gunter Hirschberg)

Through her poetic evocation of a dreamlike state which is masterfully captured in the striking lightness of alliterative verse (in the German original), Selma seems literally to push the boundaries of figurative language in an attempt to find a new vocabulary and style that can achieve a sense of liberation from the confines of a reality that stifles creativity and imagination. At no point, however, does her imaginary transgression turn into escapism. It rather seems to suggest the creation of that very space which these children were robbed of, a space that connects the past, the present, and the future, or in Ruth Klüger's words, a "timescape," i.e. a "place in time, that is, at a certain time, neither before nor after." (Klüger 2001, 67)

With the poetic evocation of a personified nature capable of empathy and compassion, and implicitly of an emotional and moral stance, together with the dreamlike crossing of borders with its restorative, liberating power, young poets like Zdeněk, Sarah, and Selma seem also to re-instate the higher authority of humanity, which they have known in the past as part of civilization. As Sarah would reflect in her diary:

[. . .] justice has no firm laws: It is more a concept based upon sensitivity, and man judges things not by some abstract measure but always in relationship to his own self and what suits him. (Fishkin n.p., 18–19)

Her last diary entry in the month of her death, May, 1942, shows that none of the Nazis' evil actions have had the power to change her own system of values – the same system humanity has cherished for generations and millennia:

I do not desire to unite with those who strive for their own good, but with people who also live for others, for the unfortunate, and keep them from falling into the pit and drowning in a deep morass of suffering from which there is no lifting them.
(Fishkin n.p., 25)

"Ver zenen mir?"

In his diary, Yitskhok Rudashevski, born in 1927 and forced to live in the Vilna Ghetto until its liquidation in 1943 when he was shot to death in the Ponary massacre, describes his feelings of despair upon being uprooted from his home: "I have been cut off from all that is dear and precious to me." (1973, 32) Whether in hiding, ghettos or camps, child victims of the Shoah experienced profound confusion, emotional degradation, and identity crises as a result of dislocation and Nazi oppression. As Kestenberg writes: "The external pressure and constant exclusion, the abandonment by peers, all had a tremendous impact on their self-esteem." (1996, 194–195) Moreover, children often ended up having to care for their parents, as the adult figures they once looked up to succumbed to despair and were no longer capable of caring for themselves. (Stargardt 1998, 226) Violence, fear, starvation, devastating isolation, and the loss of parental protection and guidance all played roles in turning these children into premature adults. The diary of survivor-author Halina Nelken (born in 1923), written in the Kraków Ghetto and another eight camps, including Płaszów, Auschwitz, and Ravensbrück, captures the adolescent's horror at the realization of the moral degradation and social isolation her community experiences during the Shoah:

Suddenly, with a terrifying feeling of abandonment, I realize that the world has forgotten us, while *they* (the German soldiers) are pushing us down into degradation and moral and physical destruction. (Nelken 1999, 104)

Yet, underlying her account is a consistent refusal to completely forsake the belief in humanity as well as a strong reliance on her religious feeling to make "sense of this utter senselessness." (Nelken 2001, 181) Her poem on hunger in Auschwitz, written in 1944, reveals a survivor-poet with a disarming sense of

the oddity and pathos of the human condition, echoing the rebellious, denunci-
atory tones of a raging Job – the only ones that seem to do her situation justice.

Untitled

Do you know what HUNGER is?
hunger
that twists your gut
sweeps thought out of brain
knives your belly?
Breath fails
the heart stops beating
in the end all thought halts
all the maddened desire
to eat! Eat! EAT!

Hours drag slowly
parched lips crave spit
the sick imagination is tormented
by a nightmare
of a loaf of bread.

If only it would fall suddenly from heaven
fresh,
warm, fragrant,
sprinkled with caraway on top . . .
runs through your crazed brain.

Oh, to tear with your teeth
chew greedily
swallow chunks
feel in your mouth
and in your throat
and in your belly
that
satiety.
Eat! Eat! Eat!

Darkness before my eyes.
God! Have pity on me.
Send me down a piece of bread!

Look – how little I need today
God
Were you ever hungry?
    (Nelken 2001, 17–18. Trans. from Polish,
            Alicia Nitecki)

In a similar vein, seventeen-year-old Itzhak Berman refuses to incorporate the
nightmare of violence and annihilation he experiences during the dissolution

of the Riga Ghetto in November 1943 into the framework of the "world" he had known before the Nazi persecution of the Jews began, and to derive meaning from estrangement, just as he refuses to resign and accept the silencing devastation of the Shoah.

> The sun went behind the clouds,
> An arctic cold has descended,
> People are wilder than animals,
> I no longer recognize the world. [. . .]
> > (Berman, in Berkowitz/Edelman
> > 1979, 48. Trans. from Yiddish,
> > Judith Berkowitz and Eve Edelman)

Writing played a vital role in raising questions about identity and collective belonging, aiding the young adolescents' "constant reworking of the notion of 'self.'" (Pollak 1988, 80) In her poem "Who are we?" (in the Yiddish original *Ver zenen mir*?) fifteen-year-old Rivka Basman, a survivor of the Vilna Ghetto and the Kaiserwald concentration camp in Riga, laments the destruction and absence of those conditions that normally aid the healthy development of a child's personality. The question she poses in the title – "Who are we?" – repeated five more times by the speaker's faltering voice, turns into a refrain that runs through the poem like a thread, yet can only be answered *ex negativo*.

Who are we?

Who are we in these dark nights, rejected and despised,
Driven from our homes, abandoned and ridiculed?
Like hurried clouds that cannot catch up with themselves,
Dispersed and dissipated in silence and without aim,
Who are we?

Who are we in these dark nights, forced to appear merry?
To tear our hearts, spill our blood,
Forced to be merry and say, "It is good!"
Who are we?

Clouds of dust obscure the spring around us,
And someplace a heart is beating . . . a bloom is blooming.
And in the deep, dark night an echo rings,
A cry of lament . . . silent night surrounds us . . .
Who are we?
> (Basman, in Kingsley 2001, n.p. Trans. from Yiddish, Eli-
> > yahu Mishulovin)

Rivka's lament of the loss of home and of beloved nature, of lost self-esteem, and loss of purpose in life, of the lost freedom that she experienced, represents a sobering or even horrifying counter-image to what the ideal conditions of a child's growing up could be.

Numerous poems and diary entries express the children's awareness of their premature aging and the "psychic closing off"-effect (Lohmann 1994, 216) as well as the pain experienced at the time of the realization that they have been robbed of their childhood. "There are no words to describe our abject lives," writes Sarah Fishkin (n.p. 17); "We are prematurely aged by dozens of years." Elie Wiesel expands on the implications of sudden maturity, explaining: "[I]n a single night, a single hour, one acquires knowledge and wisdom. The child discovers the old man within himself." (1980, 3) In a laconic contribution to the Theresienstadt paper *Vedem*, fifteen-year-old survivor-writer Peter Fischl reflects:

> We got used to undeserved slaps, blows and executions. [. . .] We got used to it that from time to time, one thousand unhappy souls would come here and that, from time to time, another one thousand unhappy souls would go away . . .   (Fischl, in Glatstein 1969, 138)

In his Theresienstadt poem "At the Crossroads," Zdeněk Ornest captures in the title imagery of the crossroads the profound identity crises he experiences at the age of thirteen:

At the Crossroads

Where can I rest my soul, where let my body carry me?
What should I toil for, where should I sow my seed?
I lean over you, I stand at the crossroads,
The wall crumbles under me, my load weighs me down.

A thousand unknown voices call me from afar,
Whatever I am at I cannot attain,
A terrible loneliness chokes me to death,
And everyone waits for the funeral pyre. . . .

Where can we turn, and to whom surrender?
Where seek salvation, in whom to believe?
Whose advice can we take, and who will return?
Oh, who will pity us, treat us with trust? . . .

I woefully ask myself, where shall I turn to?
Where is my place now, and where will I stand?
I have not gone far. Now I stand at the crossroads
And do not know what I'm to make of my life.
           (Ornest 1995, 115. Trans. from Czech, R. Elizabeth
                                                    Novak)

In twelve open questions, thematically revolving around the core question – "Where can we turn . . .?" – Zdeněk conjures up the image of a speaker in a state of complete exhaustion, prematurely aged and at the same time completely disoriented. Throughout the poem, he conveys with impressive succinctness the identity conflict experienced by an adolescent exposed to the threat to life on a daily basis, caught up between life-affirming, forward-looking moments and the presence of imminent death. Zdeněk's friend, Hanuš Hachenburg, goes one step further when in his poem "For Children" he evokes the loss of personal responsibility that threatens civilization itself:

For Children

We are all children, little ones
Playing with a coloured ball.
We cry easily with ruddy cheeks
And then, with glowing faces
We look at a silvery world
At green hillsides
At life. [. . .]
We are all people
Gambling for the globe
And the globe turns in blood
And turns and turns . . .
    (Hachenburg 1995, 177. Trans.
      from Czech, R. Elizabeth
          Novak)

While the opening lines conjure up the image of a carefree childhood, the following section skillfully denounces the actions of adults, who decline to behave responsibly. The metamorphosis of the colorful ball into the globe, the transformation of the children's game into the adults' gambling, and the transmutation of the symbols of childish innocence into symbols of chaos and destruction all gesture in the direction of the existential question regarding personal responsibility and altruism, not only concerning the individual but also the entire civilization. The same theme of personal responsibility is addressed by Ruth Klüger retrospectively, when in her memoir she draws attention to the connection between acts of goodness and the notion of freedom:

I was saved by a young woman who was in a helpless situation as the rest of us . . . . The more I think about the following scene, the more astonished I am about its essence, about someone making a free decision to save another person, in a place which promoted the instinct of self-preservation to the point of crime and beyond. . . . She saw me stand in line, a kid sentenced to death, she approached me, she defended me, and she got me through. What more do you need for an example of perfect goodness? Never and nowhere was there such an opportunity for a free, spontaneous action as in that place at that moment. It was moral freedom at its purest. . . . And so one might argue that in the perverse environment of Auschwitz absolute goodness was a possibility, like a leap of faith, beyond the humdrum of cause and effect. I don't know how often it was consummated. Surely not often. Surely not only in my case. But it existed. I am a witness.

(Klüger 2001, 106–109)

"Where is human conscience [. . .]?"

Memory, in Jewish thought and life, is a collective mandate. From the Deuteronomic imperative to "remember the days of old" (32:7, 897) and to "remember what Amalek did onto thee" (25:17, 856) to the persistent theme of remembering – "that thou wast a bondman in Egypt" (24:18, 853) – memory is re-asserted as one of the Jewish people's 613 commandments or *mitzvot*, first recorded in the Torah and recalled in the ritual settings of Passover and Shabbat. There is also the reverse of the coin found in Genesis, in the imperative to God not to forget his people, as first recorded in His covenant with Noah: "When I bring clouds over the earth and the bow is seen in the cloud, that I will remember My covenant, which is between Me and you and every living creature of all flesh; and the waters shall no more become a flood to destroy all flesh." (9:14–16, 33) In this context, Ebach argues, it becomes evident, how closely connected the two notions of remembrance and rescue are, or vice-versa, of forgetting and destruction. (1996, 106) The story of the Exodus is thus to be regarded as an "event that allowed Jewish history to begin" and also as "a paradigm of all subsequent Jewish history, or, more precisely, of all those events that, time and again, averted catastrophe." (Fackenheim 1990, 27) With this, the contemplation of history leads to the sacralization of the chain of historical events, imparting to those affected by the events a sense of identity that is connected to an understanding of collective experience decided by no other than God himself. "There is a close affinity between identity-defence and sacralization" argues Mol, as sacralization "produces immunity against persuasion similar to the biological immunization process." (1976, 5)

Some of the children-authors of the Shoah chose to draw attention to their own perception of the connection between sacralization and the endowment of their identity with meaning. Ruthka Lieblich's account of Passover on April 14, 1941, for example, demonstrates the "power of non-canonical events to trigger narrativizing even in young children," (1976, 5) and especially the relevance of the Passover-Haggadah as a "model narrative" (Bruner 1990, 81):

We didn't have special Passover dishes and utensils; neither could we prepare the customary traditional menu, for lack of food. We just ate matzoh and whatever we had. The story of two thousand years ago is applicable in our days. We, too, are in exile, among strangers, suffering beyond measure, without any prospect of liberation. Why? Isn't G-d the same Almighty as he was then? If He redeemed us then with a strong hand and an outstretched arm, why not today? In the Haggadah we read that G-d differentiated between us and other nations. (Lieblich 1993, 27)

Ruthka's attempt to inscribe the incomprehensible events of the Shoah into a wider narrative that vouches for the continuity of the Jewish people reflects just how strongly children-authors connect the two notions of memory and rescue. We are reminded of this search for connection through remembrance by Ruth Klüger herself, when she invites the reader of her memoir to become part of an "inhabited memory," the kind of personal and collective memory that secures the link between past, present, and future. (Klüger 2001, 69)

The children's poems of the Shoah remain a moving memorial to the vividness of the imagination of children in adversity. From today's vantage point, it seems legitimate to assert that the question asked by Sarah Fishkin in the diary section of the Rubzewitz Ghetto – "Where is human conscience [. . .]?" (n.p., 25) – equally makes its demands on the generations born after her perishing. The power of vision behind the evocation of the nightmare of "mnemocide," of willful erasure of memory, in the poem "The Closed Town" by an unknown young poet in Theresienstadt, may therefore resonate with all those who deem it necessary to protect the next generations from the inhumanity of forgetting the children of the Shoah:

The Closed Town

Everything leans, like tottering, hunched old women.
Every eye shines with fixed waiting
And for the word "when"?

Here there are few soldiers.
Only the shot-down birds tell of war.

You believe every bit of news you hear.

The buildings now are fuller,
Body smelling close to body,
And the garrets scream with light for long, long hours.
This evening I walked along the street of death.
On one wagon, they were taking the dead away.

Why so many marches have been drummed here?

Why so many soldiers?

Then,
A week after the end,
Everything will be empty here.
A hungry dove will peck for bread.
In the middle of the street will stand

An empty, dirty
Hearse.
      (unknown author 1993, 4–6. Trans. from the Czech
           original by R. Elizabeth Novak)

Bibliography

Aaron, Frieda W. *Bearing the Unbearable: Yiddish and Polish Poetry in the Ghettos and Concentration Camps*. Albany, New York: State University of New York Press, 1990.

Berkowitz, Judith, and Eve Edelman (Eds.). *Young Voices from the Ghetto. A Collection of Children's and Young People's Poetry Written in the Ghettos of World War II*. Waltham, Mass.: Brandeis University Press, 1979.

Bruner, Jerome. *Acts of Meaning. Four Lectures on Mind and Culture*. Cambridge, Mass.: Harvard University Press, 1990.

Ebach, Jürgen. "Schrift und Gedächtnis." *Erlebnis-Gedächtnis-Sinn: Authentische und konstruierte Erinnerung*. Ed. Hanno Loewy and Bernhard Moltmann. Frankfurt/Main: Campus, 1996, 106–120.

Eibeshitz, Jehoshua and Anna (Eds.). *Ruthka. A Diary of War by Ruthka Lieblich*. Translated from the Polish by Jehoshua and Anna Eibeshitz. Brooklyn, N.Y.: Remember, 1993.

Fackenheim, Emil L. *The Jewish Bible After the Holocaust: A Re-reading*. Manchester: Manchester University Press, 1990.

Fishkin, Sarah. *The Diary of Sarah Fishkin*. Trans. from the Yiddish by Eva Zeitlin Dobkin. Yad Vashem Archive 033.2222.

Glatstein, Jacob, Israel Knox, and Samuel Margoshes (Eds.). *Anthology of Holocaust Literature*. Philadelphia: Jewish Publication Society, 1969.

Hertz, Joseph Herman (Ed.). *The Pentateuch and Haftorahs*. London: Soncino Press, 1958.

Hilberg, Raul. *The Destruction of the European Jews*. New Haven: Yale University Press, 2003.

Hoettl, Wilhelm. *Eichmann Trial – Session 85 – Written testimonies from Germany presented to the court*. https://collections.ushmm.org/search/catalog/irn1001787 USHMM (November 17, 2021).

Holliday, Laurel (Ed.). *Children's Wartime Diaries: Secret Writings from the Holocaust and World War II*. London: Judy Piatkus Publishers, 1995.

Howe, Irving. "Writing and the Holocaust." *Writing and the Holocaust*. Ed. Berel Lang. New York and London: Holmes and Meier, 1988, 174–199.

Kestenberg, Judith S., and Ira Brenner. *The Last Witness: The Child Survivor of the Holocaust*. Washington, DC: American Psychiatric Press, 1996.

Kingsley, Gershon (Ed.). *Voices from the Shadow*. New York: Kingsley Sound 2001. https://www.milkenarchive.org/music/volumes/view/out-of-the-whirlwind/work/voices-from-the-shadow/ (November 24, 2021).

Klüger, Ruth. *Still Alive. A Holocaust Girlhood Remembered*. New York: Feminist Press at the City University of New York, 2001.

Klüger, Ruth. *weiter leben. Eine Jugend*. München: dtv, 2005.

Křížková, Marie Rút, Kurt Jiří Kotouč, Zdeněk Ornest, Elizabeth Novak. *We Are Children Just the Same. Vedem, the Secret Magazine by the Boys of Terezín*. Prag: Aventinum Nakladatelstvi, 1995.

Langer, Lawrence (Ed.). *Art from the Ashes: A Holocaust Anthology*. New York: Oxford University Press, 1995.

Lau, Ellinor, and Susanne Pampuch. *Draußen steht eine bange Nacht. Lieder und Gedichte aus deutschen Konzentrationslagern*. Frankfurt: Fischer Taschenbuch Verlag, 1994.

Lohmann, Hans-Martin (Ed.). *Psychoanalyse und Nationalsozialismus. Beiträge zur Bearbeitung eines unbewältigten Traumas*. Frankfurt/Main: Fischer (tb.), 1994.

Marton, Judah (Ed.). *The Diary of Eva Heyman*. Trans. Moshe M. Kohn. Jerusalem: Yad Vashem, 1974.

Meerbaum-Eisinger, Selma. *Ich bin in Sehnsucht eingehüllt. Gedichte eines jüdischen Mädchens an seinen Freund*. Ed. Jürgen Serke. Hamburg: Hoffmann und Campe, 1980.

Milton, Sybil. *The Art of Jewish Children: Germany, 1936–1941. Innocence and Persecution*. New York: Philosophical Library, 1989.

Mol, Hans. *Identity and the Sacred: A Sketch for a New Social-Scientific Theory of Religion*. New York: The Free Press, 1976.

Nelken, Halina. *And Yet, I Am Here!* Translated from the Polish original by Alicia Nitecki. Amherst: University of Massachusetts Press, 2001.

Pollak, Michael. *Die Grenzen des Sagbaren: Lebensgeschichten von KZ-Überlebenden als Augenzeugenberichte und als Identitätsarbeit*. Frankfurt/Main: Campus-Verlag, 1988.

Rudashevski, Yitskhok. *The Diary of the Vilna Ghetto, June 1941-April 1943*. Ed. and Trans. Percy Matenko. Tel Aviv: Ghetto Fighters' House, 1973.

Schwencke, Olaf (Ed.). *Erinnerung als Gegenwart: Elie Wiesel in Loccum*. Freiburg: Herder Verlag, 1988.

Seeskin, Kenneth. "What Philosophy Can and Cannot Say about Evil." In: *Echoes from the Holocaust*. Ed. Alan Rosenberg and Gerald E. Myers. Philadelphia: Temple University Press 1988, 91–104.

Stargardt, Nicholas. "Children's Art of the Holocaust." *Past and Present. A Journal of Historical Studies*. 161.11 (1998): 191–235.

Tauschwitz, Marion. *Meerbaum-Eisinger, Selma. Ich habe keine Zeit gehabt zuende zu schreiben: Biografie und Gedichte*. Springe: zu Klampen Verlag, 2014.

Volavkova, Hana. *I Never Saw Another Butterfly: Children's Drawings and Poems from Terezín Concentration Camp 1942–1944*. New York: Knopf Doubleday Publishing Group, 1993.

Wiesel, Elie. *Speech at the Days of Remembrance ceremony*. 2001. Washington, DC, US Holocaust Memorial Museum. Holocaust Encyclopedia https://encyclopedia.ushmm.org/content/en/article/elie-wiesel-days-of-remembrance-excerpts (November 2, 2021).

Wiesel, Elie. "Introductory Essay." Ed. George Aptecker. *Beyond Despair*. Morristown, New Jersey: Kahn & Kahan Publishing, 1980, 3–15.

Young, James E. *Writing and Rewriting the Holocaust: Narrative and the Consequences of Interpretation*. Bloomington and Indianapolis: Indiana University Press, 1990.

Daniel P. Reynolds
"Looking into a Mirror Instead of Reality." Ruth Klüger and the Problem of Holocaust Tourism

In her acclaimed memoir *weiter leben* (1992), Ruth Klüger shares serious misgivings about tourism to concentration camp memorials. Describing visitors to camp memorials with the pejorative label "das Volk der Touristen," (69) Klüger sees little chance that visitors can learn much through so-called "Holocaust tourism." Having survived Theresienstadt, Auschwitz, and the Groß-Rosen subcamp near Christianstadt from the ages of ten to fourteen, she understandably feels alienated from tourists who explore Munich in the morning and visit Dachau in the afternoon, or those who see Goethe's house in Weimar before making an excursion to the nearby Buchenwald concentration camp memorial. Disturbed by the conversion of concentration camps into musealized tourist destinations, Klüger asks, "Was haben wir davon?" (Klüger 1992, 69) – What do we get from that?[1]

Klüger's rhetorical doubt introduces the reader to her profound skepticism not only about tourism to camp memorials, but to the larger phenomenon of Holocaust memorial culture more generally. A more cursory reading of her memoir might suggest that Klüger finds the entire array of Holocaust treatments in modern popular culture – namely, in tourism, film and television, novels, online platforms – deficient. But Klüger demands more from us as readers than our first impression might suggest: she wants to argue with us, to make us think. (McGlothlin 2004, 56), I take Klüger's skeptical interjections, which recur throughout her memoir, as more than merely rhetorical, while also less than definitive of her ultimate position on popular modes of Holocaust memory. Instead, I read her doubts as a challenge to her readers to think deeply about why they participate as consumers in the market of Holocaust remembrance. Klüger's pointed questions are ultimately an invitation for further reflection, the first volley in a critical debate with her readers, with other survivors, and even with herself. (McGlothlin 2004, 61) Through her constant questioning, Klüger prods us to reflect honestly on the state of Holocaust memorial culture and what we can possibly gain from it. In

---

1 When possible, I defer throughout to Klüger's own adaption of *weiter leben* into English in her later, considerably revised version *Still Alive*, published in 2001. In this case, Klüger writes, "Yet, to what purpose," which works better in the context of her English-language memoir but loses the pointedness of her original question.

https://doi.org/10.1515/9783110793239-009

particular, she demands that we account for what rescues Holocaust memorial culture, especially through tourism, from what she later comes to call "KZ-Kitsch" – concentration camp kitsch. (Klüger 1996, 29)

In this essay, I contend that the doubt Klüger expresses about Holocaust tourism does not mean we should give up on the possibility of profoundly meaningful experiences among its participants. The fact that Klüger focuses on tourism first, then on other examples of Holocaust representation in popular fiction, film, and television, indicates an Adornian skepticism about mass culture as inherently inadequate to the task of memorializing the Holocaust, replicating as it does the very logic of instrumentalization that, in its most radical form, made the Holocaust possible in the first place. But Klüger goes to some length to distance herself from Adorno in *weiter leben*; moreover, we must ask about Klüger's own memoir, which has become an international best-seller translated into multiple languages. The problem of mass cultural representations of the Holocaust cannot be reduced to a simplistic opposition between low-brow popular culture and more esoteric artistic and intellectual efforts, even if for Klüger that can be a starting point for debate. Klüger's own view of mass culture is inherently ambivalent, even if she holds Holocaust-related works to a high standard of accountability.[2] Rather than locate Klüger's skepticism in the problem of mass culture vs. "high art," I will argue that Klüger values each instance of Holocaust representation only to the degree that it engenders critical reflection in readers, viewers, or tourists. The responsibility for meaningful Holocaust memorialization lies with authors, filmmakers, and museum curators who create Holocaust representations on the one hand, and with readers, viewers, and tourists willing to practice the same kind of skepticism her memoir so memorably vocalizes, on the other.

In the following pages, I explore how Klüger situates *weiter leben* within the broader context of Holocaust memory culture, including Holocaust tourism. Klüger's reflections in her memoir and in other texts allow us to derive a set of principles that inform her critique of "KZ-Kitsch," and help us identify its potential alternatives. I then look more closely at examples of Holocaust tourism through the lens of Klüger's critical apparatus to respond to the challenge she issues. In doing so, I approach tourism as a medium for portraying the Holocaust that, like narrative texts and visual renditions, adheres to evolving conventions of representation to make communication between the site and its visitors possible. I show how tourism, despite its potential for superficiality, also enables

---

2 In her essay "Von hoher und niedriger Literatur" (1996), Klüger admits to her love of popular movies and mystery novels, despite their status as "wegwerfbar." (6–7) She distinguishes such popular art forms from kitsch because they do not pretend to be more than what they are. Kitsch, on the other hand, is "verlogene Kunst." (27)

memory work on the part of tourists by calling upon their own agency as readers and observers on the tour. Ultimately, the question of tourism as kitsch challenges not only the intentions of museum curators or tour guides, but also the interpretive strategies deployed by tourists themselves, each of whom inevitably brings a unique personal story that informs their visit. In the end, Klüger knows that tourism to former sites of suffering will not cease, and her readers (like Klüger herself, who visited Dachau and Bergen-Belsen) will continue to visit concentration camp memorials. (Klüger 1992, 77) While the continued popularity of Holocaust tourism would doubtless fail to impress Klüger, perhaps she will have enabled some tourists to carry out a version of travel that embraces her deeply skeptical approach.

Memorialization as Redemption vs. Memorialization as Debate

Klüger's "essayistic book" engages with numerous examples of Holocaust memorial culture, ranging from theoretical considerations to narrative fiction, theater, film, and television.[3] Some of her examples are named, others are not but are easily identifiable. Almost all are subject to Klüger's critical scrutiny, with only a few emerging unscathed: Paul Celan and Peter Weiss chief among them.[4] The main thrust of her debate with Holocaust memorial culture does not aim primarily at popular culture, as her discourse on tourism might suggest, but rather with influential figures whose pronouncements on the Holocaust and its representation are so canonical as to have become dogmatic. Examples include Theodor Adorno's pronouncement on the barbarism of writing poetry after Auschwitz, or Claude Lanzmann's refusal to use archival footage as he documents sites of perpetration in his film *Shoah*. By taking on such prominent figures who have shaped debates about how to represent the Holocaust in film and literature,

---

3 Klüger refers to *weiter leben* in *unterwegs verloren*: "Eigentlich war es ein essayistisches Buch, mehr Kommentar als Handlung." (Klüger 2008, 165)

4 She also mentions Primo Levi once in passing in *weiter leben* to contrast his adult experiences at Auschwitz with those of the child she was. She later praises Levi in an important essay on the meaning of Kitsch, referring to him as "der große Klassiker der KZ-Literatur," (1996, 30) i.e. the great classic of Holocaust literature, and she contrasts his recollections, written down immediately after the war, with a Nazi who remembers him but whose memories of his own perpetration have been sanitized through the "Kitsch-Krücke der Nostalgie." ("the kitsch-crutch of nostalgia," 1996, 31 – my translation)

Klüger illustrates a contrarian perspective toward dogma. For her, and perhaps for her readers, no effort to represent the Holocaust should be spared from critique, and there are no figures, even among the survivors, with whom one may not debate – Ruth Klüger included.

Her praise of Celan comes in the form of a defense of his famous poem "Todesfuge," and indirectly her own childhood poetry, as a means to represent the supposedly unrepresentable in the "bound language" of meter and rhyme. (1992, 127) She juxtaposes poetry with the view held by many, particularly some historians, that figurative language is of lesser value in learning about the Holocaust compared to the importance of documentary evidence. She objects, insisting on the inadequacy of historical documents alone to permit any deep understanding of the camps:

> Some claim that instead of writing poetry one should only gather information, in other words read and examine documents, and do so with a composed though troubled heart. And what should readers or observers of such documents be thinking? Poems are a particular way to think about life critically and could help people in their effort to understand. Why shouldn't they be allowed? And how exactly do Allowed and Should function in this context? Morally, religiously? Whose interests are being served, who is speaking here? This topic becomes the burning bush on holy ground, which one may approach only with naked feet and subservient humility.   (1992, 127 – my translation)

Klüger follows this spirited argument against the inferiority of poetry vis-à-vis history with an admission that she has written a parody of Celan's later, famously abstruse poetry, to the shock of those who have transformed Celan into a revered icon of the Holocaust. What at first appears as a debate between two figures, Adorno and Celan, about the appropriateness of figurative language in representing the Holocaust, soon emerges as Klüger's alternative pair of principles for representing the Holocaust. First, she argues for the contribution of multiple genres, including documentary and figurative accounts, to provide a richer, if still imperfect, interpretation of the past; and second, she refuses to acquiesce to moralistic pronouncements about the Holocaust that tend to become dogmatic, as if there were no room for further debate. In comparing the roles of documents and poetry, Klüger declares the opposition to be tendentious. If documents are simply raw data, how is the reader supposed to understand them in context without the help of a narrative framework that explains their relevance to the Holocaust more broadly? Furthermore, the assumption that poetry only has an aesthetic or affective function, while historiography and theory provide bare information and rational critique, is false. As for Adorno and Celan, neither's body of work is honored by sparing them any criticism – nor, for that matter, is Klüger's own memoir.

To demonstrate her willingness to receive criticism in the same spirit in which she offers it, Klüger makes self-critique a hallmark of her prose. (Rider 2021, 60; McGlothlin 2004, 61–62) It is the device she uses to anticipate her interlocuters' objections and perform debate in her writing, but it is also an invitation to her readers to question her conclusions. In one memorable passage from the opening of Part 2 of her memoir, she recalls an encounter with two young German students at the University of Göttingen, where she is, at the time, a visiting professor. She overhears their conversation about their experiences as volunteers at the Auschwitz-Birkenau Memorial and Museum, where they have completed their alternative civilian service.[5] They worked on preservation of the camp ruins, reduced in Klüger's account to a somewhat farcical reminiscence of *Tom Sawyer*: "It was their job to white-wash the fences in Auschwitz." (1992, 69 – my translation)[6] In her typically frank manner she asks her readers, "Whatever for?" (1992, 70 – my translation), presumably having asked the volunteers a similarly pointed question.[7] After airing her concerns about preserving concentration camp sites, she admits that her skepticism may have alienated the volunteers: "Germany's hopeful young intellectuals sink their heads and awkwardly eat their soup. Now I have silenced you, that was not my intention. There is always a wall between the generations, but here there is barbed wire, rusty barbed wire." (1992, 72 – my translation) Klüger regrets the silence, but not the difference of opinion that precipitated it. At the same time, her entire memoir itself is an effort to bridge the gap of the generational divide separating her from the students to whom she has dedicated years of teaching, both in the U.S. and in Germany. Aware that her adversarial approach may alienate some, Klüger acknowledges the possibility of discord as an acceptable alternative to any overly hasty reconciliation that papers over differences; nevertheless, she pleads for debate to continue all the same.

If the generation gap is one locus for the kinds of difference that trouble simplistic conclusions about Holocaust memory and instead engender debate,

---

5 Civilian Service, or *Zivildienst*, was introduced in the Federal Republic of Germany in 1973 as an alternative requirement for German men who were excused from obligatory military service on the basis of conscientious objection. After 2011, both military and civil service became voluntary.

6 Klüger makes this reference to Twain even more explicit in *Still Alive*, where German cultural references are often replaced by American ones to better relate to her English-language readership: "Instead of serving in the military, they had whitewashed the fences at Auschwitz. I associate Tom Sawyer and his friends with whitewashed fences, and I wondered aloud whether this cheerful activity made any sense in an extermination camp." (64)

7 Klüger's translation of "Wozu nur" in *weiter leben* is rendered as "And I ask myself, why?" in *Still Alive*. (Klüger 2001, 64)

Klüger's portrayal of her own family's intergenerational conflicts prove no exception. Her unvarnished portrayal of her relationship with her mother in *weiter leben* is brutally honest and shows that even among survivors from the same family there is disagreement and possibly conflict.[8] By laying bare her frustrations (which serve as much to expose her own human frailties as her mother's), Klüger insists that Holocaust survivors have no special claim to virtue on the basis of their traumatic experiences. As she has demonstrated with her Celan parody, she prefers to view survivors as more than the sum of their traumatic experiences during the Holocaust, and she rejects the tendency to regard them as inherently heroic and noble, or as profoundly morally damaged for having survived where so many others did not. Here again she offers a way to think about approaching the Holocaust that challenges collective remembrance in its tendency to see trauma primarily in collective terms, overlooking differences among individuals: "Though the Shoah involved millions of people, it was a unique experience for each of them." (Klüger 2001, 66)

Klüger's repeated insistence on differentiation emerges in the recurring tropes of ruptures and gaps that permeate her memoir: the gap between the experience of internment and the representation of it in text; between the exception of survivors and the rule of those who were murdered; between her German readers and herself as a Vienna-born Jew living in the U.S.; between women and men, children and adults; and between the Nazi killing centers and the musealized space of the concentration camp memorials. On this last point, in the same section of *weiter leben* that opens Part 2, she refers to her own memory project, writing with her trademark self-awareness:

> It is pointless to present the camps in physical space as they were back then. But just as pointless is the effort to describe them in words, as if nothing lay between us and the time in which they functioned. (1992, 78 – my translation)[9]

Klüger blends self-questioning – her doubt that there is any point in describing the camps even as she embarks on that very effort – with an attentiveness to the limits of representation as always offering an interpretation, not a reproduction.

---

8 In *unterwegs verloren*, Klüger acknowledges the pain her mother felt upon reading about some of the revelations contained in *weiter leben*. (Klüger 2008, 210) She also lays bare her own uneasy relationship with her sons, suggesting that she, like her mother, was an imperfect parent.

9 In *Still Alive*, Klüger's observation about the past and present condition of the camps conflates physical and textual representation: "It won't do to pretend that we can evoke the physical reality of the camps as they were when they functioned. Nevertheless, I want my timescapes. Evocations of places at a time that has passed." (Klüger 2001, 68)

She invites her readers to mention what she omits, what she forgets, and to identify and engage with her "hard boiled" subjectivity. (Klüger 2001, 68) Only so can the memoir, written years after the event, serve as a catalyst for further inquiry rather than the last word.

The acknowledgment of the years that have lapsed between her imprisonment in the Nazi camps and her memoir of that experience fits perfectly into her program of embracing gaps and fragments as a forthright approach for representing the Holocaust in general. The gulf separating the self of a young girl in the Nazi camps and the adult woman who has created a new life in another country cannot be overlooked; it will necessarily lead to omissions and moments of uncertainty about the sequence of events. But those moments need to be acknowledged, as Klüger does acknowledge them, because they are generative of the memoir's commentary, not a hindrance to it. An example of this kind of commentary comes in a later essay in which she reflects on the process of writing her own memoir:

> The greater the temporal distance, the more incomprehensible the events of those years became. Sometimes it seems even to me that the recollections I carry around in my memory are foreign, meaning they are foreign to the person I have since become.
>
> (1996, 33 – my translation)

If the memoirist finds herself increasingly unable to identify with the younger self who experienced the camps, then surely readers must acknowledge an unbridgeable space separating their own comprehension of the Holocaust from the event itself. And here Klüger points to yet another pitfall in the project of Holocaust remembrance: the tendency to promote identification with the victims and survivors. To name but one example of this kind of identification in the realm of Holocaust tourism, the United States Holocaust Memorial Museum (USHMM) in Washington, D.C., gives visitors an identity card at the beginning of the tour containing the story of an individual who endured the Holocaust. The card gives tourists the opportunity to understand how the Holocaust was experienced by one individual, thereby offering a path toward understanding that might be more relatable to visitors than the effort to imagine the fates of six million different victims. (Linenthal 1995, 187) Despite that worthy goal, the card was seen initially as a gimmick that encouraged visitors to believe they understood the experiences of a victim, which worked in tandem with the museum's invitation to Americans to associate themselves with the liberators, but not with the perpetrators or bystanders. (Gourevitch 1993, 58)

Klüger's valid concern for identification with victims on the part of those who participate in Holocaust memorial cultures recalls a similar concern about identification that Marianne Hirsch describes. Hirsch develops her theory of

postmemory as the notion that trauma experienced by one generation can produce traumatic effects in the next, particularly in the case of children of survivors
who become acutely aware of their parents' trauma and feel compelled to understand it or resolve it. The intense interest in the Holocaust by the second generation becomes a kind of witnessing after the fact, a way of confronting secondary
trauma. Hirsch has called attention to the thin line that separates "retrospective
witnessing by adoption" from outright appropriation of the victims' identities.
(Hirsch 2001, 11) Retrospective witnessing means "adopting the traumatic experiences – and also the memories – of others as experiences one might oneself have
had, and of inscribing them into one's own life story." (Hirsch 2001, 10) But in-
corporating someone else's trauma into one's own life story is hard to distinguish
from the kind of appropriation from which it is supposed to differ, especially
when it applies not only to the children of survivors, but to all members of the
"second generation."[10] I wonder if Klüger would perhaps be equally suspicious
of the expansiveness of the concept of postmemory as articulated by Hirsch,
since it seems to be an invitation to appropriation of a sort, legitimated by the
notion that trauma is transgenerational on a collective scale. What is critical –
and potentially very fragile – in the distinction Hirsch raises lies in the subjunctive formulation: "experiences one might oneself have had." One did not have
those experiences; someone else did. Hirsch emphasizes the distinction between
the actual trauma of the victims and the representations of those traumas in photographs, family conversations, or even ominous silences. Hirsch and Klüger are
united in their agreement that one should "resist appropriation and incorpo-
ration, resist annihilating the distance between self and other, the otherness of
the other," (Hirsch 2001, 11) even if the concept of postmemory comes perilously
close to blurring that very distinction.

In an important departure from Hirsch's concept of postmemory, Klüger
calls into question even the notion of identification itself as a valid tool for remembrance. These two concepts merge in her radical separation from her own
young self, as already mentioned, when she admits that the experiences she recalls feel as though they happened to someone else. Perhaps it is for this reason
that she vows never to visit Auschwitz, for the place, like herself, has been fundamentally altered from its past function as an extermination camp. Rather
than seek memory in place, she insists on memory's embeddedness in an

---

10 In his study of Holocaust remembrance, *Fantasies of Witnessing*, Gary Weissman takes
Hirsch's concept of postmemory to task for suggesting that the lived experiences of one generation can be somehow inherited as memories of lived experience by subsequent generations.
He objects, observing that "[. . .] no degree of power or monumentality can transform one person's lived memories into another's." (17)

irretrievable past, an idea captured in her notion of "timescapes." Timescapes, like the remembering subject, situate the significance of place firmly in a given time that is "neither before nor after" (Klüger 2001, 67) the events recalled. The Auschwitz of her childhood is such a timescape, a place that existed in the past, forever associated not only with the physical setting, but with experiences and affects that are radically different from what any tourist can encounter as a visitor to a memorial site. The memorial site is not the extermination camp, despite the preservation of certain buildings and artefacts. In developing her idea of timescapes, she questions the value of preserving the physical remnants of the camp, now functioning as preserved ruins rather than sites of ongoing violence. She underscores this skepticism about preservation of the camp ruins by distancing herself from Claude Lanzmann, whose fixation on the ruins of the camps in *Shoah* she describes as a kind of "fetish." (Klüger 2001, 67)

Still, there is a moment of hesitation in Klüger's discounting of the camp ruins as useful memorials. The author upon whom she bestows unmitigated praise in *weiter leben* is Peter Weiss, whose 1965 essay "Meine Ortschaft" ("My Place") recounts his visit to the Auschwitz-Birkenau museum a year before he wrote his famous play of the Frankfurt Auschwitz trials, *Die Ermittlung (The Investigation)*. Like the judges who presided over these trials, Weiss makes the journey to Auschwitz to learn something about the place. And while the excursion to Auschwitz and Birkenau was of forensic importance for the trial, Weiss's visit also became a search for something more personal, an attempt to reconcile his life with the fact that, twenty years earlier, only exile spared him from the gas chambers. (Schlunk 1987, 26–30) In the end, Weiss comes to understand the unbridgeable divide that separates him from those who perished, and, as Klüger points out, separates "Gedenkstätte and Besucher" from "Gefängnis und Häftling," i.e., "memorial and visitor" from "prison and prisoner." (Klüger 1992, 75 – my translation) It is this insight into these unbridgeable gaps that leads Klüger to describe Weiss as "the best visitor one could wish for." (1992, 75 – my translation) If Weiss is the best visitor one could wish for, even though he did not experience or witness the camps as a prisoner, why does she preclude the possibility that other visitors can gain similarly valuable insights?

Despite her unabated rejection of concentration camp tourism, Klüger nevertheless provides standards by which to assess the phenomenon. She has emphasized the importance of both fictional and nonfictional texts; she champions debate over dogma, fragmented forms over closed narratives, differentiation over identification. This last point is especially relevant to her view that Holocaust tourism is kitsch, leading as it does to sentimentality. Her aim, as she so clearly states, is the appreciation of difference, not the unduly redemptive identification of future generations with the suffering of the Holocaust's millions of victims.

Speaking to her German audience, she writes: "You don't have to identify with me, in fact, I prefer that you don't." (1992, 142 – my translation) She prefaces debate on the acknowledgement of profound differences between herself and her readers; yet her memoir represents nothing if not the effort to break through the silence that separates her, a Jewish survivor, from her German readers, especially the younger generation of Germans. In her provocative comments, she challenges the tendency for new orthodoxies to arise within a German culture of Holocaust memorialization, which can take on authoritarian qualities.[11] Norbert Klages argues that Klüger's dedication to debate arises from a Jewish tradition that she opposes to the Christian discourse of reconciliation and redemption prevalent in Germany when she wrote *weiter leben*. (Klages 2010, 97) Whether or not Klages is right, Klüger is certainly keen to highlight differences between perpetrators and victims that memorialization in the service of reconciliation is too quick to pave over.

Tourism as a Mirror

While Klüger did reluctantly visit the Dachau Concentration Camp Memorial and Museum, as well as Bergen-Belsen, she vowed never to visit the Auschwitz-Birkenau Memorial and Museum (Klüger 1996, 77): "I never went back to Auschwitz as a tourist and never will. Not in this life. To me it is no place for a pilgrimage. [. . .] The place which I saw, smelled, and feared, and which now has been turned into a museum, has nothing to do with the woman I am." (Klüger 2001, 111)[12] Clearly her reasons for staying away are personal ("to me," "the woman I am"); she offers no prohibition against others going, even if she strongly doubts the value it could have. Still, as her reader, I would like to argue against her dismissals of tourism.

---

11 Klüger uses the word "authoritarian" to describe Adorno's pronouncement about poetry after Auschwitz, even after he modified his earlier formulation: "He [i.e. Adorno] later modified this pronouncement, so that it might read: let's not have any poems *about* (rather than after) Auschwitz. That's still pretty authoritarian but it gets better when it becomes a warning not to let poets and poetry readers forget about Auschwitz and when it comes in a context about the dialectical relationship of the enlightenment and barbarism and how the former can paradoxically morph into the latter." (2014, 394 – original emphasis)
12 I am grateful to Mark Gelber for drawing my attention to Klüger's visit to the Bergen-Belsen Memorial Museum, recorded in the documentary film by Renate Schmidtkunz, *Das Weiterleben der Ruth Klüger*.

Klüger's treatment of tourism seems bound up in a perception of tourism as inauthentic and superficial – a stereotype that for too long has gone unquestioned in academic scholarship and that has its origins in the advent of mass travel in the twentieth century, after tourism had for so long been the preserve of well-to-do elites. Scholars have long characterized tourists as insufficiently critical, as failing to differentiate the past event with the present commemoration of it on display at a museum or memorial. (Young 1993, 128) Tourists function as the foil to the implied readers of scholarship and eye-witness testimony about the Holocaust in this overgeneralized schema. There is an implied tourist in the scholarship on travel to Holocaust memorials whom one can characterize as uninformed, motivated by morbid curiosity (the trope of the "dark tourist"), easily swayed by curated visual displays and the narration of tour guides, and prone to sentiment rather than reflection. Tourists figure as appropriators of the victims' identities and experiences, which they mistakenly conflate with their own, failing to grasp the ways in which they can never gain experiential knowledge of the past.[13] Klüger herself provides just such an image of the implied tourist in *Still Alive*:

> A visitor who feels moved, even if it is only the kind of feeling that a haunted house conveys, will be proud of these stirrings of humanity. And so the visitor monitors his reactions, examines his emotions, admires his own sensibility, or in other words, turns sentimental. For sentimentality involves turning away from an ostensible object and towards the subjective observer, that is, towards oneself. It means looking into a mirror instead of reality. (2001, 66)

This rather harsh assessment does not explore whether the fault with such self-congratulatory tendencies lies with the curators of exhibitions or with the visitors who seek a redemptory experience. Probably she would acknowledge both as problematical. But this summary dismissal of tourists and Holocaust memorial sites as a form of self-flattery overlooks the evolving nature of both the pedagogies devised by museums, which see themselves as much as educational institutions as memorial sites, and by tourists, who have never been a monolithic demographic in the first place.

A brief overview of the history of tourism at the Auschwitz-Birkenau State Museum illustrates the evolving nature of memorialization at one site. Of course, Auschwitz is only one of hundreds of camp memorials in Europe, and there is a wide range of preservation and memorialization from place to place. But the

---

13 This point is acknowledged by Ann Rider, who addresses the problematical nature of experiential modes of learning promoted at Holocaust museums and memorials, particularly in the American context. (Rider 2021, 56)

central place of Auschwitz in Holocaust remembrance tourism, combined with Klüger's own internment there, make it an appropriate starting point.[14]

After being liberated in January 1945, survivors from Auschwitz organized themselves very quickly to preserve what remained of the site, working together with newly established Polish state agencies investigating Nazi wartime atrocities. The Auschwitz-Birkenau museum officially opened in June 1947 and was housed primarily in the brick barracks of the main camp in Auschwitz. For decades the mission of the museum highlighted Polish suffering and did little to acknowledge the unique suffering meted out to the more than one million Jews murdered there, by far the largest victim group. The memorial has since evolved with the times, from a primarily Polish site for a national (largely Catholic) audience to an increasingly international site, overseen since 1990 by the International Auschwitz Council that acknowledges the unique fate of Jews and other victim groups. To visit Auschwitz today is to encounter a palimpsest of memorialization; traces of Cold-War-inflected discourse emphasizing the Hitlerite fascists and the Soviet liberators coincide with more recent efforts to explain in greater detail the origins of anti-Semitism and other forms of racism. A perceptive visitor to Auschwitz can learn not only the history of the Nazi camp, but also the history of the memorial itself, which provides an opening for tourists to reflect on their own historical positioning in a constantly evolving process of memorialization, one that has moved increasingly from a reductive Cold War account to a more differentiated account that addresses an increasingly global audience, with tours offered in nineteen different languages. ("Guided tours options")

Along with the changes in the narratives presented to visitors at Auschwitz, the museum itself has adapted to modern times in the way it communicates with its visitors, in part by necessity. Since 1990, coinciding with the end of the Cold War era, the number of visitors each year has risen steadily from 500,000 to more than 2 million – until the COVID-19 pandemic saw a drastic decline back to

---

14 I do not mean to suggest that the establishment of the Auschwitz memorial is in any way "typical" of other camp memorials. Other extermination camps located in Poland (Chełmno, Bełżec, Sobibór, Treblinka) had been destroyed in an effort to hide the Nazi crimes and thus offered little in the way that ruins might serve as a memorial after the war. The rather early development of a memorial at Auschwitz follows the pattern of the Majdanek labor and extermination camp outside of Lublin, which had been liberated in 1944, still somewhat intact, and designated as a memorial site before the war ended. In territories liberated by the Western allies, Bergen–Belsen and Buchenwald served as emblematic memorial sites, but many other camp memorials were established only years later, reflecting the slow process of memorialization at Auschwitz II (Birkenau) more closely than at Auschwitz I (the so-called *Stammlager*). See Tim Cole's discussion of the changing status of Auschwitz in Holocaust remembrance in his book, *Selling the Holocaust*. (98–99)

500,000 in 2020. (*Report* 2020, 15) Guided tours with headsets lead tourists through the primary museum exhibits, containing numerous artifacts: prisoner uniforms, cannisters of Zyklon B, the personal belongings of the victims, and the most gruesome display, of mounds of human hair from female victims. The museum otherwise places emphasis on documentary evidence: records of transports, correspondence, reports from the SS to Berlin, and ample photographic evidence. I emphasize this multi-medial nature of the tour to recall Klüger's own insistence on the importance of multiple genres of representation contributing to the understanding of the Holocaust. Again, the site is palimpsestic and charts the evolution away from what Cornelia Brink has called *Leichenbergpädagogik*, or the pedagogy of mounds of corpses, to a more respectful approach to the victims. (Brink 1998, 204) In many ways, the Auschwitz museum is an outlier compared to other concentration camp museums that have moved steadily away from the shock of atrocity images as a viable pedagogical method. Though more "objective" approaches can hardly purge tourists' affective responses, there has been a growing understanding among many responsible for the memorial sites that affect must be paired with thoughtful reflection – much like Klüger's own insistence on the importance of both poetry and documentation in understanding the past. The absence of either would be troubling.

The careful attention to the victims at Auschwitz is simultaneously understandable, even necessary, but also vulnerable to the kind of appropriation that Hirsch warns about. Particularly in the photographs that document the arrival of Hungarian Jews to Birkenau in 1944, which are placed at various locations throughout the memorial complex, visitors see into the eyes of victims who stood at the same spot decades ago. The appreciation of the temporal distance that separates the timescape of the extermination camp from the memorial site may give way momentarily to a sense of immediacy or shared presence at the site, but any sense of immediacy or primary witnessing is quickly complicated by the phenomenology of being on a tour. The sensory input that the tourist experiences is radically different from the image contained in the black-and-white photographs. Living color in the tourist's own field of vision, the subdued ambient sounds of other tourists, even the sound of birds chirping in the trees during the warmer months, reinscribe the temporal difference separating tourists from the scene conveyed in the silent historical image, taken at a moment that was likely anything but silent.

Furthermore, the captions accompanying these photos call the tourist's attention to the original photographer. For some critics, this reliance on perpetrator photography in Holocaust tourism is deeply problematical, since it purportedly invites the tourist not only to see through the perpetrator's lens, but to tacitly endorse the power dynamics that consign the photographed subject to the status of doomed victim. Janina Struk sees the display of such photographs in museum exhibitions as a revictimization of those photographed for the sake of satisfying the tourist's morbid curiosity. (Struk 2004, 211–216) I would counter that there is immense importance in the tourist's confrontation with fact that their own gaze imitates that of the perpetrator-photographer. To the extent that identification remains part of the way that viewers consume photographs, the tourist is caught in an irresolvable dilemma: the impossibility of identifying both with the victims in the photograph and the criminal holding the camera. That alone would be sufficient to undermine any effort on the part of the tourist to usurp the victims' identities. Cornelia Brink takes up this question in her book, *Ikonen der Vernichtung (Icons of Annihilation)*, where she contrasts the critical evaluation of perpetrator images with the pedagogical intentions of memorial sites that put them on display. (Brink 1998, 209–210) Brink shows that there is nothing intrinsic in the medium of photography that insists on such easy identifications; rather, photography raises questions about subjectivity, whether taking pictures or viewing them. In the particular case of perpetrator images of victims, Brink points out that every photo has a double nature. She takes issue with critics who tend to insist that the viewer of the photograph identifies either with the photographer or the victim, arguing persuasively that both positions insist on a straightforward identificatory approach to understanding how we view photographs. Instead, Brink describes a tug-of-war between these options.

But the notion of identification itself is insufficient to understand all that takes place when looking at photographs, particularly such troubling images. Klüger's implied tourist is chiefly a consumer, not a critic or a student, and her insistence on the uncritical tourist gaze overlooks the context in which Holocaust tourism often occurs. Both the curators of the sites and the tourists who access them often invoke education as the common goal that brings them together. Tourists are agents of their own learning during the tour – they make decisions about what to look at closely, what to photograph, what to listen to, what to ignore. Tourists can ask questions, or even challenge statements made by tour guides. (I recall a tourist at Auschwitz once questioning the guide's claim that members of the SS could refuse to kill. The guide responded by providing the tourist with evidence to the contrary to consult after the tour.) Tourists arrive with varying degrees of preparation for their visits, and some may be very well informed about the site prior to their visit. Tourism becomes an opportunity to enrich their own critical engagement with the Holocaust with a stronger understanding for the space of the former camp, the distances marched, the proximity of victims to their captors, the modes of surveillance operated by the SS, and the proximity of the camp to the nearby towns.

The fact that tourists also take pictures reminds us that tourists are active agents on the tour, producing images rather than merely consuming them. Sometimes they take photos of photos, lending a citational quality to the act of photography; or they photograph other tourists, and in doing so place a critical distance between themselves and other travelers. (Reynolds 2018, 100–102) Then, of course, there is the selfie, the ultimate touristic act of looking into a mirror instead of reality. Of course, Klüger is right to object when tourists make themselves the object of the tour, as they may do when they take selfies. However, I would argue that there is more to selfies than simply a narcissistic impulse, even if I would not declare the selfie free of the more problematic aspects of tourism. More important for my argument would be to recall that tourists differ from one another in too many ways, including their approach to using a camera at a former concentration camp, to be characterized with such broad strokes. Some take no pictures at all, wondering if it is disrespectful of the site, a notion reinforced at some memorials that make restrictions on photography very clear. Touring a former Nazi concentration camp site, it becomes difficult to avoid feeling self-conscious while using a camera. Compounded with the awareness of other tourists who may look back disapprovingly, the dynamics of the tourist gaze at concentration camp memorials are too complex to be reduced to the act of self-involvement or self-admiration that Klüger describes.

The documentary film *Austerlitz* (2016) by acclaimed Ukrainian filmmaker Sergei Loznitsa, provides an interesting case study of the relationship between Holocaust tourism and the tourist gaze. Filmed on location at the Sachsenhausen concentration camp memorial in Oranienburg, Loznitsa's stationary camera lets visitors wander in and out of his frame at several locations on site. Filmed during a sunny day, the film's tourists are clad in typical summer wear – often shorts or t-shirts. Some t-shirts bear "irreverent slogans" and certainly provoke the viewer to react with disapproval; (Magilow 174) but despite showing us tourism, "warts and all," Loznitsa's film does not provide an unequivocal commentary regretting the transformation of concentration camps into theme parks, as film critic Jonathan Romney argues in his review of the film (screendaily.com). Rather, as Loznitsa's official website claims, *Austerlitz* offers itself as an "observation of the visitors to a memorial site that has been founded on the territory of a former concentration camp. Why do they go there? What are they looking for?" ("Synopsis," https://loznitsa.com/movie/austerlitz) In its contemplative long takes of visitors in all their diversity (we hear several languages spoken during the film), *Austerlitz* challenges stereotypical assumptions about them, their motivations, and their behaviors, even as it incorporates moments that affirm those stereotypes. For the most part the film shows people moving thoughtfully throughout the memorial site, pausing, reading, scanning. While most seem unaware of Loznitsa's camera, occasionally a passing tourist seems aware of the camera and stares back. The film thus draws our attention to the tourist gaze as a dynamic web of ways of looking, with the newly added layer of the documentary film's additional reversal of the gaze back onto the tourists. The film's viewers are thus now positioned as the voyeurs. One suspects that Loznitsa has kept his camera out of view, though it may have been hiding in plain sight among the many cameras carried by tourists.

Austerlitz rejects the rapid cuts, dramatic music, and startling sounds that one would associate with the aesthetics of shock, offering instead the aesthetics of quiet contemplation. While a scene of large numbers of tourists entering the Sachsenhausen memorial in casual attire might be met with initial surprise in its very matter-of-factness, the scene's length allows the viewer's attention to notice minor details and subtle differences. Rather than promote the moral condemnation of tourism, the film lets us reflect seriously on the possibility that individual tourists are in an earnest search for the memorial site's traumatic history. The drawn-out gaze of the camera lets us appreciate the tourists' own act of viewing, which is also sometimes extended, often for several minutes, as they stare at a single display. It is not possible to know, however, what each tourist is thinking. If the film is a tragedy "about the disconnection between the greatest horror of the 20th century and our inability to adequately convey it to the 21st," as film critic Michael Sicinski has stated (cinema-scope.com), then it suggests that tourism ultimately upholds one of Klüger's own tenets of Holocaust remembrance: it acknowledges the irretrievability of the past that Klüger emphasizes in her concept of timescapes. But it is important to acknowledge what the film does not – and cannot – show: the minds of the tourists. True, we see momentary displays of affect, including smiles, giggles, frowns, or arms crossed in contemplation. However, one momentary affect is preceded and followed by others, and the tourists' visit cannot be reduced to a sequence of shots in Loznitsa's film – or in our estimation of tourists' experiences. Even efforts to assess tourists' reactions through empirical research may not succeed in capturing the impact of a visit on individuals years after the tour.

Still, many of the film's reviewers claim the film condemns tourism simply by showing it. Here I am reminded of Klüger's own statement about tourists at concentration camps: "Whoever thinks they have found something there probably brought it with them in their baggage." (Klüger 1996, 75) It would seem the same could be said of tourism's critics, including those watching Loznitsa's film. The sheer variety of people, each with their own backgrounds and motivations, makes it very likely that someone will confirm our worst stereotypes. But shouldn't we notice all the others too? What Klüger rightly says of survivors – that the Shoah was a unique experience for each of the millions of victims –

could be applied to the crowds of tourists hoping to understand something about the Shoah at the places where it occurred. What irrevocably separates the two is not the moral character of the individuals involved, but the nature of their experiences. Of course, tourism does not allow its participants to be able to say that they have had an experience of the Holocaust itself. I would argue that many tourists come precisely to this recognition. By visiting these Holocaust memorial sites, tourists can understand the permanence of a loss that cannot be made whole again. Looking into a mirror can be a metaphor for precisely the kind of self-reflection on the part of tourists that denies them the consolation of a redemptory experience.

In other words, I would argue in opposition to Ruth Klüger that we should welcome the fact that tourists may be "looking into a mirror instead of reality." I would even suggest that her own project of writing a memoir is just as self-reflective in its impulse. As she has so powerfully demonstrated, there is nothing inherently sentimental or reassuring in taking a hard look at oneself. Instead, we should aim to do it as critically and as productively as Klüger herself has done.

Bibliography

Austerlitz. Dir. Sergei Loznitsa. Imperativ Film, 2016. https://loznitsa.com/movie/austerlitz (October 30, 2021).

Brink, Cornelia. *Ikonen der Vernichtung: Öffentlicher Gebrauch von Fotografien aus nationalsozialistischen Konzentrationslagern nach 1945*. Berlin: Akademie Verlag, 1998.

Cole, Tim. *Selling the Holocaust. From Auschwitz to Schindler: How History is Bought, Packaged, and Sold*. New York: Routledge, 1999.

Gourevitch, Philip. "Behold Now Behemoth. The Holocaust Memorial Museum: One More American Theme Park." *Harper's Magazine*, July 1993, 55–62.

"Guided tours options." Auschwitz-Birkenau Memorial and Museum. http://auschwitz.org (November 24, 2021).

Hirsch, Marianne. "Surviving Images: Holocaust Photographs and the Work of Postmemory. *The Yale Journal of Criticism* 4.1 (2001): 5–37.

Klages, Norgard. "A Different Voice: 'Vergangenheitsbewältigung' in Ruth Klüger's *weiter leben* and *unterwegs verloren*." *Beyond Political Correctness. Re-Mapping German Sensibilities in the 21st Century*. Ed. Christine Anton and Frank Phillip. Amsterdam, New York: Rodopie, 2010, 85–105.

Klüger, Ruth. *weiter leben. Eine Jugend*. 1992. München: Deutsche Taschenbuch-Verlag, 1994.

Klüger, Ruth. "Von hoher und niedriger Literatur." Bonner Poetik-Vorlesung Band 1. Göttingen. Wallstein, 1996.

Klüger, Ruth. *Still Alive. A Holocaust Girlhood Remembered*. New York: The Feminist Press, 2001.

Klüger, Ruth. *unterwegs verloren. Erinnerungen.* 2008. München: Deutsche Taschenbuch-Verlag 2010.

Klüger, Ruth. "The Future of Holocaust Literature: German Studies Association 2013 Banquet Speech." *German Studies Review* 37.2 (May 2014): 391–403.

Linenthal, Edward T. *Preserving Memory. The Struggle to Create America's Holocast Museum.* New York: Penguin, 1995.

Magilow, Daniel H. "Shoah Selfies, Shoah Selfie Shaming, and Social Photography in Sergei Loznitsa's *Austerlitz* (2016)." *Shofar* 39.2 (2021): 155–187.

McGlothlin, Erin. "Autobiographical Re-vision:Ruth Klügers *weiter leben* and *Still Alive.*" *Gegenwartsliteratur* 3 (2004): 46–70.

2020 – Report. Ed. Bartosz Bartyzel and Paweł Sawicki. Oświęcim Państwowe Muzeum Auschwitz-Birkenau w Oświęcimiu, 2021.

Reynolds, Daniel P. *Postcards from Auschwitz. Holocaust Tourism and the Meaning of Remembrance.* New York: New York University Press, 2018.

Rider, N. Ann. "Narrative Challenge to Cultural Cognitive Models of the Holocaust." *German Studies Review* 44.1 (February 2021): 47–66.

Romney, Jonathan. "Austerlitz: Venice Review." 7 September 2016. *Screendaily*, https://www.screendaily.com/reviews/austerlitz-venice-review/5109136.article (24 November 2021).

Schlunk, Jürgen E. "Auschwitz and Its Function in Peter Weiss' Search for Identity." *German Studies Review* 10.1 (February 1987): 11–30.

Sicinski, Michael. Austerlitz (Sergei Loznitsa, Germany) – Wavelengths. Cinema Scope Online (7 September 2016), https://cinema-scope.com/cinema-scope-online/austerlitz-sergei-loznitsa-germany-wavelengths/ (24 November 2021).

Struk, Janina. *Photographing the Holocaust. Interpretations of the Evidence.* London: I.B. Tauris, 2004.

"Synopsis." *Sergei Loznitsa. Movies: Austerlitz.* Website, https://loznitsa.com/movies/austerlitz (November 26, 2021).

Weissman, Gary. *Fantasies of Witnessing. Postwar Efforts to Experience the Holocaust.* Ithaca: Cornell University Press, 2004.

Das Weiterleben der Ruth Klüger. Dir. Renate Schmidtkunz. Navigator Film, 2011.

Young, James E. *The Texture of Memory: Holocaust Memorials and Meaning.* New Haven: Yale University Press, 1993.

Vera Schwarcz
Threads Yet to Be Spun: A China Angle on Memory and Ghosts in the Poetry of Ruth Klüger

All those who trade on sorrow
Must join together like cabbages
Must find the only possible way
To spin the pyramid around
So all four sides are bathed in light.
  Gu Cheng, "Bulin's Last Will and
  Testament."
                    (Tze 2010, 47)

There is a barbed wire of words around the poetry of the Shoah. "Too brutal!" screams Theodor Adorno. "It hurts like hell!" hurls Paul Celan. "Dare to be banished!" urges Else Lasker-Schüler. "Rebel against the Mutterland," murmurs Rose Ausländer. "Swallow speech if you must!" sings Nelly Sachs. "Keep spinning threads even in the company of unavenged ghosts!" adds Ruth Klüger.

To come near this electrified fence, one needs a roundabout route; in this essay, the journey starts and ends in China. Turning to Chinese literature about ghosts and mourning provides a useful camouflage when facing personal loss and historical trauma. It is as if Dr. Ho Feng-shan, China's Consul-General in Vienna from 1938–1940, granted a visa of safe passage out of Europe's seething cauldron. Ruth Klüger and her mother did not receive one of Dr. Ho's rescue documents. If they had, we would not have Klüger's unique window onto the darkest period of Jewish history. The depths of rage, beauty, and insight condensed in *weiter leben* might not continue to pull us toward her story, her poems.

If we had ever met and chatted at length, Ruth herself might have given me permission to bring her work into a conversation with Chinese poet-survivors. She did not view the *jüdische Katastrophe* as an isolated event. It was, and certainly is becoming in our century, part of a planetary lament for what Giorgio Agamben called "the amputation of the human experience by the dispositions of the modern state." (Agamben 2007, 54) Gu Cheng (1956–1993) was a writer who would have recognized Klüger as a kindred spirit. He, too, was at war with darkness and ghosts, but unlike the older Jewish writer, he succumbed to the

Note: I would like to thank Dr. Jan Kuehne for his help with finding and translating German sources. His own keen ear for the cadence of German poetry and the dilemmas of Shoah poetry helped shape the themes of this essay.

https://doi.org/10.1515/9783110793239-010

very nightmares he dreaded again and again. Son of a prominent Communist literary figure, Gu had been one of the millions of Red Guards who followed Mao Zedong whole heartedly only to drown in the horrors of the Cultural Revolution. Horrors – some of which the youth committed themselves by beating teachers and parents for being "reactionaries" and others which they endured after being sent down to the country side, trauma which included rape and starvation.

In 1980 Gu Cheng had just returned from the camps of enforced labor where Mao had sent the Red Guards to be "re-educated" by peasants. For the first time, it was possible to give voice to the wounds of an entire generation of youths deprived of education and family mentoring. The lowly cabbage metaphor might have appealed Ruth Klüger as a departure from the finely wrought German lyrics of her youth. She, too, after all had "traded on sorrow" – not seeking yet accepting prizes for her memoir of a traumatized childhood during the war. She might agree that there is a unity among survivors of history's viciousness despite the dramatic disparities between them. Cabbages have many leaves, densely packed, hiding a bitter core. Each leaf may be envisaged as a wrinkled narrative coaxed out of worrisome, broken words.

Gu Cheng's pyramid bathed in light is an altogether different metaphor. It harks back to the classics. It hints at the raw will to seek vision within the very bitterness inflicted by pain. We are not talking here about a self-blinded Oedipus or the even blind-seer Teiresias. These Greeks are too well known, too grandiose for victims of twentieth century atrocities. One needs to look further, deeper into the unspeakable to find a key to the ongoing quest for light by poets like Gu Cheng and Ruth Klüger. Out of the thickened tar of history, they dig up coarse diamonds. As Klüger herself put it in one of her unusually pedagogical poems:

> Alles, was leuchtet, hat Sinn
> Willst du was lernen?
> Kassiopeia, die Königin
> Ist auch nur ein Dreieck aus Sternen.
> (Klüger 1992a, 66)

Skies can be cluttered by far and near planets. Finding meaning out there is a difficult undertaking. To assert so unequivocally that the lofty queen Cassiopeia can be shrunk into a comprehensible triangle requires an act of will. Ruth Klüger, like Gu Cheng, embodies the poet's determination to know and to name.

The desire to defy conventional niceties is amply apparent. Klüger gloried in what one observer called her *indocilité,* a fierce unwillingness to bend into the winds of fate in life or in writing. (Walser 1997, iv) Aware of the myth of the three Moirai – Clotho, Lachesis, and Antropos – she came back again and again to the metaphor of spinning. Whereas the Greek story pictured humans at the mercy of these weaving women who spooled, then cut off the thread of life, Ruth Klüger was bent upon *Weiterspinnen* – holding on to fraying yarns and spinning forth despite the unravelling spool. (Schubert 2014, 501) This commitment to writing against fate may be her most compelling legacy to our generation as we face the end of the Auschwitz century.

A lachrymose acceptance of history's ravage is not permitted according to Ruth Klüger. We must pick up the unspun threads and weave our own tapestries of meaning. Disavowing the inevitable is a key starting point for this work. Gu Cheng's fellow poet, Bei Dao (Northern Island – pen name of Zhao Zhengkai, b. 1949) took up this task in a poem, entitled "The Answer." His verses aim to defy any dream of final solutions. Bei Dao's fierce iconoclasm would have appealed to Ruth Klüger. She might have claimed him as an heir in a global conversation about the dangers of blind belief:

> See how the gilded sky is covered
> With the drifting, twisted shadows of the dead . . .
>
> I came into this world
> Bringing only paper, rope, a shadow,
> To proclaim before the judgment
> The voice that has been judged:
>
> Let me tell you, world,
> I—do—not—believe!
> If a thousand challengers lie beneath your feet,
> Count me as number thousand and one.
>
> I don't believe the sky is blue;
> I don't believe in thunder's echoes;
> I don't believe that dreams are false;
> I don't believe that death has no revenge.
> (Bei Dao 2001, 27)

Here is an act of *Weiterspinnen* at its best, a poem that talks back to every kind of authority. Klüger, like Bei Dao, lived her early life with little more than paper and shadows. She, however, managed to make more of her tools, gain a more enduring hearing than Chinese dissidents of the 1980s. Tanks in Tiananmen Square in 1989, the ongoing atrocities of the Communist regime today against the Uighurs, and the harsh repression of freedom in Hong Kong make Gu Cheng and Bei Dao part of a subterranean legacy which still awaits the light of day.

For now, these poets provide a useful angle of vision upon Klüger's work. They serve as an answer to Martin Walser's interview with French radio, shortly after the appearance of the French translation of *weiter leben*. Speaking about the volume entitled "Refus de Témoigner," Walser noted: "Je ne crois pas qu'on puisse lire ce livre sans se sentir provoqué. . . . Chaque lecteur devra y répondre avec sa propre histoire." (Walser 1997, x) True, one cannot read Klüger without being irked, without being thrown back upon one's own story. It is all too common among children of survivors: flight from parental narratives into an exotic terrain. The intricacies of other tongues shield one from what was heard and seen at home.

Having grown up among Holocaust survivors in post-war Transylvania, I also sought refuge in foreign languages and distant histories. Chinese studies provided ample relief from Jewish traumas for a while. In the third decade of my work as a China historian, I arrived in Beijing to interview aged survivors of the Cultural Revolution. Through their voices, the Jewish history of the Shoah gained new dimensions. In China, I realized that children of survivors have been gifted (for better or worse) with an ability to listen to the unsayable, to read between the lines.

In Ruth Klüger's poems I hear once more my parents' nuanced command of the German language – the very tongue I fled by studying Chinese. Their proficiency qualified them for *Wiedergutmachung*, the "make-good-again" reparations that troubled my younger years. Klüger's paean to Shylock's daughter Jessica brings about a harsh re-cognition:

> Ich sitz auf der Stange
> und zerr an der Kette
> aus Gold und Wörtern
> die ihr geschmiedet.
> (Klüger 1992a, 264)

The offspring of a "usurer" gives voice to grief as well as pride by cobbling meaning out of a language debased. Shylock's daughter is a self-avowed alchemist. Not a trickster. Klüger's German poem comes through as if it were a command from Transylvania's survivors. I cannot translate her verses. Instead, here is an answer in the form of a rendition:

> Dare to sit on the shaky bench of history,
> dare to pull the chain of words.
> Language is an old-fashioned privy;
> let it flush forth poems
> as if they were gold,
> forge out of them a blessing,
> the one your father never
> gave, or savored.

Fathers die. Murdered. Brothers disappear. Murdered. The terrible toilet of history keeps getting clogged by all this death. There is no one to fix the broken chain. Words keep on coming. They appear golden. But are not.

Fireside Stories (Children Should Never Hear)

In her writings Ruth Klüger shows us how to muck about in the terrain of a soiled tongue. The twelve-year-old girl who composed poems in Auschwitz became the woman who dared to look back with an endless interest in the play of words. Far from shunning terms such as "Stacheldraht," (barbed wire), "Rauch," (smoke), "Grab," (grave), she cites her own childish verses as if they were *Kamingedichte* – a German expression which can allude to the chimneys of Auschwitz as well as to cozy fireplace readings. Her poems never paper over the fact that as a child Ruth had been cast out of home, family, and her mother tongue.

In 2001, speaking before the Parliament of Austria in Vienna, Klüger focused intentionally upon children. She had been one of many who had memorized classical German rhymes in her youth. Now, she chose to recite aloud for the first time a 1944 poem entitled "Der Kamin." Her goal was made explicit: to save her own verses from the unctuous compassion that comes when one hears about the "Jewish catastrophe." Back in Austria, sixty-six years after composing her first poems, Ruth Klüger describes herself as a girl who was forced by history to choose the topic of Auschwitz, a topic far too big to fathom then or now. Before the assembled politicians of Vienna, she declared that Jewish children had not been asleep during the war. They were, alas, fully awake. Klüger's *Kamin-Gedicht* was a "story" no child should ever have to hear:

> Täglich hinter den Baracken
> seh ich Rauch und Feuer stehn.
> Jude, beuge deinen Nacken,
> Keiner hier kann dem entgehn.
> Siehst du in dem Rauche nicht
> ein verzerrtes Angesicht?
> Ruft es nicht voll Spott und Hohn:
> Fünf Millionen berg' ich schon!
> Auschwitz liegt in meiner Hand,
> alles, alles wird verbrannt.
> (Klüger 2001, 3)

It was no mean feat for a young teen to put into flowing German rhymes the eerie ballad of the death-camp chimney. The woman who read Auschwitz verses to the Viennese parliament, however, did more than gaze backward. She was challenging her listeners beyond their well learned *Betroffenheitsgesten* – gestures, murmurings of concern – for victims of the Shoah, gestures which they hoped would gain them forgiveness for crimes committed during the Nazi regime and thereby allow both Jews and Austrians alike to move forward.

Ruth Klüger's *indocilité* shines forth. No memorialization, no "museumification" suffices for her. She holds up the mirror to those who would look away from the chimney smoke still clogging the sight, the breath, the nightmares of Jewish survivors. She reminds her listeners about Freud's well-chosen term "verdrängen" – which refers to the act of pushing aside both for the individual as well as the group. Unlike the English word "repression," "verdrängen" is not a shoving downward of memory, but rather keeping out of sight what is still raw and thorny. Children who witnessed chimney "stories" as participants can neither forget nor forgive. Klüger reminds fellow Viennese of their early war against non-Jews who were deemed "useless eaters." Nazi officers had no problem feeding their lap dogs while children with all kind of disabilities had already been thrown onto the ash heap of the Reich.

The murder of Jews was but one aspect of the "thriftiness" that covered the agenda of racial purity with its hatred of human weakness. This agenda cannot be masked by phrases such as "never again" or by increasing memorials to commemorate the Shoah. In her lectures and poems, Ruth Klüger was relentlessly ironic about *Musealisierung*. She disdained efforts to fit recollection of historical trauma onto the walls of a museum or into designated "memory sites." These convenient locations should not be allowed to contain, to tame and thereby render timeless what was so fiercely murderous in its time. Klüger was not against commemoration, but against the mumification of the past wrapped in the cloth of avoidance and forgetfulness.

An aversion to *Museumskultur* might have made Klüger a sympathetic listener to the Chinese-survivor-writer Ba Jin, who bemoaned the lack of a "truth-telling museum" which explores the Cultural Revolution. Having been imprisoned as a "renegade" in Mao's "ox-pens" – *niu peng*/(牛棚), Ba was not worried about the spatial erasure of memory. That was, and is, occurring with brutal rapidity upon the landscape of the Chinese mainland. In addition to the official amnesia imposed by the Communist Party, Ba Jin noted among his contemporaries an inner unwillingness to countenance the horror of the recent past. The goal of Chinese museums is to celebrate the achievements of the regime or to display the grandiose remains of imperial culture. Nowhere is there a site to unveil complicity in Maoist atrocities. In an essay written to commemorate the torture of his own wife, Ba Jin wrote:

It is crucial that each person fix in his mind all the words that were spoken, all the acts that he himself committed during that awful decade of 1966–1976. This call is not only to preserve wounds, but also to recall our own responsibility for what is now called simply the "great catastrophe." Whether one was victim or perpetrator . . . whether dragon, phoenix, ox or horse, there must be a place where one can take off one's face, to see what he himself did during the Cultural Revolution. (Ba Jin 1998, 292)

"Taking off one's face" is not a one-time gesture, not only an Asian worry about shame (versus guilt as some Westerners theorized). Ruth Klüger recognized the harsh honesty required to peel away rationalizations and amnesia.

Ba Jin had been declared an "enemy of the people" (人民的敌人 – *renmin de diren*), much like Klüger, who was also deemed a *Volksfeind* in her native country. Former neighbors, students, friends turned into accusers and shoved the aged Chinese writer, like the young Viennese girl, beyond the human circle. The huge difference is that Ba Jin's persecution took place on native ground, within an ever-shifting definition of who were the "people." Thus, the problem of survival, of going on with life after the death of Mao became even more daunting. Victims had been persecutors. Persecutors had been victims. No one was ready to "take off the face." Better to hide behind the new slogans of loyalty to the same old Communist regime.

Ba Jin died in 2005, "rehabilitated" – which means forgiven and forgotten by the very state which caused him and thirty million more Chinese enduring ravages. Although recent books published outside of China have sought to catalogue in detail the murderous policies of the Mao era, there has been no space within areas dominated by Beijing to really "take-off" one's face. Young men and women today do not even know about the brutal crackdown in Tiananmen Square in 1989.

A few selected Chinese educators of the younger generation have been coming to Yad Vashem in Jerusalem for the past decade to learn about the Shoah, to meet with survivors, to explore Israel. When I lectured to them in Chinese, the focus was upon the reasons why these young intellectuals were able to express such deep empathy for Jewish victims of senseless hatred. This invariably called to mind their parents and grandparents. Chinese visitors to Jerusalem have been forbidden to hear "fireside stories" in their own native country. Elders will not even whisper facts about the trauma that they endured out of dread of political authorities. The goal of these encounters is not to wound but to follow through upon a mandate entrusted to me during decades of oral history work in Beijing.

Chinese survivors of atrocity shared their narratives with me not only because I was a foreign researcher who spoke their native tongue. It was more important to them that I was a Jew, a daughter of parents who had been through the Shoah, a child who grew up under the lies-riddled Ceaușescu regime. My interlocutors often said to me: 我们有知音 – *wo men you zhi yin*; "We have a wordless understanding. You grasp the music of our hearts and souls because your people have also known historical tragedy." (Schwarcz 1989, 32) Ruth Klüger, too, had an intuitive grasp of wordless words. Even as a young girl in Auschwitz, she already voiced what aged Chinese have yet to scream out in the public domain:

> Kalt und trüb ist noch der Morgen,
> Männer gehn zur Arbeit hin,
> schwer von Leid, gedrückt von Sorge . . .
> Fern im Osten liegt ein Dunst,
> und Natur zeigt ihre Kunst:
> Sieh, die Sonne bricht hervor.
> Zeigt mir diese Strahlensonne
> eine neue Lebenswonne,
> Zieht die Freiheit still empor?
> (Klüger 1992a, 124)

Barely a teenager, the Jewish girl could not turn away her eyes from the cold and cloudy mornings which weighed down men going off to slave labor and to death. She dared to quarrel with God in their name. She shouted out a longing for freedom that never rises quietly out of the ashes of disaster.

To the sorrow of Chinese survivors, metaphors about the eastern skies and the sun breaking at dawn had been hijacked by the rhetoric of the Cultural Revolution. Mao Zedong was the only luminary who was supposed to shine in every heart. His image as the red sun has nowadays been replaced by the glowing face of the current Communist leader, Xi Jinping – an omnipresent and oppressive icon. No wonder that young Chinese are "liberated" into their own histories and grief by hearing words from Jewish survivors at Yad Vashem. Ruth Klüger might well rant against Jerusalem's vast memorializing landscape. But she would have responded with an open heart to young Chinese expressing their longing for 知音 – *zhiyin*, for some "wordless understanding" of grief which cannot yet be named on native ground.

Ghost-Seers

When language falters, a memory weaves a more diaphanous reality so that Ruth Klüger calls on her "ungelöste Gespenster." (Smale 2009, 779) These "unsolved ghosts" hark back to Freudian theory which asserts that the repressed is never quite forgotten. "Gespenster" will reappear in dark robes during liminal hours when our defenses are down, when we actually long to re-encounter those who have been irretrievably and violently lost to us.

Ruth Klüger wanted to write ghost stories, perhaps even more than poems. Had she been schooled in Chinese literature she might have been comforted by the craft that weaves poetry and ghosts together as one. Wildly popular among unlettered folk, Chinese ghost stories also enabled scholar-officials to express their own unassuaged grief when historical trauma overwhelmed the Chinese landscape. Sometime honored, mostly used and abused by autocratic authorities, these writers were spiritual ancestors of the intellectuals who became detested ghosts under the Maoist regime.

At the height of the Cultural Revolution, millions of educated cadres were labeled 牛鬼蛇神 – *niu gui she shen* ("ox ghosts and snake spirits") in order to be persecuted with less guilt. (Thurston 1984/85, 600) If one's teacher, parent, lover, or supervisor could be smeared with this demonic term drawn from the Buddhist underworld, then humiliating them, pushing their heads into toilets, beating them to death would not seem like a crime, but rather an act of loyalty to Chairman Mao as the Red Sun.

Demeaned, nearly erased from humankind, specters were depicted as both pitiful and fearsome. The ideograph for "ghost" – 鬼 *gui* – mirrored a palpable reality, an intimate "other" who could not be wished away. One of the homonyms for *gui* suggests an arc of eternal return – which may be either a promise or threat depending on how artfully the ghost story was woven into the poetry or stories of survivors. (Huang 2017, 67) Even before the great Tang dynasty (600–900 AD), a literary genre had developed called 志怪小說 – *zhiguai xiaoshuo*, "strange tales" filled with the coming and going of spirits who would have been all too familiar to Ruth Klüger. Recognizably human, skeletal like starving beggars, they call to mind the dispossessed and the detested all over the world.

In the artwork of Ming dynasty painter Zhou Chen (1455–1536), such beggar-ghosts haunt the imagination and become mirrors for the unmentionable ravages of history. (Bianchi 2017, 232)

Whereas Chinese survivors of atrocities told "spirit stories" out of hearing by political authorities, Klüger calls back her ghosts openly. Calendrically-convenient moments such as Halloween, for example, allows Klüger to bring back her brother, as if he were one, slightly more real 鬼 – *gui* standing at the door with all the other kids asking for candy. Strange yet believable, this apparition can be shaped into an English language poem, hence its pivotal presence in Klüger's English language memoir *Still Alive*.

In German, Ruth Klüger's ghosts are both more present and more demanding. No candies or English rhymes suffice for them. They hark back to earlier terrors, to a familiar and untamed tongue. Despite her aversion to religious rituals and beliefs, Klüger turns to Yom Kippur to ask herself in the *Muttersprache* some of most difficult questions about the still-not-quite-dead *Gespenster*. On this day of atonement, Klüger fasted once, in the death camps. In the poem "Jom Kippur" she alludes to her own hunger as a child as well as to the ravenous ravaging of her ghostly relatives murdered early in her life. Father and (half-)brother continue to feast upon her mind and heart, much as she begs them to let go.

She hopes to loosen the knot that ties them to her. Far from loosening, the bond tightens. As in Chinese *zhiguai*, ghosts will not let go, until the living have tasted some of the spirit's own displacement. Klüger's closing line faces up to the dark logic of this relationship: "Sind wir Lebenden den Toten Gespenster?" (Klüger 1992a, 99) If you can't bury your ghosts, can't divorce them, can't quite call them back to life, you might as well join the liminal space where they make their tenebrous home.

Some survivors of the Shoah saw themselves – and were often seen by others – as living ghosts. This was not Ruth Klüger's view. She gloried in the fullness of life after the war, refused to be reduced to a little girl who hungered, ran, hid, and was slapped harshly by a Nazi officer. Yet, in *weiter leben* she opens the gate for lost spirits wide open. She may doubt what she sees, she may question what she hears, but she refuses to run away from the company of shapeless presences, allowing them a kind of freedom that men, women, and children did not have in the darkest hours of the *jüdische Katastrophe.*

This liberty accorded to ghosts was also described by the ancient Chinese philosopher, Han Feizi, in a story about a powerful king who asked: "What is the hardest thing to draw?" No one mistook the question as an innocent inquiry about art. Rather it was a barbed way to inquire about the limits of imagination permissible to humans during the reign of an absolute ruler. Han Feizi, being a seasoned realist, suggests that dogs and horses are hardest to depict because people see them from dawn to dusk. Distortion is inconceivable (and impermissible!) when an all-powerful king controls daylight activities. Ghosts, by contrast, come and go at night. They have no fixed shape (and by implication, they need not bend into the will of autocrats) and "therefore are the easiest to draw." (Huang 2017, 58)

Catherine Smale writes about ghosts in Ruth Klüger's autobiographical project and suggests that liberation may be found through accepting an unsolved mystery. It is not simply that dogs and horses are hard to draw. Rather, the realm of spirits has a kind of fluidity (one may even say playfulness) which had been sorely lacking in Klüger's childhood and sufferings with her mother. Like Han Feizi facing a cruel king in times of ceaseless warfare, so too the

Jewish girl who grew up to write *weiter leben* had to become an inmate of *Gespenstergelände* – a terrain peopled by spirits who went up in smoke. (Smale 2009, 779) Memory-remains of the murdered are thin threads which Klüger was determined to keep on spinning without tying them down to a specific museum, a well-labeled exhibit, a photograph, or even one particular art work.

Unsolved, unfinished ghost stories carry Ruth Klüger's message toward the end of the Auschwitz century. Across the Pacific, aging survivors of Chinese atrocities spin their memorial tapestries through the internet and through massive tomes of documentation that have yet to be allowed across the Party's firewall. Disembodied spirits, however, slip through censors' iron grip. One such example is Yang Jisheng's masterful study *Tombstone*, which details the nearly thirty million "unnatural deaths" during the Great Famine of 1958–1962. It is a heart-rending account of the unremembered, whose ghosts roam the land and the public imagination to the point that China today is indeed a *Gespenstergelände,* where recollections of beatings, shaming, even cannibalism swirl unchecked upon a stench-filled terrain. (Yang 2013)

Taking both Chinese and Jewish predicaments to heart, it may be possible to vivify Klüger's unfinished ghost story with a poem of my own. She herself gave permission for this gesture at the conclusion of her essay on "Dichten über die Shoah: zum Problem des literarischen Umgangs mit dem Massenmord." (Klüger, 1992b) In this work, she actively releases spirit narratives as an offer and invitation for the next generation to *Weiterspinnen*. She asks that we pick up the endlessly unraveling spool of history in order to craft a tapestry that preserves the muted hues of survivors' nightmares while giving it a fresh look. Taking up her challenge, I wrote the following poem inspired by Chinese and Jewish "ghost-seers" alike:

> We have horse whispers, Ouija
> board readers, tea-leaf prophets,
> but few ghost-seers.
>
> One of the many slain comes
> into my classroom. She loves
> the subject of Revolution, glad
> to be thought of from time
> to time. She sits in a miniskirt,
> dangling legs like tourists
> on the Great Wall. My students
> stare sightless.
>
> I lecture passionately on unspeakable,
> humiliations in Auschwitz, in Mao's
> torture camps. The ghost wonders

why murder is beyond speech.
She doesn't speak Chinese but finds
one good German word for her death:
Genickschuss, "Shot in the neck,"
no mystery, simply a bloody mess
in broad daylight. No one wants

to talk to the ghost, the thrill
of a speech about speechlessness
is more delicious. The ghost ruminates
about the sunny day of her killing,
and the murderers, ordinary men,
not demons.
Ach! Finally, a well-dressed gentleman
sitting in the back of the freshmen sees her.

He came carrying a good heart and Party badges
found on his grandfather's desk. My power point
puts him to sleep much as he struggles to keep
his eyes open. Through heavy eyelids he glimpses
the ghost slip out of class, he is free now to leave
out the back door.

I seethe at the insult of having two
less listeners for a finely wrought talk.
The electricity cuts off, the power point arrested
before the Nazis catch Ruth Klüger and her mother,
before they kill her father and her brother.

I know the ending: She will survive,
will write an afterlife for a girl who never
got to wear miniskirts. My pupils will sigh,
sure that they understood what it means to be deprived.

The scene is Ruth Klüger's. She had faced auditorium after auditorium of students eager to hear Shoah testimony – which she always refused to give. Like Han Feizi's dogs and horses, they demanded a kind of realism she was unwilling to deliver.

In my own teaching experience, Chinese and American students are frightened by the horrific details of the Great Famine, by the Cultural Revolution of the 1960s as well as the barbaric crackdown in Tiananmen in 1989. Rightfully so. To bring home these dark events in China's history, I pull my audiences into a circle reminiscent of William Golding's *Lord of the Flies*. Half-grown children are about to murder the pitiful kid named "Piggy." My students squirm. Ruth Klüger's students were probably even more nervous, despite the fact that some of them told her that they "love the Shoah." Love?

She knew how to thrust aside such naïveté. Her goal was for us to become better *Geisterseher* – Ghost-Seers – readers more open to untold stories and unseen presences. If we can re-orient our vision a tad more, "depravation" might not be limited to miniskirts. Wordlessness need not have the last word. The old man need not slip out the backdoor carrying away with him the medals and other memorabilia connected to complicity. The specter with dangling legs may linger. Once countenanced, she may start to speak.

Pearls from the Dragon's Teeth

Would the ghost speak in verses? I am not sure how Ruth Klüger would respond. Her poems come enrobed in prose commentary, as if they were too tottering on their own. The need to versify and, at the same time to distrust what may be conveyed through common language, leads to a maelstrom for those of us inching toward the end of the Auschwitz century. Klüger herself often repeated the fact that for her poems were a talisman against madness in the camps. Recalling and writing some rhymes in German was "ein Gegengewicht zum Chaos." (Minden 2016, 164) If one could find refuge in words, madness was held at bay a little longer.

Nien Cheng, a survivor of the murderous Cultural Revolution, also writes about how classical Chinese poetry helped her maintain a modicum of sanity during incarcerations and beatings by the Red Guards. In her memoir, "Life and Death in Shanghai," Chen details the mind numbing, body pounding harangue that was her daily diet from 1966 to 1973. A highly educated woman and the widow of the manager of the Shell Dutch Company after the Communist takeover in 1949, she was an early and vulnerable target for terror. Like Klüger, Nien Cheng was deemed an "enemy of the people." She had spent early years memorizing verses from the Tang and Song dynasty poets and recited these to herself daily while being tortured. (Nien, 1987) The Red Guards neither noticed her moving lips nor heard the music of ancient words. Too busy shouting Maoist slogans and wielding their belts with metal clasps, they were sure the future was on their side. Nien Cheng's daughter, refusing to testify against her mother, was murdered.

Poetry is no defense against atrocity, but it can map a soul terrain for others who are not afraid to share the grief. This map is not easy to read, nor always reliable. Ruth Klüger warned again and again about the dangers of using aesthetics to anesthetize the cruelties of the Shoah. Speaking about the work of Ingeborg Bachmann, she discounted the possibility of poetry conveying any truth about lived events. Instead, Klüger argued, one can only hope to craft a single enduring sentence out of the messiness of life and language: *der haltbare Satz im*

Bimbam der Worte. (Minden 2016, 178) The melody of the "bimbam" is actually stronger than Klüger herself may have imagined. It invites creativity even as it strengthens the barbed wire around the unprecedented horrors of the Shoah.

To hear the darker tonalities in the music of words, it helps to turn to Chinese poetics. In Confucian culture, there was no higher vehicle for the spirit than poetry. Words – that is to say complex characters conveying ideas (hence called ideograms) – were seen not as mirrors for objective truth but rather as digging tools for the exploration of interior landscapes which would otherwise remain unseen and voiceless. A well-crafted poem has to dance between 景 – *jing* (scene, setting, nature, event) and 情 *qing* (emotion, thought, insight, wisdom). Unlike the seemingly aleatory collection of "bimbam" words, Chinese verses are called "pearls" extracted with great effort from the dragon's lair in the deepest seas. (Sun, 1995) The poet as deep-sea diver might not sound so alien to Ruth Klüger who treasured the California shore as a place to both seek and forget the harshness of history. She would have understood that the act of wrenching a jewel out of the jaws of a submerged serpent requires force and fortitude.

Survivor-poets like Klüger and Paul Celan were on intimate terms with verbal acts of violence and violation. Chinese writers, by contrast, especially those who had been incarcerated in the terror-camps of the Cultural Revolution, were more cautious, more indirect. The very indirectness of their lamentations was sanctioned by the Confucian classics. Qian Zhongshu, one of the most prominent victims of Maoist atrocities, often quoted the "Analects" to show how words may – and indeed must! – convey rancor buried in the hearts of survivors. The phrase 詩可以怨 – *shi ke yi yuan* ("poetry may be used to grieve") is attributed to Confucius, but Qian Zhongshu used it more broadly after the death of Mao. Traveling to Japan in 1980, a bent and broken man, Qian did not lecture about his own suffering. Instead, he reviewed all the great writers of the past who dared to trouble their contemporaries with sorrow-filled words. These were "noise makers," unlike refined literati who posed lyrically as troubled souls. Confident that language can indeed bear the weight of pain, Qian concluded: "The voice of the undisturbed is thin and light; that of the sorrowful refined." (Schwarcz 1996, 132)

Ruth Klüger was anything but "refined" in this Confucian sense. Yet, her own grief did come from a place of deep disturbance, somewhere near madness. Even though she had confronted (and at times invited in) the ghosts of her murdered kin, the mourning for children scorched by history remains a heavy burden. To carry it forward, Klüger used what the Chinese termed both *jing* and *qing*, a haunting landscape and a trembling heart.

A lighthouse on a dark seashore leads Klüger to portray two siblings freezing in a quarry. The boy tries to catch a lizard, the girl sobs into a cloth-covered bowl. No adults come to the rescue. When an aged couple final comes, they are speechless and barren:

> Unter eisernen Bäumen bücken sich wortlose Paare
> und sammeln metallene Frucht.
> (Klüger 1992a, 128)

Crouching in a pitiless landscape marked with iron trees, these adults harvest nothing but metal fruits. Klüger paints them with a cold, clear gaze. She also does not shy away from showing us the frozen children.

Writing about Ruth Klüger, Michael Minden likens her icy gaze to that of Anna Akhmatova, who dared to depict the horror of Stalinist camps. When asked by frozen, nearly cadaverous inmates whether she can describe their predicament in words, the Russian poet answered without hesitation: "I can." According to Minden, Klüger's *ich hab es erlebt* is the Shoah equivalent. "I have seen" is here on par with "I can" – even though Klüger had more reservations about language than Akhmatova ever dreamt of. (Minden 2016, 180) Those of us who come after these survivors of frigid landscapes must pick up their tools to map more recent atrocities. Beijing, after the violent crackdown of June 4, 1989, was my terrain – the one I had traversed on balmier days and now had to re-encounter after the bloodshed in Tiananmen Square.

Returning to China in 1991, one could still hear the echoes of an event totally erased from public memory. At a banquet following a Party-scripted academic conference, I was seated next to a prominent historian who hesitated to speak about what he had witnessed less than two years earlier. The scorpions served to us (which I resisted, grateful for kashrut regulations) opened a round about reminiscence and led me to write these verses:

> To honor foreign guests,
> recently purged academicians
> are authorized to host a banquet,
> we are served scorpions for lunch.
> They lie curled up, belly distended
> like pregnant ladies beyond their time.
>
> A grey-haired scholar who remembers more
> than the Party's ever-changing present
> urges me to taste the flesh inside the shell:
> It gives one courage.
>
> We Chinese have eaten many scorpions
> and yet . . . .
>
> And yet, the hard life after the latest crackdown
> goes on: carrying out offal in old tin cans,

brushing teeth with yesterday's rice gruel,
sweeping dust from one side of the alley
to the other, a few old ladies gossip,
as if in a dream, a young girl
cannot resist a smile.

Blood washed off the streets
lingers on the poles
of vegetable carriers,
old men sell sparrows
behind the public bathroom,
a wild chirping serenades the stench.
Scorpions grow stronger,
not men.

(Schwarcz 1993, 11)

Blood lingering on the carrying-poles of peasants was no metaphor in Beijing after 1989. Yet blood calls to blood. What cannot be spoken openly in China's public spaces is often whispered to me over meals. Chinese colleagues know that I am the daughter of Jewish survivors of the Shoah. They count on our wordless *zhiyin*.

Born after the war, I do not live like Ruth Klüger in the shadow of iron trees where couples harvest metal fruit. It is true, my mother gave away an infant in the Budapest ghetto. It is true that my father's first wife was murdered in Auschwitz pregnant. I am the after-crop, when fields were almost green again. I first went to China in 1977 when rice-sprouts of hope could be glimpsed everywhere. Now, more than forty years later, the fields of imagination and of truth-speaking are withering despite the maniacally optimistic propaganda of the Communist Party. As an outsider familiar with the many-layered grief of Chinese intellectuals, I feel obliged to carry on a task that Ruth Klüger turned down in her pivotal poem, "Aussageverweigerung."

Sprich, Ruth! Sprich!

Why bother with giving testimony? Because the threads connecting past to present are fraying. In China, memories of suffering were entrusted to me over four decades of oral history. These recollections are still being suppressed in the public realm. To ferry them across the borders of the Communist regime and get them into print abroad, I change the name of the speaker so she will not be harmed by the authorities. Sometime, my interlocutor wants his identity

known, wants some space in the writings of a Western scholar so that voiceless-
ness will not triumph on native ground.

At the same time, the ranks of the survivors of the Shoah are thinning rapidly. There is a personal and public rush to bear witness, to record, to pass on
so the next generation will not forget. Slogans about "Never Again!" do not suffice. They might even backfire by erasing the distinctive details of each victim's
narrative. Ruth Klüger was fierce in her critique of lachrymose worries about
the fate of Shoah memory:

> Relax, the living witnesses of every event in history have died and their memory has per-
> sisted thanks to writings and other recording devices. . . . What remains will be. . . . To
> put it slightly differently, what lasts is Scripture, if you will, not Holy Scripture, but an
> engraved text, on stone, on paper on a digital device, filtered by the human mind. Living
> witnesses may provide a certain frisson, sometimes even voyeuristic pleasure, but *they
> are not needed to preserve memory* (emphasis added).   (Klüger 2014, 391)

To suggest that witnesses are almost immaterial to historical memory is a radical claim indeed. As a historian, I differ with Klüger. Each voice adds depth to
our understanding of the past. Engraved texts might have scriptural weight,
but they lack the breathing room needed to re-think history in light of the
present.

Carolyn Forche, a skilled poet in her own right, also challenges Klüger's ax-
ioms about memory in her volume entitled *Against Forgetting*. (Forche, 1993) In
the introduction to this work, Forche leaves no doubt that bearing witness to
the atrocities of the twentieth century is an essential and urgent moral act. She
herself began the project in Latin America where she testified through poetry
and other writings about the murderous policies of the Nicaraguan regime.
Back on home ground, Forche collected poems by survivors of the Shoah, the
Armenian massacres, the killing fields of Cambodia, the thought-reform camps
of Chairman Mao, and the gulags of the Soviet Union. These poems taken together make for powerful, disturbing reading.

It was in Forche's volume that I first encountered Primo Levi's poem, "Voices." Written in 1981, six years before his suicide, this work describes the despair of a survivor facing a new generation eager to get on with its own life.
Klüger tells us to relax, memory will endure. Levi, by contrast, hears the ongoing muting of sounds that were raw and troubled from the start. He also dares
to describe the loneliness of those of us who need to listen to witnesses at the
end of this cacophonous Auschwitz century:

> Voices mute forever, or since yesterday, or just stilled;
> If you listen hard, you can still hear the echo.
> Hoarse voices of those who can no longer speak,

Voices that speak, and can no longer say anything,
Voices that think they're saying something,
Voices that speak and cannot be understood . . . .
I speak to you companions of revelry,
Drunk like me on words,
Sword-words, poison-words,
Key-words, lockpicker-words,
Salt-words and nepenthe.
The place we are going is silent.
Or deaf. It's the limbo of the lonely and the deaf.
You'll have to run the last lap deaf,
You'll have to run the last lap by yourself.

(Forche 1993, 377)

I carried Primo Levi's poem in my mind during all my time in China. As I listened to and recorded the sufferings of Chinese intellectuals during the Mao era, I was aware that this was a Jewish mission. I was taking testimony from those who were not allowed to speak, those who had fallen mute, those who had no access to "lockpicker-words" to frame recollections of recent terror.

In order to bring Chinese survivors into the conversation, it helps to build upon Ruth Klüger's legacy of reticence. She was worried about the "frisson" that our generation might savor while listening to survivors. Testimonies that find their way into broken words are, in fact, rugged enough to withstand various fads. Encouraged by writers like Primo Levi, we are running this lap alone. Crossing cultural, historical, and linguistic boundaries expands our mission. No one would dare to say that the Shoah was like the Cultural Revolution in China. Instead, both atrocities are in danger of being covered over by over-used words. Klüger's labor with threads not yet spun helps the post-Auschwitz generation to look afresh at the jumbled and shredding tapestry of the past and start to re-weave a more durable cloth for the future.

A vivid example of such weaving may be glimpsed in the painting and calligraphy of the Chinese artist Shi Lu (1919–1982). The scion of a wealthy family, he studied classical painting before becoming a Communist and a supporter of the Party's victory in 1949. Commissioned to paint a large-scale mural for the Great Hall of the People, Shi Lu made the "mistake" of evoking a grand landscape of mountains and valleys in which Mao Zedong stands front and center. The Communist chief is looking out upon his troops ready to defeat the Nationalist enemies. The proportions of this painting were traditional, the subject new, and the oils used represented a revolutionary departure from Chinese ink drawings. Applauded for his masterful work at first, Shi Lu was violently attacked during the Cultural Revolution. He was accused of willfully diminishing the stature of Chairman Mao. Imprisoned in a cage, beaten, forbidden to touch a calligraphy brush for over three years, he managed to cling to his own artistic talent despite the oncoming of madness.

In 1971, while his inner and outer demons still multiplied, Shi Lu managed to paint a magnolia lily which mirrored his sufferings. (See Fig. 1) this was a fresh perspective intended to protest the ravages of the Cultural Revolution. As art-historian Shelly Drake Hawks put it: "Shi Lu's personality infuses his flower subjects. Though physically injured, they are spiritually buoyant, even acrobatic. Something has knocked this lily to the ground, but its dangling stem, twisted upside down is not defeated." (Hawks 2017, 168)

The agitated, scattered, uneven calligraphy above the dangling stem bears witness to Shi Lu's vision of how atrocity may be endured with dignity. The key theme here is "injured beauty" not simply in terms of classical aesthetics, but also in terms of contemporary ethics. The violation of the human spirit and body – experienced by Klüger and so many other Jewish victims of the Shoah – might be glimpsed afresh through the art of a Chinese survivor. The flower may be trampled but cannot be erased. The disjointed characters above the pliant blossom promise linguistic rescue. They create a wild lace-work of words, a *bimbam* Ruth Klüger would have recognized and appreciated.

Despite her personal refusal to give testimony about the Shoah, either to Dori Laub's Fortunoff Archives at Yale University or Steven Spielberg's collection in California, Klüger kept travelling to Germany to "gift" her friends with shards of language every bit as cutting and challenging as Shi Lu's characters above the magnolia lily. Klüger's poem "Aussageverweigerung" may be read as a cry of defiance against the Moirai, not unlike that of Shi Lu.

The Fates will not have the last word here. Instead, in the words of Michael Minden, "Klüger mends a tear in the intertextual fabric of literature, finding her own form of words as a contribution to the *Traditionen des Entsetzens, für die es immer schon die richtigen Worte gegeben habe.*" (Minden 2016, 181) The horrors of history cannot be buried in wordlessness. Language, for better or worse, is capacious enough for the darkest realities, even when the mind balks at its intelligibility. Shi Lu's characters may not all be legible, but they are recognizably linguistic and painted with the same instrument as the acrobatic blossom which springs up from below.

Poetry has become my own "brush" for evoking the harsh cliffs of history. I turn to its promises and foibles by drawing Ruth Klüger out of the corner that she paints herself into with the verses of "Aussageverweigerung." I get it: She feels hounded by crowds wanting to listen to her testimony. I get it: She does not want to be locked down to the witness chair. I get it: She hates interrogations. She would rather label herself a liar among liars than speak again about

Fig. 1: Shi Lu, "Magnolia Lily" In 1971. (In: Hawks 2017, 142)

the horrors of the past. Only the most personal ghosts are allowed to command her voice.

What follows is not such a command. It is an invitation to talk across time and space. As Primo Levi understood so well, there is no way but to hobble onward into the century after Auschwitz. As Klüger showed us, poetry may serve as a bridge across broken time. Using her own words, I am moved to create this envoi in place of a conclusion about the Shoah – an event which has no artful ending:

Sprich, Ruth! Sprich!

Speak to us, Ruth! Please, speak.
You are no longer a hunted, haunted
witness to events you want no part of.

Mein Steckbrief klebte an jeder Wand,
unter mehreren Namen war ich bekannt.

You have only one name now,
the Jewish one you chose,
a Moabite princess who joins a famished,
almost vanquished folk. Your face is not
on every wall, the gracefully-aged profile
just yours, not shared with a frightened child
who sings rhymes to stave off the night,
questioning gendarmes and the restless dead.
No need to give any more evidence in court.

Alle Gendarmen haben mich ausgefragt,
Wo ich ging und stand, nach den Toten.

We know where you were. We know where
you stood. We know where you ran,
we know the winds and the ocean
which took you in, covered your tracks.
Why then so much self-blame
in the witness chair?

Aber die allerverlogensten Zeugen
Sind nicht so unzuverlässig wie ich.

The most unreliable amongst the lying?
It cannot be! I don't need you to verify
truths embedded in lengthy words.
Aussageverweigerung.
Nineteen letters just to hide
a voice that aches to speak.

I am listening Ruth! I am not one
of your wandering ghosts. I am
a reader, a daughter of *weiter leben*,
ongoing rush of life after the war,
the after-child who does need to wake
reciting names of every death camp.

But I know them. You have taught us well:
Sorrow, singer and the song are one. We
keep on spinning threads you left unspooled.

Bibliography

Agamben, Giorgio. *Infancy and History: On the Destruction of Experience*. Trans. Liz Heron. New York: Verso Books, 2007.

Ba Jin. "Wen Ge Bowuguan." (Museum of the Cultural Revolution). Cited in Vera Schwarcz. *Bridge Across Broken Time: Chinese and Jewish Cultural Memory*. New Haven: Yale University Press, 1998, 210.

Bei Dao. *The August Sleepwalker*. Trans. Bonnie McDougall. New York: New Directions Press, 2001.

Bianchi, Alice. "Ghost-like Beggars in Chinese Painting: The Case of Zhou Chen." In: Vincent Durand-Dastès and Marie Laureillard (Eds.). *Fantômes dans l'Extrême-Orient d'hier et d'aujourd'hui*. Paris: Presses Inalco, 2017, 225–250.

Forche, Carolyn. *Against Forgetting: Twentieth-Century Poetry of Witness*. New York: Norton Press, 1993.

Hawks, Shelly Drake. *The Art of Resistance: Painting by Candlelight in Mao's China*. Seattle: University of Washington Press, 2017.

Huang, Minwen. "From Cultural Ghosts to Literary Ghosts: Humanization of Chinese Ghosts in Chinese Zhiguai." In: Maria Fleischhack and Elmar Schenkel (Eds.). *Ghosts – or the (Nearly) Invisible. Spectral Phenomena in Literature and the Media*. Lausanne: Peter Lang, 2017, 66–74.

Klüger, Ruth. *weiter leben: Eine Jugend*. Göttingen: Wallstein, 1992a.

Klüger, Ruth. "Dichten über die Shoah: Zum Problem des literarischen Umgangs mit dem Massenmord." In: *Spuren der Verfolgung: seelische Auswirkungen des Holocaust auf die Opfer und ihre Kinder*. Ed. Gertrude Hardimann. Berlin: Bleicher, 1992b, 203–21.

Klüger, Ruth. "Parlamentsrede." https://www.parlament.gv.at (2001).

Kluger, Ruth. *Still Alive. A Holocaust Girlhood Remembered*. New York: Feminist Press at the City University, 2001.

Klüger, Ruth. "The Future of Holocaust Literature." In: *German Studies Review*. 37: 2 (2014): 391–393.

Minden, Michael. "Dichtung and *weiter leben*: Ruth Klüger's Autobiography as Literature." In: *The Modern Language Review*. 111: 1 (January, 2016): 163–182.

Nien Cheng. *Life and Death in Shanghai*. New York: Grove Press, 1987.

Schubert, Katja. « Des images qui s'excluent et qui se complètent: « Relire Ruth Klüger et Grete Weil sous le signe de la « normalisation de la mémoire.» *Revue d'Histoire de la Shoah*. No. 201. 2014: 499–521.

Schwarcz, Vera. "Memory, Commemoration and the Plight of Chinese Intellectuals." In: *The Wilson Quarterly*. 13:4. 1989: 92–97.

Schwarcz, Vera. "Scorpions for Lunch." *Hudson Valley Echoes*. No. 1. Summer, 1993: 11.

Schwarcz, Vera. "The Pane of Sorrow: Public Uses of Personal Grief in China." In: *Daedalus*. 125:1. Winter, 1996: 119–148.

Smale, Catherine. "Ungelöste Gespenster? Ghosts in Ruth Klüger's Autobiographical Project." In: *The Modern Language Review*. 104: 3. July 2009: 777–785.

Sun, Cecile Chu-chin. *Pearls from the Dragon's Mouth: Evocation of Scene and Feeling in Chinese Poetry*. Ann Arbor: University of Michigan Press, 1995.

Sze, Arthur. "Gu Cheng." In: Arthur Sze and Edward Hirsch (Eds.). *Chinese Writers on Writing*. Hartford, Ct.: Trinity University Press, 2010, 92–101.

Thurston, Ann. "Victims of China's Cultural Revolution: The Invisible Wounds." In: *Pacific Affairs*. 57:4. 1984/85: 599–620.

Walser, Martin. "Preface." *Ruth Klüger. Refus de témoigner*. Trans. Jeanne Étoré. Paris: Renaud Bray, 1997.

Yang Jisheng. *Tombstone: The Untold Story of Mao's Great Famine*. Trans. Guo Jian. New York: Penguin Books, 2013.

Notes on Contributors

Stephan Braese is Ludwig Strauß Professor of European-Jewish Literature and Cultural History at RWTH Aachen University. He has been a fellow at the Franz Rosenzweig Research Center at The Hebrew University, Jerusalem and at the Center for Advanced Judaic Studies in Philadelphia, Pennsylvania. He is the author of *Die andere Erinnerung – Jüdische Autoren in der westdeutschen Nachkriegsliteratur* (^{3}2010), *Eine europäische Sprache – Deutsche Sprachkultur von Juden 1760–1930* (2010) and of *Jenseits der Pässe – Wolfgang Hildesheimer: Eine Biographie* (^{2}2017). He co-edited with Holger Gehle *Ruth Klüger in Deutschland* (1994).

Heinrich Detering (Ph.D. Göttingen University) is Professor of German and Comparative Literatures at the University of Göttingen, a member of the Academies of Science in Göttingen, Mainz, and Copenhagen, and of the German Academy of Language and Literature (Darmstadt). He has been a Visiting Scholar at the University of California at Irvine, Washington University Saint Louis, New York University, HUST University Wuhan (China), Aston University Birmingham (England), Bergen University (Norway), Aarhus University (Denmark), at the Villa Massimo (Rome, Italy), and a Fellow at the Wissenschaftskolleg Berlin and the Thomas Mann House in Pacific Palisades. In 2009, he received the Leibniz Prize, the highest scientific award in Germany, in 2011 the Heisenberg Award, in 2012 the Hans Christian Andersen Prize, among others. His books include critical editions and monographs on Thomas Mann, Nietzsche, Brecht, and Bob Dylan. He first met Ruth Klüger during her visiting professorship in Göttingen and was among the first readers of the manuscript that was to become her book *weiter leben*. They continued their literary discussions and exchanges until Ruth Klüger's last years.

Mark H. Gelber (Ph.D. Yale University) is Professor Emeritus and former Director of the Center for Austrian and German Studies at Ben-Gurion University of the Negev in Beer Sheva, Israel. He established and directed the International Summer University for Hebrew, Jewish Studies, and Israel Studies for German-speaking students in Beer Sheva. He has written, edited, and co-edited twenty books and authored one hundred academic essays, book chapters, and scholarly articles. He has been a Visiting Professor and Honorary Guest Researcher in Austria, Belgium, China, Germany, New Zealand, Slovenia, and the United States. Mark Gelber was elected to membership in the Deutsche Akademie für Sprache und Dichtung (Darmstadt). The Republic of Austria selected him to receive the Austrian Medal of Honor in Science and Art, First Class (Österreichisches Ehrenkreuz für Wissenschaft und Kunst, 1. Klasse). He was a close friend of Ruth Klüger for almost forty years. They first came into contact with each other in the early 1980s when she was editor of the *German Quarterly*, and she accepted one of his early scholarly essays for publication. Subsequently, he invited Ruth Klüger to visit and to speak in Israel several times. The first time he hosted her, she read in his living room to a small group of some ten colleagues from a manuscript she was working on, tentatively entitled "Stationen." Later, it became *weiter leben*.

Sander L. Gilman is a distinguished professor of the Liberal Arts and Sciences emeritus, as well as emeritus Professor of Psychiatry at Emory University. He was a friend, colleague, and collaborator of Ruth Klüger beginning in the 1960s. A cultural and literary historian, he is the author or editor of over one hundred books. His *"I Know Who Caused COVID-19": Pandemics and Xenophobia* (with Zhou Xun) appeared with Reaktion Press (London) in 2021; his most

https://doi.org/10.1515/9783110793239-011

recent edited volume is *The Oxford Handbook of Music and the Body* (with Youn Kim) published in 2019 with Oxford University Press. For twenty-five years he was a member of the humanities and medical faculties at Cornell University where he held the Goldwin Smith Professorship of Humane Studies. For six years he held the Henry R. Luce Distinguished Service Professorship of the Liberal Arts in Human Biology at the University of Chicago. For four years he was a distinguished professor of the Liberal Arts and Medicine at the University of Illinois at Chicago where he created the 'Humanities Laboratory.' He has been a visiting professor at numerous universities in North America, South Africa, The United Kingdom, Germany, Israel, China, and New Zealand. He was elected president of the Modern Language Association in 1995. He has been awarded a Doctor of Laws (honoris causa) at the University of Toronto in 1997, elected an honorary professor of the Free University in Berlin (2000), an honorary member of the American Psychoanalytic Association (2007), and made a Fellow of the American Academy of Arts and Sciences.

Irène Heidelberger-Leonard is Professor Emerita of the Université Libre de Bruxelles (1980–2009) and Honorary Professorial Fellow at Queen Mary College, University of London since 2009. Member of the Deutsche Akademie für Sprache und Dichtung (Darmstadt) since 1999. Author and editor of books on Günter Grass, Alfred Andersch, Ruth Klüger, Jean Améry, Jurek Becker, Peter Weiss, Thomas Bernhard, Ingeborg Bachmann, W. G. Sebald, Imre Kertész. Her biography on *Jean Améry. Revolte in der Resignation* (2004), was the "Sachbuch des Jahres von der Deutschen Bundeskulturstiftung," the winner of the Raymond Aron Preis, and was awarded the Einhard Preis for "hervorragende internationale Biographik" in 2005. She is the General Editor of the nine volume edition of *Jean Améry, Werke*, (2002–2008). Her latest book is *Imre Kertész. Leben und Werk* (2015). She was a close colleague and friend of Ruth Klüger since 1985 and is currently writing her biography.

Ulrike Offenberg is a rabbi and historian living in Berlin. She wrote her doctoral dissertation on the history and the political role of the Jewish congregations in former East Germany. Ordained by Hebrew Union College-Jewish Institute of Religion in Jerusalem in 2016, she serves as a rabbi for the Jewish congregations of Hameln and Stuttgart. Also, she is a research fellow at the Hochschule für Jüdische Studien in Heidelberg, and she is very active in Jewish-Christian and Jewish-Muslim dialogue. She frequently writes for radio, print, and online media about Jewish, feminist, and interfaith issues. She recently translated Rabbi Dalia Marx's volume, *Durch das Jüdische Jahr* from Hebrew into German. Currently, she is researching the rabbinical work of Regina Jonas, the world's first woman rabbi, during her incarceration in the Theresienstadt concentration camp.

Daniel P. Reynolds (Ph.D. Harvard University) is Seth Richards Professor of Modern Languages at Grinnell College, Iowa, where he has taught since 1998 in the Department of German Studies. His book, *Postcards from Auschwitz. Holocaust Tourism and the Meaning of Remembrance* (2018), explores tourism to sites of Holocaust perpetration and remembrance in Poland, Germany, Israel, and the United States. The research for this book was supported in part by the U.S. National Endowment for the Humanities. He has written articles on German literature and culture from the late nineteenth century to the present, including essays on Rainer Maria Rilke, Bernhard Schlink, and Günter Grass. He also researches the legacies of German colonialism, particularly through literature that recalls the genocide of the Nama and Herero people in the former colony of German Southwest Africa, today's Namibia.

Vera Schwarcz, a China historian and poet, Professor Emerita of History and East Asian Studies at Wesleyan University (Connecticut), was born in Romania to parents who survived the Shoah. She was awarded several distinguished fellowships, including a Guggenheim, a Fulbright, and a Lady Davis Fellowship. She is the author of nine books about Chinese intellectual history, including *Bridge Across Broken Time: Chinese and Jewish Cultural Memory* (1989), which was nominated for the National Jewish Book Award, as well as *Colors of Veracity: A Quest for Truth in China and Beyond* (2014). She has also written six books of poetry, among them *The Physics of Wrinkle Formation* (2016). Her latest book – *In the Crook of the Rock* – focuses on the theme of Jewish refuge in Shanghai during the Shoah. (2018)

Monica Tempian (PhD, Université de Genève) is a Senior Lecturer in German at Victoria University of Wellington, New Zealand. Her research interests focus on the literature of the Shoah, questions of Jewish displacement, memory, and migration, with special emphasis on the experience and memory of the young victims of the Nazi regime. Her recent book publications include *Maria Dronke. Glimpses of an Acting Life*; an English translation of Minnie Maria Korten, *Ein Schauspielerleben rund um die Welt* (2021); Manfred Winkler. *Haschen nach Wind. Die Gedichte* (Co-Ed. with H. J. Schrader, 2017); and *The Young Victims of the Nazi Regime: Migration, the Holocaust, and Postwar Displacement* (Co-Ed. with S. Gigliotti, 2016).

Index

https://doi.org/10.1515/9783110793239-012